The Fiction of

Angela Carter

EDITED BY SARAH GAMBLE

Consultant editor: Nicolas Tredell

ICON BOOKS

Published in 2001 by Icon Books Ltd.,
Grange Road, Duxford, Cambridge CB2 4QF
e-mail: info@iconbooks.co.uk
www.iconbooks.co.uk

Sold in the UK, Europe, South Africa and Asia by Faber & Faber Ltd.,
3 Queen Square, London WC1N 3AU or their agents

Distributed in the UK, Europe, South Africa and Asia by Macmillan
Distribution Ltd., Houndmills, Basingstoke RG21 6XS

Published in Australia in 2001 by Allen & Unwin Pty. Ltd.,
PO Box 8500, 83 Alexander Street, Crows Nest, NSW 2065

Distributed in Canada by Penguin Books Canada, 10 Alcorn Avenue,
Suite 300, Toronto, Ontario M4V 3B2

Consultant editor: Nicolas Tredell
Managing editor: Duncan Heath
Series devised by: Christopher Cox
Cover design: Simon Flynn
Typesetting: Wayzgoose

ISBN 1 84046 267 1

Printed and bound in Great Britain by
Biddles Ltd., Guildford and King's Lynn

Contents

INTRODUCTION   7

A brief summary of Angela Carter's life and career, and an outline of the
main areas of debate to be dealt with in this Guide.

CHAPTER ONE   12

Shadow Dance (1966), *Several Perceptions* (1968) and
Love (1971)

Begins with Marc O'Day's influential classification of these three novels
as the 'Bristol Trilogy', and goes on to examine the links traced between
them by Lorna Sage, Sarah Gamble and Linden Peach. It then offers examples of textual analyses of each of the three novels in turn: Sarah Gamble
argues that *Shadow Dance* is distinguished by its stress on female victimisation, Linden Peach and Aidan Day examine the carnivalesque conclusion
of *Several Perceptions*, and Lorna Sage and Patricia Juliana Smith consider
Love's relationship to the Gothic mode.

CHAPTER TWO   32

The Magic Toyshop (1967)

Opens with Olga Kenyon's interview with Carter, in which she outlines
her view of the novel's heroine. Two early feminist analyses of *The Magic
Toyshop* – one by Paulina Palmer, the other by Sara Mills, Lynne Pearce,
Sue Spaull and Elaine Millard – are compared, with particular stress on
their problematisation of the issue of the male characters' treatment of
the women in the text. The discussion then moves on to a consideration
of discussions of the novel published from the 1990s onwards, by Lorna
Sage, Jean Wyatt, Aidan Day and Linden Peach, which adopt a much
more tolerant stance towards the male characters in *The Magic Toyshop*.
However, the chapter concludes with Lucie Armitt's analysis, which
returns to the issues raised by the feminist critics of the 1980s in its reading of the text as a novel about women's sexual and social subordination.

Heroes and Villains (1969)

The first extracts cited in this chapter are taken from an interview that Angela Carter gave to Les Bedford in 1977, in which she identified *Heroes and Villains* as marking an alteration in her fictional themes and techniques. It continues with Roz Kaveney's discussion of the novel's relationship to the science-fiction genre, which is followed by David Punter's classification of the text as Gothic fiction. The debate then moves on to Robert Clark's condemnation of the novel for apparently condoning the act of rape, and Paulina Palmer and Elizabeth Mahoney's exploration of the same topic, which interprets Carter's intention as ironic and deconstructive. It concludes with Gerardine Meaney's exploration of the novel's temporal structure, and Anna Katsavos's 1988 interview with Carter, in which she discussed her portrayal of myth and history.

The Infernal Desire Machines of Doctor Hoffman (1972) and Fireworks (1974)

Opens with Sarah Gamble's and Lorna Sage's discussion of the relationship between the short stories published in *Fireworks* and the period Carter spent in Japan in the early 1970s. It then cites analyses of *The Infernal Desire Machines of Doctor Hoffman* by Lorna Sage, Elaine Jordan, Sarah Gamble, Aidan Day, David Punter, Susan Rubin Suleiman, Linden Peach and Cornel Bonca, examining such topics as pornography, the relationship between reality and fantasy in the text, and the extent to which it can be considered a postmodern novel.

The Passion of New Eve (1977)

Begins with extracts taken from a critical review of the novel by Peter Ackroyd, followed by Carter's defence of it in interviews with Olga Kenyon and John Haffenden. Elaine Jordan and David Punter read the novel as a complex and challenging analysis of gender identity, and Alison Lee examines the reader's relationship to a text in which the identity of the narrator is in constant flux. Heather L. Johnson argues that it is a work which anticipates the rise of transgender theory, while Lucie Armitt offers an interpretation which utilises the postmodern techno-theories of Jean Baudrillard and Donna J. Haraway. Finally, examples of the discussion around the novel's ambiguous conclusion are offered by Lucie Armitt, Sarah Gamble, Elaine Jordan and Aidan Day.

CHAPTER SIX   110

The Sadeian Woman (1979) and *The Bloody Chamber* (1979)

Firstly, Lorna Sage and Merja Makinen consider Carter's views concerning the meaning and importance of the fairy tale, followed by Carter's
own statement on the issue, given to Helen Cagney Watts. The chapter
then moves on to look at debates concerning the influence of the work of
the Marquis de Sade upon Carter's work. Sally Keenan looks at the critical
reception *The Sadeian Woman* received upon its publication, and Carter's
attitude towards de Sade, as well as the extent of his influence on *The
Bloody Chamber*, is debated fervently by Nanette Altevers, Andrea
Dworkin, Susanne Kappeler, Patricia Duncker, Margaret Atwood and
Robert Clark. Elaine Cronan Rose is cited as an example of an early feminist analysis of *The Bloody Chamber* stories, and is compared with Lucie
Armitt's more recent postmodern reading. Extracts from Cristina
Baccheliga's discussion of postmodern fairy tales end the chapter.

CHAPTER SEVEN   135

Nights at the Circus (1984) and *Black Venus* (1985)

Opens with favourable reviews of *Nights at the Circus* by Robert Nye and
Carolyn See, followed by Merja Makinen's examination of the reasons
for Carter's rise in popularity in the 1980s. It continues with an extract
from Angela Carter's interview with John Haffenden, in which she
talked of the intentions behind the writing of the novel, as well as
Paulina Palmer's influential reading of the novel through Bakhtinian
theories of the carnivalesque – an interpretation questioned by Aidan
Day. Substantial extracts are included from Mary Russo's book on the
female grotesque, in which Russo analyses the heroine Fevvers as an
example of the contradictions inherent in the figure of the female
grotesque. Aidan Day and Jill Matus offer different readings of Carter's
short story 'Black Venus', Sarah Gamble examines 'The Fall River Axe
Murders', and Day also argues that 'Overture and Incidental Music for *A
Midsummer Night's Dream*' anticipates the main themes to be found in
Carter's final works of fiction.

CHAPTER EIGHT   163

Wise Children (1991) and *American Ghosts and Old World
Wonders* (1993)

Begins with extracts from reviews of *Wise Children* written by Lynne
Truss, Joyce Carol Oates and Salman Rushdie. It also includes examples
of Carter's interviews given at the time of the novel's publication to Peter

Kemp, Susannah Clapp and Lorna Sage. Kate Webb and Gerardine Meaney examine *Wise Children*'s literary antecedents – particularly Shakespeare. Clare Hanson questions interpretations of Carter's later work as unproblematically utopian, while Beth A. Bohem looks at the relationship between comedy and death in Carter's last novel. The chapter concludes with critical analyses of the short stories in *American Ghosts and Old World Wonders* by Sarah Gamble and Aidan Day.

NOTES   186

SELECT BIBLIOGRAPHY   201

ACKNOWLEDGEMENTS   214

INDEX   215

A NOTE ON REFERENCES AND QUOTATIONS

Where the author of a cited extract has given a simple reference to a text as an end/footnote, I have incorporated their reference system into the Notes at the back of this Guide. More involved notes are announced as those of the appropriate author at the beginning of each note.

In any quotation, a row of three dots in square brackets [...] indicates an editorial ellipsis within a single sentence or paragraph, and a row of six dots in square brackets [... ...] (that is, two ellipses) indicates an editorial omission of a paragraph break. All editorial insertions have been made in roman, not bold.

INTRODUCTION

A NGELA CARTER was born Angela Stalker in 1940 in Eastbourne, Sussex, her mother having moved from London to escape the Blitz. The family then spent the rest of the war with her grandmother in Wath-upon-Dearne in South Yorkshire, returning to London after the war. When she was eighteen, Angela's father Hugh, a journalist, found her a job as a junior reporter for the *Croydon Advertiser*, where she was later to say that her career was hampered by a 'demonic inaccuracy as regards fact'.[1] She was only twenty when she married Paul Carter and moved to Bristol, gaining a degree in English at Bristol University in 1965.

It was in 1966 that Carter published her first novel, *Shadow Dance*, and she began to win literary prizes with her second, *The Magic Toyshop*, which was awarded the John Llewellyn Rhys Prize in 1967. However, although Carter was well on the way to being a successful novelist, she left Britain altogether after winning the Somerset Maugham Award for *Several Perceptions*, published in 1968. Her decision to live in Japan for three years removed her from her by now failing marriage, but it also separated her from the British literary scene; and although she remained a prolific and ambitious novelist, it took a long time for her to regain her early success. On her return from Japan in 1972, Carter had no permanent base in Britain and no publisher; the novel written during her stay in Japan, *The Infernal Desire Machines of Doctor Hoffman*, did not sell particularly well, and *The Passion of New Eve*, published in 1977, did little better.

In fact, it was not until the 1980s that Carter's career began to take an upward turn. In 1979, she published her second volume of short stories, *The Bloody Chamber*, a collection of subversively rewritten fairy tales, which not only attracted the attention of reviewers and the general reader, but also initiated some of the first critical examinations of her work by feminist critics. By the publication of her eighth novel, *Nights at the Circus*, in 1985, Carter was an established and reasonably well-known writer. Now happily settled in Clapham, south London, with a new partner and a baby, she not only wrote prolifically, but also took up short writer-in-residence posts at universities in America and Australia. An additional boost to her popularity was the entry of her work into other media – 'The Company of Wolves' was turned into a film, directed by

Neil Jordan, in 1985, and *The Magic Toyshop* was made for Granada TV the following year.

Carter's last novel, *Wise Children*, was published in 1991, only a few months before she died of lung cancer; it was, ironically, probably her most accessible and popular piece of work. However, it has frequently been pointed out that Carter did not attain *real* fame until after her death. As Paul Barker observes in an article published in 1995:

■ She dies untimely, and everyone suddenly bursts out weeping. The obituaries give her better notices than anything she ever wrote received in her lifetime. Her books sell out within three days of her death. She becomes the most read contemporary author on English university campuses. Her last story, finished during her final illness, sells 80,000 copies in paperback. She has arrived. But she is dead.[2] □

The very existence of this book, a guide to the criticism published on Carter's work, testifies to Carter's continuing importance within the field of English studies. Assembling it has been a daunting task, as the amount of critical material generated by Carter's work is large and growing ever larger. A few pioneering pieces were published in the early-to-mid 1980s by critics such as David Punter, Gina Wisker and Ellen Cronan Rose, but that trickle became a steady flow by the beginning of the next decade, and a flood following Carter's death. However, if a date can be assigned to the advent of 'Carter studies' as a fully-fledged discipline, it would be 1994. This was the year in which Lorna Sage published the first monograph on Carter's work, as well as the first collection of critical essays, *Flesh and the Mirror: Essays on the Work of Angela Carter*. 1994 was also the year in which the first major academic conference on Carter was held at the University of York.

Angela Carter is popular with critics because she gives them so much to work with. For a start, she is the author of an impressively wide-ranging *oeuvre*. In twenty-six years, she published nine novels, four collections of short stories and three volumes of non-fiction; not to mention radio plays, film scripts, poetry, children's fiction and journalism. In response to the variety of this extensive body of publication, the criticism of her work spans a number of academic disciplines, such as literary theory, gender studies, film theory, cultural theory and philosophy.

However, her attraction does not just lie in the variety and volume of her work, but in its depth. Carter's writing is never just 'merely' entertaining, but also showcases her formidable intellect and her love of ideas. For all the fabulous variety and inventiveness of her plots, Carter always remained dedicated to the idea that the role of literature was to instruct as well as to divert. As she said in 1984: 'I do put everything into a novel to be read – read the way allegory was intended to be read, the way you are supposed to read *Sir Gawayne and the Green Knight* – on as many levels as you can comfortably cope with at the time'.[3]

This means that any critic of Carter's texts is presented with plenty of material for thought, since her narratives habitually draw on an enormous range of sources. Lorna Sage, Carter's friend and one of her earliest academic critics, described her once as having 'taken over the sub-genres (romance, spies, porn, crime, gothic, science fiction) and turned their grubby stereotypes into sophisticated mythology'.[4] However, although Carter delighted in playing with less 'respectable' forms of fiction, she was equally capable of throwing in references to so-called 'high' culture – her writing is peppered with allusions to the theories of Mikhail Bakhtin, Jacques Derrida and Michel Foucault, the novels of Dostoyevsky and Balzac, the magical realism of Gabriel García Márquez and Jorge Luis Borges, Jacobean tragedies, the plays of Shakespeare, Dadaism, surrealism, psychoanalysis, Hollywood film and experimental European cinema, to name but a very few. Indeed, one of the things she did throughout her career was to challenge the very divisions of taste which deemed some genres or forms superior to others: 'I think I must have started very early on to regard the whole of Western European culture as a kind of folklore. I had a perfectly regular education, and indeed I'm a rather booksy person, but I do tend to regard all aspects of culture as coming in on the same level'.[5]

This eclectic borrowing from a variety of different sources, genres and modes was a perfectly deliberate strategy on Carter's part. In a particularly important essay published in 1983, 'Notes from the Front Line', she summarised her authorial intentions in a typically deft aphorism: 'I am all for putting new wine in old bottles, especially if the pressure of the new wine makes the old bottles explode'.[6] The fact that Carter came of age in the 1960s is something to which both she and her critics attach a great deal of significance. In 'Notes from the Front Line', Carter describes the end of the sixties as a time 'when, truly, it felt like Year One, that all that was holy was in the process of being profaned and we were attempting to grapple with the real relations between human beings'.[7] It could be argued that this was a spirit she strove to keep alive in her work, which never stopped questioning and challenging consensual beliefs of any kind.

Her writing itself is unconventional, full of tense couplings between the old and the new, the 'high' and the 'low', all conveyed in a highly mannered and stylised prose. (Indeed, she said that she did more than merely 'embrace' opportunities to overwrite, but would 'half-suffocate them with the enthusiasm with which I wrap my arms and legs around them'.[8]) However, she sought more than literary innovation. It has frequently been observed that a central conundrum lies at the heart of Carter's work. She has variously been described as an author of science fiction, magical realism, speculative fiction and fantasy, but the one thing she could never have been accused of was being a realist writer. Yet, as the journalist Nicci Gerrard has observed, those who view her as some kind of fey fantasist are way off the mark:

■ [M]any of the women who so adore Angela Carter have attempted to reduce her mocking iconoclasm into something more comfortable and less dangerous. Because she rewrote fairy stories, made her female heroines fly, played freakishly with notions of magic and metamorphoses, they look to her now as a New Age role model, an earth mother. (I remember a colleague of mine once asking Carter to write something on the summer solstice and Stonehenge; Carter looked at her pityingly and said in her soft, reedy voice: 'You just haven't got me, have you dear?')[9] □

Or, as she once acerbically put it, 'I'm a socialist, damn it! How can you expect me to be interested in fairies?'[10] In fact, at the base of all of Carter's fiction lies a hard-nosed awareness of reality and a desire to compel the reader to face up to their responsibilities in a harsh material world. To use her own words once again, it is

■ the product of an absolute and *committed materialism* – i.e., that *this* world is all that there is, and in order to question the nature of reality one must move from a strongly grounded base in what constitutes material reality. Therefore I become mildly irritated (I'm sorry!) when people, as they sometimes do, ask me about the 'mythic' quality of work I've written lately. Because I believe that myths are products of the human mind and reflect only aspects of material human practice. I'm in the demythologising business.[11] □

This description of herself as a 'demythologiser' is the key to Carter's perception of her role as a writer, for she creates her stories in order to shatter the fictions that regulate our everyday existences. Put more simply, she writes to make us think.

This desire to disrupt has, however, aroused a good deal of controversy amongst critics. The issue that is perhaps most hotly debated is Carter's relationship with feminism. She always described herself as 'a very old-fashioned kind of feminist'[12] who was primarily concerned with investigating 'the nature of my reality as a *woman*. How that social fiction of my "femininity" was created, by means outside my control, and palmed off on me as the real thing'.[13] Yet she was a feminist who subjected the pornographic writings of the Marquis de Sade to serious scrutiny, who frequently placed her heroines in situations of sexual violation, and who resolutely refused to conform to any kind of what we would now term 'political correctness'. Carter's supporters would argue that she indulged in such risky strategies in order to deconstruct the power structures which render women vulnerable to such sexual exploitation, whilst others assert that it is impossible to play with such representations of women without falling into the trap of perpetuating them. She was also a feminist who liked men, and who was therefore, she claimed, 'less dismissive of the entire gender than some of my sisters'.[14] She often, particularly in the early part of her career, wrote from a male point of view, and she never lost interest in 'describing men as objects of desire'.[15]

This Guide is concerned with charting critical discussions of Carter as a feminist, as a materialist and as an artistic innovator. It also aims to demonstrate that although each piece of writing has generated its own particular areas of discussion, certain themes run throughout the criticism, such as Carter's portrayal of sexuality, her depiction of gender, and her self-proclaimed role as a demythologiser. Another topic which will recur throughout this Guide is the interest displayed by most of Carter's critics with tracing the web of intertextual references in her fiction, an exercise which inevitably leads to a consideration of how generic classifications apply to her work. The question of what we are reading – science fiction, magical realism, postmodernism, fairy tales? – is one which is frequently posed in studies of Carter's work.

However, although it casts its net widely, a publication of this length and breadth cannot cover all the arguments surrounding Carter's writing in detail. Its intention is to function as an accessible introduction to the main debates, but readers are nevertheless urged to turn to the Bibliography at the back, where they will find a list of additional sources which, if followed up, will further their understanding of Carter's writing.

Part of the pleasure, however, of reading and analysing Carter's writing is that, as an author who was as interested in ideas as in invention, she is always one step ahead of you and can therefore never quite be pinned down and satisfactorily anatomised. Elaine Jordan has put this nicely: 'Whether reading Carter stimulates delight or revulsion (as sometimes it must do), it is always an intellectual activity'.[16] Thus, her work continues to generate lively and stimulating arguments – something which would have pleased Carter. A critic herself, she understood the pleasures of criticism and was not a writer who attempted to dictate how her work should be read. As she once said: 'One of the functions of fiction is to try to present a set of ideas in fictional prose, but at the same time, fiction should be open-ended; you bring your own history to it and read it on your own terms'.[17]

CHAPTER ONE

Shadow Dance (1966), *Several Perceptions* (1968) and *Love* (1971)

A NGELA CARTER'S first published novel was *Shadow Dance* (1966), followed in quick succession by *The Magic Toyshop* (1967), *Several Perceptions* (1968), *Heroes and Villains* (1969) and *Love* (1971). However, at the time when Carter was gaining a reputation in academic circles, three out of these first five novels – *Shadow Dance, Several Perceptions* and *Love* – were out of print. This certainly affected the way in which Carter's work was assessed in early criticism which, taking its cue from her radical retelling of fairy tales in *The Bloody Chamber* (1979), tended to present her primarily as a feminist fabulator.

A revised edition of *Love*, to which Carter had appended an Afterword, was published in 1987, but it was not until after her death in 1992 that *Shadow Dance* and *Several Perceptions* found their way back into print. The fact that all three of these early novels were not easily available until the critical evaluation of Carter's writing was already well underway has placed them in a slightly anomalous position, for although they were amongst her earliest published novels, they are in a way latecomers to the field of Carter criticism. A consequent feature of academic considerations of these texts is the amount of time spent on putting them into context, considering their relationship to the rest of Carter's work and to each other, although *Love*, a text which was revised and reissued in 1987, has inspired criticism on its own merits.

The first prolonged consideration of these three neglected works was Marc O'Day's essay 'Mutability is Having a Field Day: The Sixties Aura of Angela Carter's Bristol Trilogy', published in the first collection of critical essays on Carter in 1994. As his opening section makes clear, O'Day's argument has two objectives. Firstly, he is concerned with tracing the connections between these three novels in order to establish them as a clearly distinguished group of linked works. Secondly, he regards such a group of works as a vantage point from which to reassess Carter's concerns as a writer.

■ We have become too used to characterising Angela Carter's fiction by the shorthand label 'magical realism'. The term began to be applied to her writing, apparently with the author's blessing, in the early 1980s, and it took a firm hold with the publication of *Nights at the Circus* in 1984.[1] Later, in some of the tributes and reassessments which followed her death, it was retrospectively applied to the whole of her *oeuvre* from the sixties onwards.[2] This is inaccurate: several of the early novels actually invite readings in terms of quite traditional literary realism. True, it is a sixties realism saturated with domesticated gothic and psychological fantasy elements, but 'magic', in the sense of supernatural or fantastic violations of the laws of everyday life, hardly comes into it.

The works I have in mind here are the little-known *Shadow Dance* (1966), and *Several Perceptions* (1968), and the much better known *Love* (1971). These three novels, it seems to me, clearly belong together within Carter's *oeuvre*, because of the many formal and thematic elements they share. I label them collectively 'The Bristol Trilogy', for though Bristol is never named as the city in which they are set, external evidence makes the autobiographical connection clear.[3] The Trilogy novels offer realist representations of the 1960s 'provincial bohemia' which Carter herself inhabited. They deploy a similar motley array of characters, plot structures which can be read as variants of one another, comparable forms of narration, and a wide variety of themes and motifs concerning the sixties counterculture in which Carter moved. In all, they exude a fascinating period aura and are full of charming and nasty contemporary 'notations' – to use Roland Barthes's term for those descriptive details which construct the 'effect' of reality.[4] This essay aims to show that reading these early novels literally affords us valuable insights into the particular cultural and social moment from which Carter's writing derives much of its style, energy and historical vision.

How do these books produce their reality effects? Taking setting first, the events of the Bristol Trilogy 'happen' – very much in the sixties sense of 'happening', where art and life mingle so that life itself is often a form of art – in a variety of everyday, local private and public spaces. These include bedsits, flats and houses (derelict as well as occupied), cafés and coffee bars, pubs and shops, auction rooms, museums, libraries, hospitals, the Zoo and the Labour Exchange, and outdoor locations like the streets, the park and the Down. The locations are not identical. In *Shadow Dance* the auction room, the junk shop and the derelict houses are foregrounded; in *Several Perceptions* it's the Down, the (anti)hero's bedsit and a large, shabby mansion; and in *Love* the park, the ballroom (must be a Mecca) and, most of all, the protagonists' two-room flat. There is, nevertheless, a strong sense that Carter is representing the same place over a period of time.

One American commentator describes the milieu of *Shadow Dance* as 'a British slum where streets smell of urine, vomit, and stale beer'.[5] Carter quoted with amusement reviewers' responses to her chosen locale, which certainly isn't all urine and vomit, though it's undeniably, gloriously seedy. She'd insist that the novel concerned 'a perfectly real area of the city in which I lived',[6] while London-based reviewers tended to view it as 'a completely other world', nothing like the one with which they were familiar.[7] Of course, this was partly due to her use of gothic codes. Her implied criticism of the reviewers, too, is no doubt partly tongue-in-cheek, but it also conveys a truth about the mainstream metropolitan insularity of the reviewing Establishment.

The Trilogy's locations, then, are a fictional mediation of and an imaginative response to the particular place where the author lived, in marked contrast to the fictional worlds of the speculative fictions. Similarly, too, the motley, marginal, deviant and mainly counter-cultural characters in each of the novels are partly composites drawn from the people among whom she lived. Fashionable youth in various phases provide the core: if they aren't students at the university or the art school or pupils at the comprehensive school, they're liable either to be doing short-term jobs to earn a bit of cash or to be living on the dole. Some have 'square' jobs, like factory worker or teacher, but many are engaged in more self-consciously arty and bohemian pursuits, such as the second-hand trade, or art, or jewellery and handicrafts. (No one, as far as I can remember, is a writer.) Then there are other, often older, people whose lives have marginalized them from middlebrow society: an ageing prostitute, a faded actress, a former music-hall artiste, a tramp, as well as the locals who work in the shops and cafés. Authority is represented by parents who put in an occasional appearance, or lurk in the minds of their offspring; and by psychiatrists, who are increasingly prominent as the decade proceeds. But youth is at the centre of things and Carter, like anyone under thirty in the sixties (and, indeed, like many people over thirty), was intensely conscious of the sexiness of youth: witness her feeling that she was a 'has-been' when she published her first novel at the ripe old age of twenty-six.[8]

The plots of these novels are also similar: they circulate around youthful death. *Shadow Dance* and *Love* are particularly close to one another, since in each a love triangle involving two young men and a young woman is at the centre of events which conclude with the woman's death. In the earlier novel, the exhibitionistic, polymorphously perverse Honeybuzzard – bird of prey, sweet thing, bastard – tyrannises those closest to him, the weak, neurotic Morris Gray and the masochistic Arthurian moonchild Ghislaine, whom he has (probably) scarred and whom he finally murders in a blasphemous ritual.

Honey and Ghislaine are 'twins for blondness and prettiness, with a wild innocence in their playing bred of sheer perversity ... two golden beloved children destroying each other' (p. 168),[9] while the unhappily grey Morris is often dangerously close to the locals whom Honey despises: '"They are all shadows. How can you be sorry for shadows?"' (p. 83). The title switch between British and American editions, from *Shadow Dance* to *Honeybuzzard*, reflects a shift of attention from the supporting cast to the monster himself.

Love represents, with frank intensity, the sadomasochistic and emotionally cannibalistic triangle involving two half-brothers: narcissistic school teacher Lee and his unstable brother Buzz (self-named, truncated descendant of Honeybuzzard), and Lee's equally unstable wife Annabel. It ends with Annabel's suicide. She's tried at least twice before, though each brother feels that the other is responsible.

Several Perceptions works the other way round, in a double sense: here death haunts a young man, Joseph Harker, instead of a woman; and his suicide attempt, in part a response to his girlfriend Charlotte's departure, occurs in the novel's first chapter, not its last. Joseph's preferred mode, like Annabel's when she is finally successful, is gas (Morris, too, briefly contemplates a similar fate in the opening chapter of the first novel), but he fails. The remainder of the novel charts, among other things, his uneven recovery, and it closes with a positively carnivalesque and miraculous party. It's by far the most optimistic conclusion of the three.

The narratives that make up the Bristol Trilogy are set in a very precise cultural and historical moment – or rather, several moments within the wider history of the counterculture and the sixties. *Shadow Dance* – drafted in 1963 and/or 1964, but not published until 1966 – belongs to the 'post-beatnik, pre-hippie phase'.[10] *Several Perceptions* is signed 'March–December 1967' on the last page: this is the moment 'when things were peaking'.[11] *Love*, written in 1969 and revised in the winter of 1970, captures and grotesquely magnifies the waning of the sixties.[12] Carter herself once claimed that she initially thought of herself as a 'social realist'.[13] She may have been joking, but there is no doubt that these novels work over the terrain of the emergent counterculture in a recognisably realist form. More than this, however, they explore the relationship between the 'alternative' people and the postwar consumer society which also 'took off' fully in the 1960s.[14] ☐

As the above passage makes clear, O'Day's rationale for connecting these three novels together is firmly rooted in a consideration of the time and place within which they were written – a conclusion that moves away from the notion that Carter is a writer primarily concerned with myth and fairy tale. O'Day quotes extensively from two of Carter's essays in which she writes about her experience of the sixties, 'Notes from the Front Line' and 'Truly, it Felt Like Year One', in order to argue that

■ what the Trilogy novels give us [...] which we don't get so recognisably elsewhere in her *oeuvre* is a sense of at least a part of the milieu from which Carter's ongoing revaluation of the boundaries between the valued and the valueless – whether in terms of forms and kinds, ideas, people and things – proceeds. It's long been customary to notice that postmodern aesthetics involves the renegotiation – though not, surely, the effacement – of the boundary between the high and the low, the serious and non-serious or frivolous, art and kitsch, the durable and the rubbish in the arts, the media, and culture more generally. The Trilogy mixes realism and gothic, in a way that fits quite neatly into the revival of a domesticated gothic in the sixties; but more than this, it shows clearly how the sixties were a laboratory – or perhaps, rather, a battlefield – in the relativisation of all kinds of values: aesthetic, moral, spiritual, economic, political.[15] □

O'Day's presentation of these novels as a trilogy rooted in sixties Gothicism set the tone of subsequent discussions, and arouses a response from the writers of most of the critical treatments of Carter's early work. In the same year as she edited the collection of criticism in which O'Day's essay appeared, Lorna Sage published a short study of Angela Carter in Northcote House's 'Writers and Their Work' series, in which she comments on O'Day's essay – with certain qualifications.

■ Marc O'Day calls *Shadow Dance*, *Several Perceptions*, and *Love* [Carter's] Bristol trilogy, and certainly grouping the three novels together makes sense. They share a stylised but none the less recognizably contemporary setting, they quote and borrow and beg and steal, they are half in love with death, and derive an indecent energy from the images of decay and boredom and disillusion. They are, as O'Day argues, in a sense realist texts – except that you have to remember that reality has been infiltrated by fiction, so that these novels that represent it have the extra density of fiction squared.[16] □

Sage, however, makes this observation at the end of a chapter in which she has not treated these three novels as a distinct trilogy, but linked them with Carter's other early novels, *The Magic Toyshop* and *Heroes and Villains*. It is also obvious that she is not entirely comfortable with O'Day's use of the term 'realism'. For Sage, what connects all of Carter's early works is their relationship to the past, which they rework, recycle, and represent in playful, subversive forms, blurring the boundaries between reality and fantasy in the process. It is *Shadow Dance* which sets the tone, evoking

■ a whole world of leftovers, quotes, copies, *déjà-vu*: 'life imitating rotten art again, as Honey always said it did' (p. 10).[17] Morris, who is supposed to be a painter, but despises his own work and has settled for collecting junk instead (the borders between art and trash are busily dissolving), admires Honeybuzzard for his pitiless playfulness. Honey is as beautiful as Ghislaine was, but he is a sadistic joker and power addict [...] He becomes a toy-maker, making jumping-jack caricatures of the other characters (anticipating sinister Uncle Philip Flower in *The Magic Toyshop*), and fantasizing about the freedom of role-playing:

> 'I like – you know – to slip in and out of me. I would like to be somebody different each morning. Me and not-me. I would like to have a cupboard bulging with all different bodies and faces ... There was a man, last night; we were in a club and there was this man, singing blues, and he had a red rose stuck in his shirt. It was red as the cap of liberty ... I would like to wear him, tomorrow morning'. (p. 76)

Honey plays tirelessly and cruelly, like a big cat; anything and anyone is fair game. He shares the vampire imagery with Ghislaine – but the reference (above) to the 'cap of liberty' worn in the French revolution signals that he is no ordinary monster. Like the Marquis de Sade,[18] he is a radical pornographer, who strips away the mystifications of sex and sentiment to reveal the workings of power underneath. He camps it up, too: '"Never been so embarrassed, darling." He made a mincing gesture with his right hand and tittered' (p. 60) – and is regularly described in androgynous terms. He bows to no conventions about masculine Nature.

It is Camp with a capital 'C' that matters here, though, and to understand Honeybuzzard's dubious charm for his creator, as well as for characters in the book, you have to recognize that he alone belongs to two worlds, in gender terms and, in terms just as vital to Carter the writer, the real (life) and the shadow (art). He is on that fault-line, an early embodiment of her conviction that the fantastical and the actual can exist on the same plane. The Gothic need not be locked away in a separate genre. Honey is in the real world, very much the kind of figure [Susan] Sontag described, 'a dandy in the age of mass culture': 'Camp taste transcends the nausea of the replica ... The relation between boredom and Camp taste cannot be overestimated. Camp taste is by its nature possible only in affluent societies, in societies or circles capable of experiencing the psychopathology of affluence.'[19] When Honey and Morris strip old houses, sell beaded frocks and chipped Staffordshire china and kitsch loo-chains, they are located securely in their Sixties moment, they are 'realistic' figures. But they also, like Ghislaine, point to the pull of the past, the spectre that faced Carter from the very beginning of her writing career – the thought that there was nothing new to do, or be: 'I am the pure product of an advanced, industrialised, post-imperialist country in decline'.[20] *Shadow Dance* dramatizes the paradoxical advantages of living in a belated world – you can see people as constructs, not born but made; you have to piece together your own myths, in the absence of God-given truths.[21] □

Sage does not accord *Several Perceptions* much room in her analysis, but she is more expansive when she comes to *Love*, which she presents as Carter's farewell to the sixties:

■ [S]he rounded out the sixties with an extraordinary elegy for utopia, *Love* – not published until 1971, but written in 1969. It is a bitterly perfect book, a bleak celebration of the emptiness you arrive at if you rubbish the real too thoroughly. In a sense it's a rewrite of *Shadow Dance*, with the shadows (images, unrealities) taking over yet again. Glamorous, sinister Honeybuzzard from her first book has been split into two, the 'Honey' reborn as beautiful Lee, the Buzzard as Buzz, his dark half-brother. The girl who is their go-between ends up as a blasphemous sacrifice to fantasies of power in both books – though Ghislaine is murdered, and Annabel in *Love* kills herself, the difference is not so great as it sounds, since both girls die of delusion, overdosed on role-playing, and complicit in their own destruction.

There is no patriarch or puppet-master character in *Love*, however. The text's propensity for violence is distributed amongst the three central figures, who form a lethal love-hate triangle. The half-brothers are orphaned sons of a mad mother, rootless products of a lost working-class culture, Annabel is a middle-class drop-out, and they meet in the new no-man's land of Sixties Bohemia, where they proceed to mutilate and misread each other. The writing has a beauty – a glowing patina of craft and indifference – that exactly fits the artificial 'nature' of the people: Annabel's craziness and second-hand Art School images; Buzz's alienated, jealous insistence on seeing everything through a camera lens; Lee's goodness, which is really self-love, his niceness which is perhaps merely a chronic eye infection that makes him weep easy tears. Lee is the failed folk-hero, a handsome, confident Jack-the-lad who finds himself lost in the fun-house. Annabel and Buzz both desire him, and conspire with each other against him, leeching away his anyway shaky sense of identity. Or that is one way of looking at it. The narrative point of view is Lee's more than anyone else's, but, given the coolness of the tone, that isn't saying a great deal. Once upon a time Lee would have delivered a sexual redemption, now he does not. Sex is turning out to be an exercise in alienation, not the stuff of revelation and intimacy. Bodies have lost the innocence and materiality we used to attribute to them, and flesh has revealed itself as culturally conditioned, a kind of costume or disguise.

So one of the novel's crueller structural refinements (again reminiscent of *Shadow Dance*) is that Lee is allowed a brief midsummer night's idyll with earthy, street-wise Joanne at the very same time that vampire Annabel is slipping into her coma. There is a glimpse of a happy ending – a loose end, an open door – except that we already know (though he does not) the guilty truth. The writing takes on an air of conscious unreality, dramatic irony, the poignancy of paradise lost:

> The silver-plated trees cast barely visible shadows on the grass and each blade and daisy, each bud and blossom, shone with an individual, clear, distinct brilliance. The south side of the park was far more luxuriantly wooded than the north and the man and his girl stepped off the path and walked through the moist undergrowth between the bleached trunks of trees, in and out of the stippled light, until they glimpsed before them the serene white pillars of the miniature temple. All was calm, all was bright. The pale light magically rendered Joanne's gaudy dress as a brief tunic of vague, leopard-like blotches and a few twigs and leaves caught in her hair. (pp. 121–2)[22]

Lee and Joanne simply cannot sustain the classic, timeless simplicity of 'the man and his girl' ... and in any case, dead Annabel has taken possession of the final scene – 'a painted doll, bluish at the extremities ... . Flies already clustered round her eyes' (p. 124). This is Carter's Camp triumph, experience transformed into theatre, with nearly nothing left over once the curtain falls.[23] □

The notion that Carter's early, rather more naturalistic, works are linked by a camp sensibility is central to my own argument in *Angela Carter: Writing From the Front Line*, in which I contend that *Shadow Dance* and *Several Perceptions*, in particular, are 'both texts which draw overtly on the concept of a counterculture, and which celebrate ... [the sixties'] devotion to narcissistic spectacle'.[24]

■ I would argue that *Shadow Dance* and *Several Perceptions* are linked by a similar camp sensibility, embodied most obviously in the iconic figure of the dandy. Dandyism, however, is an attribute also shared by Carter's narrative itself. According to Andrew Ross, in its ironic valorisation of the artefacts of consumer culture, camp 'represented a direct affront to those who governed the boundaries of official taste' by 'problematizing the question of *taste* itself'.[25] Put this statement in a literary context, and you have an apt summary of Carter's approach in both these narratives, which are an eccentric and eclectic assemblage of references and techniques drawn from a wide variety of 'high' and 'low' literary forms in which the likes of Shakespeare and Keats are placed on an equal level with references to Hammer Horror, folk-tale and the Marquis de Sade. In this way, the method by which mainstream culture allocates categories of value, taste and morality is systematically dismantled.[26] □

I thus follow O'Day and Sage in my tracing of a direct connection between the texts and the period in which they were written. The character of Honeybuzzard, for example, may be approached as a personification of Bakhtin's 'Romantic grotesque', a malcontent from Jacobean drama or a monster out of gothic horror, but he is also 'a creature of the sixties cultural hinterland'.[27]

■ Within his setting, Honeybuzzard is no anomaly, but an expression – as well as an exploiter – of the larger camp culture within which he moves. According to Andrew Ross, an inherent characteristic of camp is its 'rediscovery of history's waste … [which] retrieves not only that which had been initially excluded from the serious high cultural tradition, but also the more unsalvageable material that had been picked over and left wanted by purveyors of the "antique"'.[28] This is an apt summary of the situation evoked by Carter in *Shadow Dance*, for as well as *being* camp, Honeybuzzard is also a knowing purveyor of sixties camp taste. Together with Morris he deals in junk, plundered from the debris of the past in nocturnal excursions to abandoned houses that are on the point of demolition. Here they find the personal flotsam and jetsam of long-gone people's lives, which they clean, polish and sell for a profit to Americans 'as conversation pieces' (p. 90).[29]

Floating free of any historical or aesthetic value system which might give them meaning, scruffy artefacts can be turned into profit by such cultural scavengers, giving an added ingenuousness to Carter's statement in 'Truly, It Felt Like Year One' that the people of the sixties were 'early into recycling'.[30] Morris frequently feels a certain nostalgia for the past, often trying to decipher clues about the lifestyle of the original owners from the items they find. No such emotions bother Honeybuzzard, however, for centred as he is around the self and the moment, such relics can have only two possible uses: either to make money, or to act as props in his ever-changing production of himself.[31] □

One critic who has moved away from discussions of the sixties and of camp with regard to these three novels is Linden Peach. He endorses

O'Day's classification of them as a trilogy, but whereas for O'Day what sets them apart from Carter's other work is their location within a recognisable 'sixties' milieu, Peach focuses on the literary associations between them, arguing that they are indebted to a mode of writing which considerably predates the sixties.

■ There are further reasons why these novels may be regarded as a trilogy [...] Each novel, at various levels, including parody, is indebted to Euro-American Gothic. In particular, through a combination of Gothic and psychological fantasy, Carter pursues themes and motifs from nineteenth-century American writers, especially Herman Melville and Edgar Allan Poe. Carter's view of American Gothic writing was undoubtedly mediated through Leslie Fiedler's *Love and Death in the American Novel* (1960) which quickly became required reading for students of literature. One of the epigraphs to *Heroes and Villains* (1969) is from Fiedler's book and suggests that Carter was particularly interested in his perception of Gothic American literature: 'The Gothic mode is essentially a form of parody, a way of assailing clichés by exaggerating them to the limit of grotesqueness.' Certainly many of the characteristics of Carter's early writing recall Fiedler's summary of the principal features of Gothic writing: the substitution of terror for love as a central theme; the vicarious flirtation with death; an aesthetic that replaces the classic concept of 'nothing-in-excess' with 'the revolutionary doctrine that nothing succeeds like excess'; and a dedication 'to producing nausea, to transcending the limits of taste and endurance'.[32]

Each of the novels constituting the Bristol trilogy explores the negative aspects of the psyche – a project which leads inevitably to the Gothic tale, traditionally a vehicle for ideas about 'psychological' evil rather than evil as a force exterior to the mind. In the afterword to the first edition of *Fireworks* (1974) Carter makes clear that even in the mid-1970s this was how she thought of European Gothic tales although, as [Marina] Warner points out, she removed it from subsequent editions having become by then more interested in the connection between folktales and the imaginations of 'ordinary' people:

> cruel tales, tales of wonder, tales of terror, fabulous narratives that deal directly with the imagery of the unconscious – mirrors; the externalised self, forsaken castles, haunted forests; forbidden sexual objects ... . Characters and events are exaggerated beyond reality, to become symbols, ideas, passions. Its style will tend to be ornate, unnatural – and thus operate against the perennial human desire to believe the word as fact. Its only humour is black humour. It retains a singular moral function – that of provoking unease.[33]

Carter's early novels, however, are not simply Gothic in the traditional sense of the term. The Gothic genre is itself subversive, giving expression to what is culturally occluded such as sexual fantasy and female desire. However, Carter's novels are frequently subversions of the genre; themes and ideas first explored – albeit however crudely – in Gothic writing are re-examined, challenged and expanded. The Gothic becomes a mode of awareness within the novels which challenges, contradicts or confirms other perspectives as diverse as social realism, Jungian psychoanalysis and 'projection' theory, and is in turn subverted and/or expanded by them. This hybridity creates different possible ways of reading the texts, giving them the 'extra density of fiction' to which [Lorna] Sage refers. However, the dominance of the Gothic mode of writing within these early novels subverts the close relationship between word and referent which characterises realism. As Elizabeth MacAndrew (1979) points out, the all pervading symbolism of the Gothic tale is 'almost, though not quite allegorical' – the 'referents are deliberately hazy'.[34] In the early novels – as in the later non-realistic, philosophical fiction – Carter exploits the hybridity of Gothic writing and its capacity for ambivalence and ambiguity.

In this trilogy, Carter appears to be re-visioning the sequence novel which according to [Steven] Connor (1996) underwent a remarkable revival after the Second World War. As he points out:

> The world of the sequence has the self-sufficient density it supposes of the 'real' world. It is closed and complete in itself, a parallel universe or working simulacrum of the real not only in the encyclopaedic abundance of its narrative detail but also in its plethora of different possible perspectives; typically the novel-sequence will combine and juxtapose not only different experiences of different characters but also the same experiences revisited from different points of view.[35]

Unlike the conventional novel-sequence which Connor describes, and more like [Samuel] Beckett in his Trilogy [*Molloy/Malone Dies/The Unnamable*, published 1951–3], Carter's sequence resists offering the reader a complete, coherent and self-sufficient world. Each of the novels in the Bristol trilogy enacts a complex, repetitive and paradoxical narrative.[36] □

Like Sage, Peach, whilst acknowledging that the novels that make up the trilogy share a superficial adherence to the realist mode, also regards it as adopting an interrogative stance towards that realism:

■ It is plausible, then, to read *Shadow Dance*, *Several Perceptions* and *Love* as a trilogy based on fictional mediation of bohemian life at various points in the 1960s Bristol which invites reading from a realist perspective. However, it is no coincidence that when Joanne takes Lee home to her bed in *Love*, they pass through the wrought iron gates of the park which 'neither permitted nor denied access' and seemed to negate a moral problem 'by declaring it improperly phrased' (pp.110–11).[37] Throughout each of the three novels, Carter is concerned with the significance of how things are 'phrased', that is conceptualised. A range of different frameworks provide different ways of approaching and pursuing issues as the hybrid nature of the novels and the myriad of intertextual references provide different pointers as to how they should perhaps be read. Realism in these novels, as in all Carter's work, offers one way of looking at things but it is disrupted by, and in turn destabilises, a combination of American Gothic and Freudian, Jungian and even object relations psychology.

Although these novels do not have the characteristics often associated with 'magic realism' that we find in the later novels [...] they demonstrate Carter's interest in the fictionality of realism and of much that we regard as non-fiction. In each novel, the boundaries between reality and illusion and between fact and fiction become blurred. Although each novel is a third-person narrative, they are identified, especially in the case of *Shadow Dance* and *Several Perceptions*, with a specific male consciousness. It is impossible to accept this consciousness as that of the author. And, even if we accept it as a construction, it is invariably a slippery, incoherent fiction which is difficult to map adequately. Carter appears to have become interested in these novels in the different means which have been available at different times for mapping the mind. The reader soon becomes aware that ways of conceptualising the mind have a literary as well as a psychoanalytic history. In these early novels they are dehistoricised – perhaps because, as *Several Perceptions* illustrates, Carter is interested in the collage, a non-linear way of constructing fictions. Joseph's wall is covered with photographs of different periods:

There were some pictures tacked to the wall. Lee Harvey Oswald, handcuffed between policemen, about to be shot, wild as a badger. A colour photograph, from Paris Match, of a square of elegant houses and, within these pleasant boundaries, a living sunset, a Buddhist monk whose saffron robes turned red as he burned alive. Also a calendar of the previous year advertising a brand of soft drinks by means of a picture of a laughing girl in a white sleeveless, polo-neck sweater sucking this soft drink through a straw. And a huge dewy pin-up of Marilyn Monroe. (p.15)

In Joseph's room, these photographs exist in new spatial and temporal relationships with each other. The pictures of the monk and of the houses from the French magazine, for example, have been lifted out of the framework in which the reader would normally encounter them, creating a new context in which the viewer might now 'read' both differently. In other words, conventional ways of 'phrasing' these events have been challenged. The ahistorical arrangement of these photographs is echoed in the early novels in Carter's use of intertextuality [a term which describes the creation of texts from references to other texts]. For example, in *Love*, we are told that Lee 'looked like Billy Budd or a worker hero of the Soviets, or a boy in a book by Jack London' (p. 12). Here, Carter juxtaposes three pieces of representation which readers may not have thought of connecting in such a concentrated way for themselves. Lifted out of their usual cultural, geographical and temporal frameworks, and placed in this new special and temporal sequence, these references pose a problem for the reader. Which of these references is to be privileged over the others? To give priority to one rather than another may take our reading of Lee in a different direction from that suggested by the others. The association of Lee with Billy Budd would more than likely emphasise the feminine nature of his beauty and lead the reader to consider the ambivalence in the representation of Lee's relationship with his brother. On the other hand, placing Lee in context with idealised portraits of Soviet workers would invariably lead the reader to consider the importance to the narrative of the left-wing aunt with whom he was brought up; his own working-class origins and how they are betrayed (probably in both senses of the word); and how he represents himself in class terms, including his relationships with Carolyn and Joanne and his marriage.

The intertextuality in the Bristol trilogy may involve us in studying specific allusions, in tracing particular references and in comparing sources. At another level, it may encourage us to think in more general terms – recalling characters, plots, images and convention from literary traditions which in the novels are appropriated, challenged or transformed. Thus through their intertextuality, the novels may transform the way in which we think about intellectual frameworks – encouraging us to be more aware of, and open in, how we read, think and conceptualise within frameworks; and in the way in which we consciously and unconsciously police boundaries between fiction and non-fiction.[38] ☐

As demonstrated above, the debate surrounding these three novels has taken its lead from O'Day in focusing on the linking elements between them. Most critics have also observed, however, that each of these texts has a distinct identity. *Shadow Dance*, for example, is a bleak and excessively violent novel: as James Wood writes in a review of the novel upon its reissue in 1994, it 'is not remotely likeable, and, like a hated teacher, it shows no interest in being likeable'.[39] My own view of this book is that, for all its stress on theatricality and performance – themes which were to become dominant tropes in Carter's subsequent fiction – its bleak humour fails in the face of the extreme unpleasantness it metes out to its female characters:

■ [W]here the camp burlesque of *Shadow Dance* falters badly is over its treatment of women, which could come as a nasty shock to any reader accustomed to thinking of Carter as a feminist writer. Although Carter appears to be trying to create a world in which you make your own rules unfettered by the traditions or moral assumptions of an outmoded past, it is a freedom that the text often seems only to extend to men. Furthermore, the treatment meted out to Ghislaine makes some kind of moral response to the text on the part of the reader unavoidable.

To be fair, it would be incorrect to try to force this narrative to conform to contemporary feminist views that were not in the author's mind when she wrote it, for at this period in her career Carter 'didn't see the point of feminism'.[40] One should also take into account her tendency towards wilful perversity, which delighted in toppling belief systems of any kind; an iconoclastic process from which nothing was exempt.

It is also possible to argue, as Lorna Sage does, that Honeybuzzard is an early example of Carter's 'radical pornographer', who 'strips away the mystifications of sex and sentiment to reveal the working of power underneath'.[41] In this context, his violent treatment of Ghislaine – and thus by implication the violent treatment meted out to many of Carter's female characters in her early fiction – can be justified as a kind of (anti)morality play which aims to undermine through exaggeration.

It was nevertheless an element in her writing for which Carter later apologised, claiming in 1992, for example, that 'It took me a long time to identify patriarchal bias in my discourse'.[42] It is in *Shadow Dance* that this bias is most disturbingly obvious, for this is a text in which women are resolutely denied the privilege of a narrative voice. By excluding them from the formation of discourse, they are rendered figments of a fevered male imagination, and become the targets of a disturbing blend of violence and eroticism. [...]

Ghislaine, of course, is the most extreme example of this process. When Morris meets her in the bar at the beginning of the book, his extreme reaction to her is partly revulsion at her ugliness, combined with guilt at 'the memory of her naked, threshing about beneath him' (p.5). He is also patently annoyed at her 'unfeminine' display of economic independence: 'Shall I buy a drink for you, Morris? Have you no money? Always penniless, poor Morris' (p. 1). Yet he can transfer his guilt for both emotions onto Ghislaine herself by classifying her as the monstrous representative of a voracious, predatory, female sexuality. Infinitely malleable to any number of interpretations, Ghislaine's scar again becomes the focus of this symbolism, where it is transformed into a grotesque image of the female genitalia; open, grinning and never satisfied. Later on in the book, for example, Morris dreams of Ghislaine as 'a vampire woman, walking the streets on the continual qui vive, her enormous brown eyes alert and ever-watchful, and the moment she saw him she would snatch him up and absorb him, threshing, into the chasm in her face' (p. 39). This description of himself as 'threshing' chimes yet contrasts with his earlier use of the verb. Then, it was applied to Ghislaine, but now its transferral to himself signals her transformation from sexual prey to street-walking predator.

Although Honeybuzzard is the person who finally kills Ghislaine, Morris recognises his own complicity in the crime, for all Honey has done is to dare to act out what Morris 'had always wanted but never defined. ... choking out of Ghislaine her little-girl giggle ... filling up her voracity once and for all by cramming with death the hungry mouth between her thighs' (pp. 178–9). As a statement of murderous misogyny, this could hardly be bettered, but the elaborate mythology which is built up around Ghislaine tends to obscure the fact that she has done very little, if anything at all, to deserve it, apart from becoming the repository of the guilty secret of Morris' own adultery. And as Mary Russo has noted, misogyny and the grotesque spectacle have always had a certain affinity, enabling woman to be 'cruelly observed in intricate detail, but never allowed to make words'.[43] In later books, Carter will give her female characters the power to appropriate and subvert that process, but it is not a power shared by poor Ghislaine.[44] □

Several Perceptions, on the other hand, does not place quite the same stress on violence and abuse. Linden Peach's description of the novel highlights the similarities between *Shadow Dance* and *Several Perceptions*, while also pinpointing the significant difference between them:

■ Like *Shadow Dance*, *Several Perceptions* (1968), written between March and December 1967, is a third-person retrospective narrative. Again the focalisation is through the consciousness of a single, male character, Joseph Harker, who, like Morris, is prey to dreams and phantasies. He is haunted like Morris, but by death rather than a woman. Whilst Morris contemplates suicide, Joseph attempts it. The narrative charts his recovery, culminating in a miraculous party at the end of the novel.[45] □

Whereas the climactic moment of *Shadow Dance* is a murder, in *Several Perceptions* it is a party, which presages the celebratory function of theatre which will become such a dominant feature of Carter's last novels. Some reviewers of the novel have expressed disappointment at such an apparently optimistic conclusion. Writing in the *New York Times Book Review*, Richard Boston argues that the novel can be seen as a study of fashionable theories concerning schizophrenia: that 'in a mad society (such as ours) the only people who are sane are those that "normal" people call mad. If society has deviated from sanity, those who deviate from society are sane'. However, Boston finds the novel's ending 'rather disappointing', at odds with its earlier 'powerful account of the horror, the logic and the poetry of the schizophrenic's world'. 'Perhaps short of Joseph's successfully committing suicide, the novel had to have some such ending to round it off. One has no quarrel with Angela Carter's decision to end affirmatively. But after her early tough-mindedness, one had hoped for a more telling denouement than the Spirit of Christmas.'[46]

Academic critics have, however, interpreted this ending in a variety of ways. Linden Peach sees the conclusion's apparent incongruity as completely intentional:

■ At the end of *Several Perceptions*, illusion intrudes to subvert the 'realism' of loss, pain and suffering [...].

[I]n reading the final pages of *Several Perceptions*, we might also think of those plays by Shakespeare, such as *The Winter's Tale*, in which the world itself is turned into a theatre. Towards the end of the miraculous part in *Several Perceptions*, as towards the end of Shakespeare's last plays, the reader is made aware of the theatricality of the event [...]. Realism as the dominant mode of the text dissolves and threatens to disappear altogether. [...] The party which closes the novel, is more than just a carnivalesque conclusion. It returns us to the David Hume epigraph[47] and the notion of the theatricality of the mind. [...] The ending of the novel is meant to appear theatrical and contrived; a fitting conclusion to a text which from its very epigraph deliberately confounds illusion and reality.[48] □

Aidan Day, however, sees in the novel's ending Carter's celebration of the utopian spirit of the sixties:

■ The special happenings recorded in this concluding chapter of *Several Perceptions* take place within the 'floating world' (p. 128)[49] of the counterculture. Generosity and creativity in human relationships are figured as the key to the counterculture, which is celebrated as an alternative model of human relationships to that of the old order of fathers and wars. The counterculture of the 1960s – in its general opposition to the Vietnam War and specifically, in this novel, through Joseph's instruction by Mrs Boulder on the irrelevance of father figures – is being identified by Carter as anti-paternalistic in character and hence as creative and regenerative.[50] □

Such optimism does not carry on over into *Love*, however, published two years later. Lorna Sage's opinion that *Love* and *Shadow Dance* share many similarities has already been cited above. The implication is that, rejecting the notion of utopia, Carter has returned to the bleak world of sexual victimisation. Sage views *Love* as rounding off not merely a trilogy set in 1960s provincial bohemia, but all the novels Carter wrote during this decade. In her book *Women in the House of Fiction*, she argues that sexual fixation is the dominant theme in all these texts, a concept which *Love* takes to its absolute, horrific limits.

■ There's a recurrent Carter plot from these years which, if you translated it into more or less realistic terms, would go like this: a middle-class virgin bewitched and appalled by the fictions of femininity falls in love with a working-class boy, a dandified, dressed-up tramp who's meant to make sense of her desires, but doesn't. [...] In *Love* (written in 1969, published in 1971, revised and reissued in 1987), the theme of sexual fixation plays itself out with cold brilliance, like the last act in a firework display.

The backdrop is a municipal park, once the landscaped garden of a great house, only its follies still standing to mark out Classical south and Gothic north, though its gates are still in place:

> ... a massive pair of wrought-iron gates decorated with cherubs, masks of beasts, stylised reptiles and spearheads from which the gilding flaked, but these gates were never either open or closed. They hung always a little ajar and drooped from their hinges with age; they served a function no longer for all the railings round the park were gone long ago and access everywhere was free and easy. (p. 2)[51]

This studied and beautifully ominous opening description marks the threshold of a place of ambivalence. The lord of this manor is long-departed, and our trespasses will neither be forbidden nor forgiven. Inside and outside, self and other, lose their definition. The central love-triangle composed of Annabel, her husband Lee and his dark, deranged half-brother Buzz, is a fight to the death over this amorphous space. They construct their selves, cannibalistically, out of each other, and inscribe their meanings on each other's flesh. Lee seems the most innocent of the three, though that is because he is the most thoroughly narcissistic [...]. Moreover his point of view is privileged by the authorial voice, whereas Annabel [...] and Buzz are described in terms of the alien ways they perceive the world. [...] Their intimacy is a mutual violation, like intercourse between creatures from different species: 'she gazed at him with wonder, as if he might be magic, and he looked at her nervously, as if she might not be fully human' (p. 34). Ironically, this distance derives from the very thing that brings them together, their lack of purchase in the world, in which they are alike ('as though both could say of the world: "We are strangers here"', p. 17). Sexual love, though, depends on a certain complementarity (a *domesticated* difference, you might say), which these two can't contrive. They are at once too different and too similar ('strangers'), and their love-making estranges them further. Buzz compounds the obscenity ('they often woke in the morning to find him perched on the end of the bed, clicking away', p. 25).

The marriage comes to a bitter end with a 'mutual rape' (p. 97) which demolishes Lee's good opinion of himself and perfects Annabel's despair. Her final gesture [...] is to make herself over into a parody-woman (a blonde, painted doll) and then, by logical extension, a dead one:

> ... she could not draw anything any more and so was forced to make these imaginative experiments with her own body which were now about to culminate, finally, in erasure. (p. 103)

It's a nastily plausible conclusion, rendered all the more disturbing by the narrative's refusal to blame Lee (or even the horrible Buzz). Carter's 1987 revisions to the text are interesting in this connection. She remarks wryly in her Afterword on 'its almost sinister feat of male impersonation' (p. 113); she has also deleted several passages which in the original made Lee Annabel's victim. For example: 'since he loved her, he did not wish to believe his occasional intuitions that she was obscurely calculating and malign' (p. 84);[52] and 'She filled him with revulsion; her curiously pointed teeth might be those of a vampire' (p. 107). In 1971, Annabel 'slavered' kisses on him in her final doomed attempt to force sex to have a meaning, whereas in 1987 she 'lavished' them, and so on. The effect of these changes is to diminish the amount of subjective sympathy Lee is allowed, and so reinforce what was anyway the original implication: that 'the hero' has no power to redeem.[53] □

In a particularly interesting essay published in 1994, Patricia Juliana Smith adds an intriguing twist to this debate, drawing what at first seems a rather incongruous comparison between Carter and Jane Austen in order to argue for *Love* as a novel which critiques emotional excess, or 'sensibility'.

■ In this [novel], Carter effectively scrutinizes the moral ambivalences of sensibility, particularly the sinister motivations lurking behind the external display of emotionality constructed as a sign of heightened sensitivity and refined benevolence. Simultaneously, she mercilessly illustrates the similarities between the excesses of the period that gave rise to Romanticism and those of the period that gave us the sexual revolution. Through the medium of the ménage à trois comprised of Lee, Annabel and Buzz, she takes stock of our cherished and reviled conventional gender roles and to what extent they have, while changing drastically, nonetheless stubbornly remained the same.

In a retrospective assessment of the cultural and social significance of the sixties, Carter speculated that 'manners had not been so liberal and expressive since the Regency – or maybe even since the Restoration, with the absence of syphilis compensated for in the mortality stakes by the arrival of hard drugs'.[54] Indeed, the sex and drugs that seem synonymous with sixties culture were simply elements of a greater phenomenon, the youth culture's valorization of total freedom (or, more precisely, license), of boundless physical and mental sensation, and of a Rousseauistic 'natural' goodness unrelated to traditional social mores [...]. Likewise, if less demotically, the eighteenth-century cult of sensibility prized emotional susceptibility, heightened sensitivity, and a tremendous capacity for suffering, all regarded as the outward signs of a highly refined moral character. The novel of sensibility, as Janet Todd explains, was originally a didactic mode that 'showed people how to behave, how to express themselves in friendship and how to respond decently to life's experiences', but it soon devolved into a popular form that 'prided itself more on making its readers weep and in teaching them when and how much to weep'.[55] Yet Carter, incorporating this mode into a postmodern pastiche, inverts this paradigm. *Love* is more likely to invoke fear and revulsion than tears and sympathy – and is, in its fatal consequences, a study in how *not* to deport oneself.[56] □

As Smith points out, the Gothic novel and the novel of sensibility are closely related, and she argues that Annabel functions as an exaggeratedly Gothic heroine, exemplifying 'the "feminine" traits of physical and mental frailty and passive victimage'[57] to a horrific degree. Regarded in this light, the conflict between the novel's three main characters is 'for the distinction of having the acutely tortured sensibility' – for, as we are reminded, 'sensibility has never been the exclusive property of imperiled heroines'.[58] Smith sees Carter's later revision of the book as indicative of its didactic role as a critique of the excesses of the period in which it was written:

■ As the adolescent Jane Austen demonstrated in her parodic 'Love and Freindship' (*sic*) two centuries before, sensibility is often nothing more than a façade to disguise a refusal to accept responsibility, a means by which to 'check out' and feign ignorance of cause-and-effect relationships that govern one's environment. Through the 'almost sinister feat of male impersonation' (p. 113)[59] from which she demurs in retrospect, Carter creates a telling and painful parody of the mores of her own generation. [...] In all, Carter's characters approximate, in their self-created emotional fragility, the condition of moral dubiousness characteristic of Austen's self-styled heroines [...].[60] □

For Smith, therefore, the morbid masochism of *Love* assumes a cautionary function, carrying an implicit critique of sixties dissipation. It is an opinion which is echoed in O'Day's conclusion concerning *Love*, that it pinpoints the moment when the sixties counterculture self-destructs: 'Annabel's and Buzz's sickness, however defined, may have its origins in the family and early childhood, but the heady aura of their quintessentially sixties lifestyle provides an ample theatre for its development'.[61] However, neither O'Day or Smith pays a great deal of attention to the violence that takes place within the novel. In Smith's discussion, Annabel is categorised as 'a passive-aggressive' sadist,[62] who assumes the role of victim in order to inflict pain on others; and while O'Day acknowledges that 'it's worth noting that there's a high degree of sexual and other violence towards women'[63] in both *Shadow Dance* and *Love*, it is not an aspect of his argument that he develops to any great degree. As the following chapters of this study will show, however, discussion of Carter's treatment of women, which forms only a subtext in the criticism on the so-called 'Bristol Trilogy', comes to the fore in much of the criticism on the other two novels Carter wrote in the sixties, *The Magic Toyshop* and *Heroes and Villains*.

CHAPTER TWO

The Magic Toyshop (1967)

T HE MAGIC *Toyshop* was Carter's second novel, and her first commercial success, winning the John Llewellyn Rhys Memorial Prize for the
most promising novel of the year (although according to Catherine
Stott's interview with Carter for the '*Guardian* Woman' page in 1972, 'all it
meant, she said, was £100 and something useful for later dust-jackets'[1]).
Given that *The Magic Toyshop* is probably the most widely-read of her
early works, it is surprising that a greater number of detailed critical
analyses of it have not been published. Of the three major anthologies of
essays on Carter's work now in print, only one includes an essay specifically on this text: Jean Wyatt's 'The Violence of Gendering: Castration
Images in Angela Carter's *The Magic Toyshop*, *The Passion of New Eve*, and
"Peter and the Wolf"', which will be discussed later in this chapter. *The
Magic Toyshop* does make an inevitable appearance in surveys of Carter's
career, however, where it tends to be viewed as the novel in which Carter
began explicitly to voice the themes and narrative techniques that were
to become her trademark. What these were, exactly, is highlighted in an
interview with Olga Kenyon:

■ *K:* ... The novel of yours which first made its name is *The Magic
Toyshop* which was published in 1967. You take a fairly simple story
and put your pubescent heroine through baroque events.

C: I usually put my adolescent heroines through the mangle. She's a
bourgeois virgin, a good screamer, like the Hammer films I enjoyed as
a child.

K: And she's a woman in peril, like the heroines of all good gothic
novels.

C: She's quite silly and overprivileged, there seems no reason she
shouldn't find out about real life.

K: You don't seem to feel any special fondness for your characters?

C: I start from the basic premiss that fiction is fiction. I specialised in medieval literature [at Bristol University], which gave me enormous delight. I now realise that certain kinds of medieval and fabulous narrative are close to folktales which attract me – some of which I weave into *The Magic Toyshop*.[2] □

The themes that come out of this exchange with regard to *The Magic Toyshop* are a problematic interest in female victimisation – Melanie, the heroine, is 'a good screamer' – and intertextuality, which is the process whereby new texts are created through the reworking of older ones. Paulina Palmer's article 'From "Coded Mannequin" to Bird Woman: Angela Carter's Magic Flight', a pioneering survey of Carter's work up to 1984, analyses both these aspects of the text:

■ *The Magic Toyshop* is a text of particular interest to the feminist reader. It illustrates Carter's skilful use of the device of intertextuality to analyse femininity and female subordination as cultural constructs. In it, she reworks episodes and motifs from not just one text but three. These are the biblical story of the Garden of Eden, E.T.A. Hoffmann's tale *The Sandman* and Freud's account of the psychic structures relating to the family unit (the primal scene, the Oedipal configuration and the castration myth). Thus her novel becomes, in the words of Barthes, 'a multi-dimensional space in which a variety of writings, none of them original, blend and clash'.[3] The deliberately subversive reworking of the three texts which she achieves accords with the deconstructive approach to fiction which she endorses in the essay 'Notes from the Front Line'; here, she concludes that:

> reading is just as creative an activity as writing and most intellectual development depends upon new readings of old texts. I am all for putting new wine in old bottles, especially if the pressure of the new wine makes the old bottles explode.[4]

Carter's reworking of the three texts mentioned above highlights the part played by myth and culture in the construction of the subject. Culture, she suggests, assumes primacy over subjectivity. The hero Melanie finds herself trapped, against her will, in conventional family roles and structures. While in bed with her lover Finn, with her little sister Victoria playing in the room, she has a sudden disquieting sense that she and Finn 'might have been married for years and Victoria their baby' (p. 177).[5] Involuntarily, she finds herself slotted into the roles of wife and mother. In a similar manner Finn, occupying the place usually taken by Uncle Philip at the breakfast table, is greeted by Victoria as 'Daddy' (p. 183). In rebelling against his uncle's authority, he discovers himself usurping his position. Throughout the narrative, images of mutilation and castration (Melanie's fantasy of the severed hand, and Finn's bee-stung eye) advertise to the reader the elements of violence at the heart of the patriarchal family unit. They also highlight the violent nature of the myths which perpetuate its existence.

Carter's reworking of all three texts is skilfully contrived. However, it is her reinterpretation of motifs from Hoffmann's tale *The Sandman*[6] that deconstructs the patriarchal social hierarchy most effectively. Freud, in his psychoanalytic analysis of the tale, foregrounds male experience. He interprets it as symbolic of male fears of castration and marginalizes the motif of the female puppet Olympia.[7] Carter, on the contrary, makes the puppet central. She treats the relations between puppet-master and puppet as symbolic of the control exerted by a patriarchal culture on women and the roles available to them. The roles to which Melanie is introduced, in her uncle's toy theatre or in other episodes of the novel, include wood-nymph, bride or victim of rape. In representing them, Carter pinpoints the ambiguities in woman's position. She foregrounds the contradiction between the romantic images of femininity reproduced in culture and art, and the facts of sexual violence. She also creates a lively interplay between art and nature, theatrical representation and 'real life' in typical 'magical mannerist' fashion.[8]

Another subversive feature discernible in Carter's reworking of motifs from Hoffmann is the way she allows certain cracks and fissures to become visible in patriarchal structures and roles. Her treatment of the motif of the *double* is notably ambiguous. On the one hand, it advertises the apparently immutable nature of patriarchal roles, by illustrating the primacy which culture and myth exert over subjectivity. On several occasions in the novel, the artificial double is presented as equalling in importance or even claiming precedence over the real-life original. The portrait of the bull terrier, Melanie thinks, stands guard over the house while the actual dog is absent (p. 60). And Uncle Philip tends to prefer the company of his puppets, which are obedient to his will, to his flesh and blood relatives who challenge it (pp. 132, 167). On the other hand, the motif simultaneously carries opposite implications, evoking ideas of liberation and change. Carter's introduction of it suggests the concept of the split subject. This challenges the notion of unified character, pointing to the existence of multiple identities and the possibility of change they contain.[9]

Carter's treatment of the motif of the *eye*, another one she inherits from Hoffmann, is similarly ambiguous in meaning. Her description of the peephole which Finn constructs in the wall of his room in order to spy on Melanie while she is undressing, introduces the theme of voyeurism. It draws attention to the power exerted by the male gaze. The gaze is a practical means for men to impose control on women, as well as a symbol of sexual domination.[10] However, the fact that Melanie responds with indignation to the intrusion on her privacy and retaliates by using the peephole to spy on Finn back (p. 109), complicates the meaning of the image. On peering in it, she catches sight of him walking on his hands. This results in a momentary instance of role-reversal. She becomes the observer and he the observed. She represents the norm while he, in his odd position, becomes the freak and 'spectacle'. These are roles which, in a patriarchal society, are generally reserved for women. Thus, in her treatment of both motifs Carter indirectly reveals that, despite appearances to the contrary, the roles adopted by men and women are, in fact, flexible. They are open to change.

Carter's analysis of the roles allocated to woman in the family unit, discussed above, is accompanied by the problematisation both of relations between the sexes and of heterosexual sexual practice. Probing beneath the ideology of romantic love and familial affection, she discloses the contradictions which exist in these relations. She also reveals the element of violence in male-defined models of sexual pleasure. The connection between sex and violence is a theme which confronts writers of fiction with notable difficulties, and Carter's treatment of it is by no means free from ambiguity. It raises questions of vital concern to feminist readers and writers. Is it possible to represent a female protagonist as a victim of sexual harassment or violence while, as the same time, portraying her as an autonomous individual? Can a writer represent a male protagonist as perpetrating acts of violence without either glamorising him or depicting him as an inhuman monster? What is the distinction between representations of violent sex which constitute a serious inquiry into the topic, and ones which have to be classed as pornographic?[11] □

The Magic Toyshop is, as Palmer says, 'of interest to the feminist reader'; but it is not, as the rhetorical questions with which this extract closes demonstrate, a text in which feminist ideologies are unproblematically endorsed. As will be discussed in later chapters, this becomes an area of controversy in Carter's work, with critical opinion split between those who believe Carter falls into some kind of salacious trap, and those who read her portrayal of male/female relationships as ironic and deconstructive.

In *Feminist Readings/Feminists Reading*, Sara Mills, Lynne Pearce, Sue Spaull and Elaine Millard offer an interpretation of *The Magic Toyshop* which has been heavily influenced by Palmer's essay. However, their analysis lacks much of Palmer's interrogative stance, delivering a more simplistic view of the novel as a cautionary feminist fable about the horrors of patriarchy.

■ [Melanie's] quest for self-definition is at the centre of the novel. Yet that quest is strictly limited by the roles and potential assigned to her by her cultural heritage, her socialisation and the overbearingly patriarchal world she inhabits. Looking into the mirror, the images she sees are those previously inscribed there by male authors, painters and women's magazine writers. The boundaries of Melanie's adolescent imaginings are thus marked by thoughts of her future roles as lover, wife and mother.

Immediately she enters the confines of her uncle's house, Melanie's loss of autonomy becomes apparent. Recognising her powerlessness, she feels herself to be like one of her uncle's puppets [...]. Her feelings of powerlessness intensify, in relation to both her Uncle Philip and her cousin Finn. She no longer has a mirror in which to see herself, a further factor contributing to her loss of subjectivity. 'She was seized with panic, remembering that she had not seen her own face for so long' (p. 103).[12] Control of her identity is taken over by Finn and Uncle Philip. She begins to see herself as she is seen by others. Discovering the spy-hole into her room from Finn's, she realises that 'all the time, someone was watching her' (p. 109). Later, she sees the picture Finn has painted of her through the spy-hole, undressing: an image of an idealised, pale, pure virginal girl, which is how he sees her and 'not precisely as she saw herself' (p. 154). She recognizes herself, uncannily, in one of her uncle's toys on her first day in the shop: '... a sylphide in a fountain of white tulle. She had long, black hair down to the waist of her tight bodice' (p. 67). Finally, she must literally fit the image Uncle Philip has of her, forced to take part in one of his puppet shows alongside his puppets. He complains: '"I wanted my Leda to be a little girl. Your tits are too big"' (p. 143). Melanie is thus denied her own sexuality. She must take on the role of angel – passive and virginal.[13] □

According to this argument, Melanie's role is principally that of functioning as the 'object of exchange'[14] between Uncle Philip and Finn, a tug-of-war over which she has no control. The ending of the novel signals the resolution of this conflict between the two men, but only confirms Melanie's powerlessness as she

■ gradually resigns herself to the prospect of sex and marriage with Finn: she accepts the roles of lover, wife and mother assigned her by society. Melanie's enclosure within patriarchal structures is thus complete, and Finn has finally 'won' her from his Uncle Philip. In Carter's vision of this patriarchal nightmare world, it would appear that there is no escape.[15] □

Melanie, therefore, serves no liberatory purpose at all: she exists in the text only to enact the role of submissive female. However, the authors of this discussion allocate a potentially more redemptive role to Melanie's Aunt Margaret, whose dumbness is interpreted as a covert act of rebellion and anger. For although Margaret's silence appears to confirm her as another victim, they argue that

■ Margaret's silence represents more than her submission to patriarchal authority. It is in Margaret that we should perhaps identify Carter's 'double', her 'covert authorial rage'. Like Bertha, the madwoman in the attic in *Jane Eyre*, it is Margaret who finally challenges the patriarchal order depicted in the novel. And, like Bertha, it is Margaret who is responsible for the fire which destroys the toy shop in the closing scene. Just as in Susan Gubar's analysis of [Isak] Dinesen's story 'The Blank Page', blankness was shown as 'an act of defiance',[16] so Margaret's silence hides her secret and her ultimate defiance of Philip's authority.[17] □

Palmer's analysis of *The Magic Toyshop* appeared in 1987: Mills, Pearce, Spaull and Millard published theirs in 1989. However, reading the criticism of the novel published through the 1990s, one is struck by a change of mood, for the majority of the text's critics are happy to rationalise its treatment of Melanie and the other female characters. Uncle Philip is regarded as a character too grotesque ever to be taken seriously, and Finn becomes Melanie's comrade in oppression, demonstrating – in true postfeminist fashion – that men as well as women are patriarchy's victims. Lorna Sage's treatment of *The Magic Toyshop*, for example, glosses over the provocative questions raised by Palmer's analysis in order to paint a picture of a book which is an idiosyncratically charming adaptation of fairy tale.

■ *The Magic Toyshop* simplifies things wonderfully. It is deservedly the most popular of the early novels, a classic rite-of-passage book which contrives to orphan its heroine Melanie twice over, once from her middle-class 'real' family, and a second time from her ogre uncle, Philip Flower. He is a parody-patriarch who rules over the same sort of shadow world that ate up Ghislaine, Honey, and Morris in Carter's first book, and adolescent Melanie finds herself in his power as a result of stepping over the boundary between reality and fantasy. One moonlit night she tries on her mother's wedding-dress and – as if by horrible sympathetic magic – her parents are killed in a plane crash on the other side of the Atlantic.

This 'wedding-dress night, when she married the shadows' (p. 77),[18] exiles her and her younger brother and sister from their comfortable, liberal, middle-class home in the country, to live in a dark, narrow house above Uncle Philip's toyshop in south London. They exchange prosperity for poverty, country for city, and indulgent present for the authoritarian past, and – most important – a world of common-sense realism for one which works according to the laws of dreams, fairy-tales, folktales, myth, and magic. Aunt Margaret, they are told, was struck dumb on the day she married Uncle Philip; she and her two brothers, Francie and Finn Jowle, were orphans themselves, and are unwilling Irish captives in the toyshop. Uncle Philip has made images of them as toy monkeys, they are in his power, and now Melanie, Jonathan, and Victoria join them in this house where there are no mirrors and no books, *because it is the world you find in books and mirrors*, the regions of copies and images and representations.

So humans, animals and toys inhabit the same dimension in this text. Uncle Philip specializes in kitsch artefacts which deliberately insult both 'life' and 'art' by mixing up the two, like the scary jack-in-the-box he once sent Melanie – 'a grotesque caricature of her own face leered from the head that leapt out at her' (p. 12) – or the toyshop cuckoo clock which houses 'a real cuckoo, stuffed, with the sounding mechanism trapped, somehow, in its feathered breast' (p. 60). Melanie feels 'withered and diminished' when she contemplates the cuckoo, a very mild foretaste of her humiliation and terror when Uncle Philip recruits her to play the part of Leda and be 'raped' by his huge puppet swan. In 'Flower's Puppet Microcosm' flesh and wood, images and originals, share a sinister equality: '"He's pulled our strings"', says Finn (p. 152). All the same, this cruel factory of simulacra is where you find yourself.

Plunged into want and fear and dirt and dreams, Melanie avoids the bright bourgeois future that was in store for her, and is initiated into the uses of magic. She might, we're told, have grown up to be like the silly 'expensive woman' who comes into the shop looking for '"something little and gay"' – 'the sort of woman who used to come for the weekend at home … with a suitcase full of little black dresses for cocktails and dinner' (pp. 95–6). Instead, she is drawn into the Jowles' occult rebellion, conducted through music, images and incest. She learns to dream prophetically. She rescues her brother Jonathan from the fire that consumes the shop by dreaming him in advance into the scenery of Uncle Philip's stage, 'the painted water … swirled and splashed … . The ship was ready to sail away' (p. 176). And she herself survives to start the world with smelly and sensuous Finn – both of them subject to a sudden vertigo and uncertainty now that the old man has been dethroned.[19] □

Such a summary of the book makes it seem fairly unthreatening and straightforward. However, a far more detailed analysis of *The Magic Toyshop*'s portrayal of patriarchal oppression was published by Jean Wyatt in 1996, in which she uses psychoanalytical theory in order to argue that Carter creates a picture of female acculturation into patriarchy which is perturbing in its viciousness:

■ The violence of gendering is usually masked by the dynamic of love that produces it: according to the feminist theorists cited by Nancy Chodorow, a father 'bribes' his daughter with 'love and tenderness' when she exhibits the passive feminine behaviours that please him and so gradually trains her to derive self-esteem from his praise rather than from her own actions – to become, in the familiar phrase, the apple of his eye, the submissive object of his affection.[20] The idealisation of the father as powerful subject in relation to a passive and independent self 'becomes the basis for future relationships of ideal love, the submission to a powerful other who seems to embody the agency and desire one lacks in oneself'.[21] By stripping the oedipal conversion from subject to object of compensatory fatherly affection and condensing a process of adaptation that usually takes years into the space of a single scene, Carter dramatises the violence of the father–daughter relations which force the identity of passive object on a girl – a violence already implicit, if unexplored, in [Simone] de Beauvoir's description of a daughter's normal oedipal resolution: 'It is a full abdication of the subject, consenting to become object in submission [to the father]'.[22]

The oedipal stage which transforms an active girl into a passive object is always governed by the deeds of a male-dominant social order;[23] but the social dimension is usually hidden by the family's enclosure within a seemingly private space. Carter emphasises that the closed space of the family doubles as cultural space by superimposing the myth of Leda and the Swan on Melanie's oedipal initiation. At a founding movement of Western civilisation – for the rape of Leda engendered Helen, hence the Trojan War, hence the master epic of the Western tradition, Homer's *Iliad* – as in every girl's oedipal experience, Carter implies, woman's subjectivity is erased as she is inserted into the patriarchal order. As the exaggerated conventionality of his patriarchal traits suggests, Philip's puppet workshop represents more than a family business: it doubles as a cultural site where the myths that sustain patriarchy are fabricated. (Philip's other puppet plays also dramatise a particular idea of womanhood: in 'The Death of the Wood-Nymph', for instance, his chiffon-draped ballerina puppet is exquisitely graceful and then in death, exquisitely graceful, silent and quiescent.)[24]

If Philip's imagination is crude, incapable of reaching beyond the terms of brute power, so, Carter implies, is the patriarchal imaginary.

Rape is a basic trope of our Western cultural heritage: by Amy Richlin's count, Leda's is one of fifty rapes in Ovid's *Metamorphoses* alone.[25] And Yeats's modernist update of 'Leda and the Swan' manages to celebrate rape as an act of power and beauty by eliding, again, the woman as subject. Leda is reduced to a body part, her sensations of pain and feelings of violation dead-ended in a synecdoche [a form of figurative language, when a part of something is used to signify the whole]: 'How can those terrified vague fingers push/The feathered glory from her loosening thighs?' Carter's clumsy swan is a joke on patriarchal mythmakers who dress up the principle of male domination in grandiose poetry – but it is a serious joke. Yeats mystifies rape as a moment of divine transcendence ('Did she put on his knowledge with his power?'); Carter shows it to be an act of brute force.[26] □

This is uncomfortable stuff: however, Wyatt ultimately affirms the text's allegiance to a revitalising utopian vision, in which Carter's heroine is permitted to escape patriarchal structures and enter a world of gender equality. While Uncle Philip's power goes up in smoke, his apprentice Finn remains; representative of a maleness which does not define itself through the domination of others.

■ *The Magic Toyshop* offers an alternative as well as a critique of patriarchal sexual relations. Melanie forms a romantic alliance with Finn, her counterpart in age, status, and subordination to the father – her 'brother', in a word, in this family structure. Choosing the more egalitarian structure of the brother–sister bond defeats the aim of the father–daughter relation, which is meant to shape female desire to the passive responsiveness that sustains male dominance. It is not that Melanie suddenly changes from the impressionable girl that I have been describing into an autonomous and self-defining heroine; rather, it is Finn who makes the revolutionary gesture of forfeiting the privileges of masculinity, opening up the possibility of a different relationship between man and woman.

During the night following the play, Finn comes to Melanie's bedside asking for comfort. He has destroyed the puppet swan, he says, and he is trembling with shock at his own audacity and with fear at the terrible vengeance that awaits him – for Philip loves all his puppets inordinately, especially the newly-created swan. Finn describes chopping up the swan and carrying the pieces to a park nearby to bury:

'First of all, I dismembered [the swan] ... with Maggie's little axe ... the swan's neck refused to be chopped up; the axe bounced off it. It kept sticking itself out of my raincoat when I buttoned it up to hide it and it kept peering around while I was carrying it, along with all the bits of the swan ... It must have looked, to a passer-by, as if I was indecently exposing myself, when the swan's neck stuck out. I was embarrassed with myself and kept feeling to see if my fly was done up ... it seemed best ... to bury it in the pleasure garden.' (pp. 171–3)[27]

It is from his own body that the false 'phallus' pokes out, so in chopping it off Finn refuses the masquerade of masculinity: he acknowledges his own castration. In the family structure, Finn is in the position of son to Philip, 'apprenticed' to him ostensibly to learn the art of toymaking, but implicitly to learn the art of male dominance. 'He is a master', says Finn, referring to Philip's skills as dollmaker; but in the field of gender relations as in woodcraft Finn is meant to identify with the father figure, become 'master' in relation to woman. (Before the play, for instance, Philip sent Finn to 'rehearse' Melanie in the role of Leda – in other words, to play the part of the rapist swan; Finn initially complied, but bolted in the middle of the act.) Severing and throwing away the paternal symbol is equivalent to refusing the phallic function. In Lacan's terms, Finn acknowledges the lack that is everyone's inevitable lot. He presents himself at Melanie's bedside as castrated – that is, as incomplete, insecure, in need of comfort: 'Sick and sorry, he came creeping to her bed ... "Melanie ... can I come in with you for a little while? I feel terrible"' (p. 170). Finn not only derails the family agenda; by rejecting 'the affirmation central to our present symbolic order that the exemplary male is adequate to the paternal function'[28] Finn subverts the power relations of patriarchy.

A remark dropped during an interview suggests what Carter was up to when she staged this male castration:

'But you see, one of the things I love about Charlotte Brontë, about Jane Eyre, is that she won't look at Rochester until she's castrated him ... [Then] she's very nice to him, she can afford to be, this is where she can start behaving like a human being. Actually, in Freudian terms (not Freudian, Freud would be terribly upset) what she's done is to get him on an egalitarian and reciprocal basis, because in fact she hasn't castrated him at all, she's got rid of his troublesome *machismo*.'[29]

Carter's nod to Freud's discomfurture [sic] suggests that she is aware of the revolutionary potential of shifting castration from woman to man. Freud would be 'terribly upset' because he inscribed his notion of gendered power relations across the genitals, with the active penis representing the triumphant male subject and the corresponding blank representing a necessarily passive female space. Fixing the sign of castration on the male body, dispensing with a 'troublesome *machismo*', with the aspiration to invulnerable masculinity – with the phallus, not the penis – would shift the balance of power to which Freud subscribed, opening the way for an 'egalitarian and reciprocal' relation between man and woman.

Indeed, Melanie responds to Finn's display of neediness with a new set of responses:

> He must have been through a great ordeal … . 'I have been in that place, too,' she thought. She could have cried for them both … . 'You must have had a time of it, poor Finn.' She felt that somehow their experience ran parallel. She understood his frenzy. 'Poor Finn.' (pp. 172–3)

Finn's refusal to disavow castration has started a general collapse of the fortifications that defend the system of sexual difference. Melanie's recognition that she and Finn are alike undermines gender hierarchy. A founding principle of the sex/gender system, Gayle Rubin shows, is 'the idea that men and women are mutually exclusive categories'; that social fiction contradicts 'nature', where 'men and women are closer to each other than either is to anything else – for instance, mountains, kangaroos, or coconut palms … Far from being an expression of natural differences, exclusive gender identity is the suppression of natural similarities'.[30] Jessica Benjamin, analysing the principles governing erotic dominance in 'The Story of O', finds that each act of the master 'signifies the male pronouncement of difference over sameness'.[31] Absolute mastery depends on absolute differentiation from the subjugated woman, especially on a denial of mutual dependency. In less extreme cases of male dominance as well, a man's fear of being demoted to the feminine position safeguards the system of sexual difference from an admission of similarity. 'Psychological domination is ultimately the failure to recognise the other person as like, although separate from oneself.'[32]

Finn is released from the fear that he will be reduced to similarity, he is already there. And Finn's renunciation of all claim to phallic sufficiency necessarily releases Melanie from the task of patriarchy's good woman – seeing and desiring a man 'only through the mediation of images of an unimpaired masculinity'.[33] The dangers to gender hierarchy of admitting resemblance are immediately clear, as Melanie moves from empathy to a geometry of equality: 'their experience ran parallel' (p. 173). The image of lives lived along parallel lines implies the replacement of hierarchy by a lateral relationship, 'egalitarian and reciprocal'.[34] □

Wyatt's conclusion is echoed by Aidan Day, who similarly regards Finn as representing 'Carter's persistent interest in the way in which men as well as women may be negatively affected by patriarchy and seek to resist it'.[35] Uncle Philip, he argues, 'is almost a caricature of the patriarch',[36] whose all-encompassing authority also makes him the personification of imperialist power.

■ It is possible to see Melanie and Finn, when they escape from the burning house, as examples of a different kind of human being – a kind where relationship is defined not in terms of oppression and subservience but in terms of equality. They have passed through an initiation rite into adulthood of a different kind to normal. They can mature in a new world because they have both resisted and thrown off the sexist oppressiveness of the old. In a 1992 interview Carter observed that 'The shop in *The Magic Toyshop* gets burnt down, the old dark house, and adult life begins'.[37] Throughout *The Magic Toyshop* there have been allusions to the biblical fable of the Garden of Eden, and the fall of humankind and its expulsion from Eden. When, at the very end of the novel, Melanie and Finn stand ready to leave the garden – the metaphoric garden – of a neighbour's house, they are not about to leave as the sinful children of a wrathful, patriarchal God. The mythology of sin has been purged. The fire in Uncle Philip's old house has consumed him, leaving the young adults free on the threshold of a world that will not be constrained by an archaic mythology. The toyshop was not divinely ordained. Neither was it magic. It was – like Uncle Philip's swan, which Melanie at one point described as 'a ludicrous thing' (p. 174)[38] – a ludicrous *representation* of the way things are, not the essence of the way things are. In adulthood, Melanie as a woman is not to be treated as a child. The fire, not unlike Emily's burning of Honeybuzzard's possessions in *Shadow Dance*, has purged both Uncle Philip and the childhood – represented by Melanie's toy bear – that he ruled over.

> A floor caved in inside the house with a gush of fire. All burning, everything burning, toys and puppets and masks and chairs and tables and carpets ... Edward bear burning, with her pyjamas in his stomach.
> 'All my paintings,' said Finn faintly. 'Such as they were.'
> 'Even Edward Bear,' she said.
> 'What?'
> 'My bear. He's gone. Everything is gone.'
> 'Nothing is left but us.'
> At night, in the garden, they faced each other in a wild surmise.
> (p. 200)

That wild surmise – that wild imagining of a new future – alludes to Keats's picture, in 'On First Looking into Chapman's Homer' (1816), of the sixteenth-century Spaniards' first sight of the Pacific Ocean. Carter's imagination seems to have been caught by Keats's poetic evocation of the glimpsing of a new world, a new order of being:

> Then felt I like some watcher of the skies
> When a new planet swims into his ken;
> Or like stout Cortez when with eagle eyes
> He stared at the Pacific, and all his men
> Looked at each other with a wild surmise –
> Silent, upon a peak in Darien. (ll. 9–14[39])[40] □

An alternative perspective on the undeniably ambiguous conclusion of *The Magic Toyshop* is provided by Linden Peach, who does not read its ending quite so positively as Day. Peach's discussion is focused less on Carter's depiction of male oppression, and more on the novel's intertextual elements. He is particularly concerned with Carter's adaptation of fairy tale motifs, which, he argues, anticipates *The Bloody Chamber* collection of stories.

■ Although *The Magic Toyshop* is not a fairy tale as such [...] it reclaims a number of elements from the genre. The word 'reclaim' is used deliberately here, for the fairy tale has been marginalised as a literary form, relegated to the non-serious world of children's fiction. In *The Magic Toyshop*, Carter rediscovers its imaginative potential, especially for the feminist writer. The storyline of the novel itself is reminiscent of a fairy story. Its heroine Melanie, her brother Jonathan and sister Victoria are orphaned; the death of their parents in a plane crash is linked in Melanie's mind to an act of transgression – Melanie secretly trying on her mother's wedding dress one night – and the children are forced to live with a relative they hardly know who turns out to be an ogre. The stock fairy tale motifs adapted by Carter include: the arduous journey – the children travel from their comfortable home in the country to their uncle's toyshop in south London; the dumb mute – their aunt in London has been struck dumb on her wedding day; metamorphoses – Uncle Philip's evil is revealed gradually in the course of the narrative; and even the winged creature – in the form of the swan puppet which Philip makes for the show in which Melanie takes part. [...]

[The novel] anticipates how in her later collection, *The Bloody Chamber and Other Stories*, Carter adapted the form to criticise the inscribed ideology and to incorporate new assumptions. The novel incorporates the reactionary element of the fairy story in the consequences which befall Melanie borrowing her mother's wedding dress.

However, it also undermines this inscribed ideology by emphasising what the misogynistic fairy stories suppressed, an adolescent girl's excitement about her body and the discovery of her emerging sexuality.[41] □

Peach's allusions to the novel's intertextual referents comprise an important element of his remarks regarding the novel's conclusion. He, too, picks up on the Garden of Eden allusions, but is less inclined than Day to read a utopian future into them.

■ At the end of the novel, Melanie and Finn escape from the toyshop, like Adam and Eve from the Garden of Eden, returning the reader to the biblical myth which is employed in the earlier description of Melanie's sexual awakening. In fact, Carter herself has said that she saw the novel in terms of the 'Fortunate Fall': 'I took the Fortunate Fall as meaning that it was a good thing to get out of that place. The intention was that the toyshop itself should be a secularised Eden'.[42] The 'Fortunate Fall' is not only from the toyshop but the cultural myths which have contributed to women's intellectual, emotional and sexual oppression.

The theme of a new Eden and the human race reduced to an elemental pair was common in science fiction of the 1950s and 1960s. Carter's adaptation of it is ambiguous and possibly influenced by the art of the time, especially collage work that suggested that desire, as Thomas Crow (1996) maintains, is 'held hostage' by the Adam and Eve myth.[43] In Richard Hamilton's collage, *Just what is it that makes today's homes so different, so appealing?* (1956), for example, Charles Atlas, the model body-builder of comic-book back pages is the naked Adam and the pulp pin-up is Eve. In Hamilton's collaborative contribution, the same year, to the installation art exhibition, *This is Tomorrow*, the primal male is the robot from *Forbidden Planet* who holds a Jane-like figure in his arms. Next to him is Marilyn Monroe in a still from the pavement grating scene in Billy Wilder's film, *The Seven Year Itch* (1955). The latter, in which a married man has a fling with the girl upstairs, suggests through a series of dream sequences that desire is structured by the dominant fictions in society. At the end of *The Magic Toyshop*, Carter appears to imply, as she said, that the Fall was fortunate, but also that Melanie and Finn are trapped by the Genesis myth. It is ironic that in the fire 'everything is gone' but that the myth remains.[44] □

One of the most recent studies of *The Magic Toyshop*, however, eliminates any sense of ambivalence from its analysis, and the result is a reading reminiscent of the feminist interpretations published in the 1980s. In her book *Contemporary Women's Fiction and the Fantastic*, Lucie Armitt analyses the novel as an example of a modern Gothic text open to psychoanalytical interpretation. A particularly important source for her in this regard is Freud, and both his essay 'The Uncanny' and the narratives surrounding his most famous patient, Dora,[45] crucially inform Armitt's view of the novel, which displays little of the tolerance towards its male protagonists evident in most recent criticism.

■ Dora's so-called hysteria is brought on by a complex set of inter-familial relations in which taboos are breached by more than one party, but always from behind a veneer of social respectability. In *The Magic Toyshop* the same paradigms are followed. Three potentially nuclear families interconnect and, in the process, interrupt their respective nuclear orientations. The first family comprises Melanie, Jonathan, Victoria and their parents, the second Uncle Philip and Aunt Margaret, and the third Margaret, Francie and Finn. This structure sets up Uncle Philip as the totemic father to an extended tribal network, who will be dispatched at the end of the text to enable Finn and Francie to take possession of the women they desire.[46] □

As this extract reveals, Armitt reinstates Melanie as the hapless object of patriarchal competition – Uncle Philip's authority is frighteningly absolute, and it will be perpetuated, not eliminated, by the younger male inhabitants of the house. While in the work of critics such as Wyatt and Sage, Finn, in particular, is portrayed as an incipient New Man who functions as Melanie's equal in subordination, here he is Uncle Philip's successor – a role which Armitt argues is apparent from his first appearance in the text:

■ The dialogue in the taxi between Finn and Melanie, though terse, is important. Watching the fare mount, shilling by shilling, and already starting to feel her throat and nostrils constrict against the smell of Finn and Francie's unwashed flesh, Melanie asks a seemingly literal question: '"Is it very far, still?" ... "Still farther," said Finn abstractedly ... "Still farther," he repeated. "It is beginning to get dark," she said, for the light drained from the streets ... "And will get darker," responded Finn' (pp. 36–7).[47] The first element of the conversation implies that what Melanie reads as a literal journey, Finn knows to be symbolic too. He has, of course, taken this road himself, accompanying Margaret and Francie just as these three children travel together, and again, their own orphan status is inferred to be one motivation behind the change. Two inferences cohere in Finn's choice of the words 'still farther'. The first is that he still has a way to go before his own 'journey' with regard to the toyshop is complete and, in these early words, we hear the goal for which he aims: the supplanting of Uncle

Philip, 'still father' to the household. Reading closely, we realize that once in the toyshop Finn immediately starts to put his plan into action, for it is he, not Philip, who imposes a strict dress code upon Melanie, even though he purportedly does so on behalf of another patriarch: 'No, you can't wear them! ... He can't abide a woman in trousers ... No make-up, mind. And only speak when you're spoken to. He likes, you know, silent women' (pp. 62–3). Nor should we miss the fact that the minute he verifies Melanie's identity at the railway station, the first words he speaks to her are 'Let me take the child off you' (p. 35). Uncle Philip is not the only businessman on the premises, and, despite his squint, Finn has a keen eye for a bargain and a keener one for profligacy: '"A whole pound went on chocolate?" "And magazines ... One called *Sea Breezes* for Jonathan and the *Beano* annual for Victoria ... " "Nevertheless, it is a lot", he said' (pp. 35–6).

Though the toyshop is a far cry from the aristocratic gothic mansion, being 'a dark cavern ... so dimly lit one did not at first notice it', situated next to 'a failed, boarded-up jeweller's' (p. 39) [...] the interior is gothic in its most conventional sense. Resistant to intruders, including customers (which raises the obvious question of what, exactly, is 'for sale' and to whom), Finn has to push hard against the resistance of the door as, in the second important threshold moment of the text, it 'momentarily' refuses to open and allow them in. Once across the threshold all will change for Melanie, as her role of interloper in this female gothic text situates her indoors and thus controlled by the presence of a more powerful, sexualised masculine figure.[48] □

However, Armitt's subsequent statement that 'the triangular power dynamics in *The Magic Toyshop* always revolve around the still centre of Uncle Philip as he fights Melanie's father for possession of Melanie's mother, Finn for possession of Melanie and Francie for possession of Aunt Margaret' widens the arena of conflict still further.[49] Whereas the triangle formed by Uncle Philip, Finn and Melanie is a fairly obvious one, Armitt argues that the novel contains a tangle of incestuous desires which involves all the female members of the family, be they living or dead:

■ Underlying what proves to be the revelation of the secret of Francie and Margaret's incestuous relationship is a matching desire that never finds full, uncloseted articulation. This is the latent incestuous fascination felt by Uncle Philip for Melanie's mother, which erupts on several occasions as an example of trans-generational haunting, concretised by the omnipresence of the wedding photograph. Standing 'alone' as her mother's 'only living relative' (p. 13), Uncle Philip apparently acts as auctioneer at the sale, but is actually forced to give away the only 'lot' he wishes to keep, one who will become de-'Flowered' in the process.[50] □

As far as Armitt is concerned, the role of women as objects of exchange is not resolved into anything more comforting at the end of the novel:

■ As in the Dora story, then, parental relations and their displacement onto other figures are crucial aspects of the incest motif. But what of Melanie's own Oedipal relations? Fleeing with Finn from the burning toyshop, Melanie recalls her own father's playful nursery song:

Sally go round the stars,
Sally go round the moon,
Sally go round the chimney pot
On a Sunday afternoon.
Wheeeeeeee! (p. 199)

Again, as in Freud's essay, issues of flight are directly related to a choice between 'flying *with*' or 'fleeing from' and involve running from the arms of one father figure into the arms of another. But, as we said from the start, though psychoanalytic relations are crucial here, so are the social circumstances in which they are situated. Melanie has little choice but to fly with Finn because she does so in order to flee Uncle Philip. As Finn and Melanie face each other in the garden, the 'wild surmise' (p. 200) on their faces makes it clear this is no Edenic, utopian escape. All evidence points towards Melanie's life with Finn following the same pattern as the other transactions [in the novel]. Finn and Philip do not just share a phonetic similarity of names, they also share a fascination with women as spectacular commodity. Hence Finn's 'Atlantic-coloured regard' washing over Melanie (p. 34) in Chapter 2, just as Philip will later 'size her up' with his eyes as he casts her in the role of Leda to his swan. Right from day one, Finn controls Melanie's movements and appearance, practising his puppetry skills with one squinty eye always on his own inheritance.[51] □

Although Armitt's interpretation may be more theoretically sophisti-cated, in its basic premise that this is a novel about women's sexual and social subordination, it returns to the arguments aired by Palmer and the authors of *Feminist Readings/Feminists Reading*. And the fact that Carter continued to portray women as currency within a patriarchal economy in her next novel, *Heroes and Villains*, has, as the next chapter will show, initiated similar debates amongst her critics.

CHAPTER THREE

Heroes and Villains (1969)

IN HER 1977 profile of Carter, Lorna Sage says that 'Angela Carter herself dates a turning-point in her career from *Heroes and Villains*: one of the reviewers, she said, observed, while relishing the book, that she wouldn't be winning any more prizes'.[1] Carter identified *Heroes and Villains* as a point of departure for herself in other interviews too. In the same year as her meeting with Sage, she gave an interview to Les Bedford for Sheffield University Television, where she was particularly expansive on the issue of this novel. She professed herself 'very irritated at the Gothic tag' that reviewers had applied to the three books she had previously published, and so decided to show them 'what a Gothic novel really was':

■ I knew it was all owls and ivy and mad passions and Byronic heroes who were probably damned, and I knew I wasn't writing them. Even though some of my heroes were quite emphatically damned, they weren't damned in the Byronic fashion, and that was why, when I set about writing my fourth novel, I very consciously chose the Gothic mode, with owls and ivy and ruins and a breathtakingly Byronic hero.[2] □

However, she also identified *Heroes and Villains* as marking a methodological shift in her work; the point at which she began to move away from 'being charming', and 'consciously trying to seduce, and perhaps attempt to rape my readers', towards a more detached and intellectual approach:

■ I was beginning to regard the work that I was doing as external to myself and in no sense fantasy wish-fulfilment or working through personal problems, personal situations in the form of a novel. I was beginning to perceive text as text, as Barthes would say, and since the work was external to me, it was a place where I could engage with ideas, and with characters – well, with ideas, rather, characterised as characters and as imagery.[3] □

In her essay 'New New World Dreams: Angela Carter and Science Fiction', Roz Kaveney regards this interest in 'text as text' as one of the novel's features which link it to the science-fiction mode. As many critics have observed, for all of Carter's claims for it as an ostentatiously Gothic piece, *Heroes and Villains*, set in a post-holocaust world, is also a futuristic novel. Kaveney describes it as

■ a version of the post-apocalyptic novels of the fifties, in which an older sort of decline-of-civilisation novel which goes back to Mary Shelley's *The Last Man* (1826) or Richard Jefferies's *After London* (1885) is blended with specific fears that it is our own civilisation whose distorted tatters will be handed down among radioactive ruins. The Cold War fifties were a golden age for novels about the aftermath of atomic war and other collapses, both inside and outside the SF [science-fiction] world; one can oversimplify this issue, but English examples tended to be about return to a safer pastoral existence, 'back, beyond our father's land'; while American examples tended to be far more about a continuation of legitimacy – Walter Miller's *A Canticle for Leibowitz* (1960), with its monks making illuminated copies of electronic schematics, is the obvious prototype.

It is almost beside the point whether Carter had actually read much of this material, or absorbed it as the air which one then breathed: *Heroes and Villains* is a book which participates in these debates.[4] □

Kaveney argues that what drew Carter to the genre was its intrinsically postmodern aspects – not 'the hardware of science-fiction and genre fantasy', but 'the freedom it gave its practitioners [...] the freedom to play with causality and to regard character in a way less linked to Leavisite moral fictions or a bourgeois myth of identity which is three-dimensional and self-determined'.[5] Kaveney defines science fiction and genre fantasy as having 'their admirably formalist aspect, where iconic material is shuffled in pleasing patterns, with something new added from time to time as an improving spice', and argues that this coincided with 'the formalist aspects of Carter's work – the extent to which she combined stock motifs and made of them a collage that was entirely her own'[6]

However, Kaveney stops short of categorising Carter as a science-fiction writer, identifying Carter's relationship with the British science-fiction community as simultaneously tangential and influential:

■ Angela Carter was at no time a science-fiction writer, but she wrote several stories for one of the major British science-fiction magazines, and rather regretted never having published in the most important of the others. Angela Carter was not a science-fiction writer, but she was

Guest of Honour at SF conventions and taught writing to a number of young and later influential figures in the SF world. She was one of the crucial influences on a whole generation of British SF writers, yet she was never a writer of science fiction.[7] □

Kaveney's analysis draws attention to the assemblage of influences drawn from science-fiction sources in *Heroes and Villains*: the 'New Wave' fiction of J. G. Ballard, Michael Moorcock and John Sladek combined with the post-apocalyptic surrealist visions of Max Ernst's paintings, Shakespeare's *The Tempest* and Sir Philip Sidney's *Arcadia*.

Critics such as David Punter, however, focus more explicitly on the novel's Gothic elements. In his study of Gothic fiction, *The Literature of Terror*, Punter attempts to 'arrive at some kind of contemporary "land-scape" of Gothic',[8] placing *Heroes and Villains* alongside such books as Isak Dinesen's *Seven Gothic Tales* (1934), Mervyn Peake's *Gormenghast* trilogy (1946–59), J. G. Ballard's *The Atrocity Exhibition* (1970) and Thomas Pynchon's *Gravity's Rainbow* (1973). What makes this novel 'Gothic' for Punter, however, is not owls, ivy, mad passions or Byronic heroes, but its adherence to a heavily ironic form of parody:

■ One of the epigraphs to Carter's *Heroes and Villains* [...] is from Fiedler's *Love and Death in the American Novel*: 'The Gothic mode is essentially a form of parody, a way of assailing clichés by exaggerating them to the limit of grotesqueness.' The opening sentences establish the tone of fake innocence by means of which this particular kind of parody is to be achieved:

Marianne had sharp, cold eyes and she was spiteful but her father loved her. He was a Professor of History; he owned a clock which he wound every morning and kept in the family dining-room upon a sideboard full of heirlooms of stainless steel such as dishes and cutlery. Marianne thought of the clock as her father's pet, some-thing like her own pet rabbit, but the rabbit soon died and was handed over to the Professor of Biology to be eviscerated while the clock continued to tick inscrutably on. She therefore concluded the clock must be immortal but this did not impress her. (p. 1)[9]

The central convention of *Heroes and Villains* is certainly a cliché:[10] a world divided between tribes of new barbarians and the over-intellectualised relics of an effete civilisation, and Marianne's explora-tion of the realm of the barbarians, but it is a convention transcended by the authorial tone. Marianne is no innocent heroine: if she is some-times shocked by the barbarians' worst excesses, this is not because they offend her purity but because they do not conform to her idea of the reasonable. Again, the barbarians are not quite the tough, colour-ful people they first appear, but a motley collection of incompetents and poseurs, admirable more for their reactions to the immense diffi-culties they continually face than for any particular innate heroism.

The scene where Marianne is raped by the barbarian Jewel is typi-cal. She has run away and he pursues her, finding her up a tree; his behaviour is a bizarre blend of half-remembered *politesse* and not wholly convincing violence. Marianne is particularly incensed when, covered in amulets and charms, he points out in a managerial tone that 'we'd have to establish common ground to communicate as equals'. What she is upset by is both the reminder of her educated past envi-ronment and also, it seems, the *lèse-majesté* implied in Jewel's use of civilised forms of address. She springs upon him, but predictably loses the battle:

> Afterwards, there was a good deal of blood. He stared at it with something like wonder and dipped his fingers in it. She stared at him relentlessly; if he had kissed her, she would have bitten out his tongue. However, he recovered his abominable self-possession almost immediately. She began to struggle again but he held her down with one hand, half pulled off his filthy leather jacket and ripped off the sleeve of his shirt, as he had done before when he had treated her snakebite. This repetition of action would have been comic had she been in a mood to appreciate it. He held the rag between her thighs to sop up the bleeding, a bizarre piece of courtesy. (pp. 77–8)

The conflict, here in particular and in the book in general, is a multi-valent parody: of class relations, of relations between the sexes, of the battle between rational control and desire. And it is also a conflict within Marianne herself, but one which only becomes clear progres-sively. She has no conscious aims: indeed, her discourse is half-traumatised, not by her escape into barbarism but rather by the veneer of civilisation which she has acquired earlier. She is impressed by Jewel, but only in a limited way, and it gradually becomes clear why: because she is herself stronger than the barbarians, and has only to realise this to seize power for herself. They may play at being violent but Marianne grows, precisely through her female experiences, through her first-hand knowledge of repression, into a force far more effective than they, more pragmatic and less bound by ritual and superstition. In the end, both male-dominated worlds look like differ-ent aspects of the same nursery.

There are, obviously, no heroes and no villains; only a set of silly games which men play. Thus to call *Heroes and Villains* parodic is not to say that it parodies the real world but rather that it exposes some of the ways in which the real world habitually parodies itself: some of the ways in which people exaggerate their own conflicts, attempt at all costs to construct a distinctive life-style even if it is radically inappropriate to the surroundings. Nor is the fact that Marianne is partially exempt from this process particularly encouraging: what protects her is not insight but psychological blockage. Carter ironically suggests that the Gothic vision is in fact an accurate account of life, of the ways we project our fantasies onto the world and then stand back in horror when we see them come to life.[11] □

Punter's focus on parody in the extract above, however, does not lead him into what has become one of the most focused-on areas of the novel: the extent to which it endorses male violence – and specifically sexual violence – against women. The last chapter mentioned how *The Magic Toyshop* has frequently got off rather lightly on this score, for in spite of the fact that its heroine is extensively victimised to the point of attempted rape, critics have tended to read this as an allegorical critique of patriarchy. One dissenting voice stands out, however: that of Robert Clark, who in 1987 published a highly critical essay on Carter's focus on sexual violence in her work. Clark casts his net wide, condemning most of Carter's fiction for its adherence to

■ liberal late-bourgeois criticism, founded somewhere in the implicit assumption that criticism leads to correction and to a healthier life, but founded so long ago and on such shaky premises, and now so heavily institutionalised that criticism appears a purely abstract virtue. The linkage between criticism and action has been lost.

   The importance of this rupture is that it deprives Carter's work of any way of including within its own critical representation an understanding of the complicity of that representation with the social forces it appears to reject.[12] □

Unlike many other critics, Clark is not prepared to read Carter's writing allegorically. Rape, he argues, 'is a patriarchal topos because even when it is not successful the act signifies the subjection, humiliation and reduction of women': therefore, any writer who wishes to represent rape in their work has to take extreme care to 'unambiguously situate the practice in its wider moral and political history', otherwise they will fall into the trap of 'unwittingly support[ing] masculinist assumptions'. The parodic and highly artificial nature of Carter's writing, however, leads her into a form of 'literary sensationalism'[13] which reduces her readers to the passive role of voyeurs, rather than actively inviting them to critique the patriarchal ideologies which lead to acts of sexual violence. Although

Clark's discussion encompasses several of her novels, as well as the short story 'The Company of Wolves', his analysis of both *The Magic Toyshop* and *Heroes and Villains* is relevant here, because it has provoked such a strong response from other critics:

■ There are innumerable rapes or near rapes in Carter's writing, as there are moments when women are subjected to male power, sometimes turning the tables by discovering the power vested in their own sexuality. Her early Freudian parable *The Magic Toyshop*, for example, centers on the experiences of the adolescent Melanie whose parents are killed in a plane crash and who then goes to live with her Uncle Philip.[14] [...]

The novel establishes an ambiance that becomes typical for Carter, an ambiance of ambiguous attraction and repulsion constituted by Melanie's fascination with Finn's physical grace and animal sensitivity, and repulsion by his malodorous lack of hygiene; by the repressed gentleness of her Aunt Margaret and the ruthless autocracy of the patriarchal Philip. The world of the everyday domestic interior is revealed as a stifling network of repressed emotions, the antidote to which is the escape into a world of all that is illicit, incestuous, pagan, animal, sensuous; in literary terms, a world of the gothic and of the romance. In this antithetical world female sexuality becomes more potent, but whether in one world or the other the threat of rape is constantly enticing.

Carter's next novel, *Heroes and Villains*, is an allegory of the post-holocaust future and of the late-sixties hippy opposition to conventional life. Compounds of Professors, Workers and Soldiers maintain a dull and orderly civilisation in a land otherwise populated by roaming, regressive tribes. The Professor of History kills himself; his daughter, Marianne, elopes with Jewel, the beautiful barbarian, and goes to live with the savages. Before she marries Jewel she is threatened with rape, and like Melanie [in *The Magic Toyshop*] before her and Eve after her she deals with the experience by abstracting herself:

As if his laughter were a signal, the three beside the fire began to move towards her and the man on her left, Johnny, or perhaps it was Jacob, deliberately put his hand beneath the opening of her embroidered shirt and felt her right breast. Firelight shadow monsters galloped along the walls. All gasped and came closer.

They directed her inexorably towards the table. Mrs Green wrung her hands and emitted small mews of distress but she, too, was ambivalent; she would be distressed but also perhaps obscurely satisfied at what would certainly take place. Marianne discovered she was not in the least frightened, only very angry indeed, and began to struggle and shout; at this the brothers laughed but did not cease to crowd in on her. So she closed her eyes and pretended she did not exist.

But this desperate device for self-protection proved unnecessary ...

'They're brave, grant them that,' said the giant. 'It's a well-known fact that Professor women sprout sharp teeth in their private parts to bite off the genitalia of young men.' (p.49)[15]

The usual response of the character to such situations is to abstract mind from body, a willed self-alienation that may imitate actual human behavior, but which effectively means that the victim can offer neither physical nor moral resistance. The individual becomes very like one of those half-animate automata that recur throughout Carter's work and which might be read as displaced symbols of the status of people under capitalism. But this interpretation, although it is one Carter herself has entertained, must be qualified by her warning that such a meaning is unconscious rather than conscious:

> I would like to say that the clockwork prostitute and the puppets are man under capitalism, but it's not consciously been so ... that sort of parodic imitation of life, the closed system, the clockwork prostitute going through the motions and being dependent on someone else for their motive power ... I think if I think about it I may spoil it.[16]

An author's fear that she (or he) might spoil her work by thinking too deeply about it tends in the twentieth century to command a sympathetic response. It signifies a suspicion of analytic reason, and a commitment to the imagination as a way of penetrating mystifications that Reason has in some measure been responsible for perpetrating. Such a credo, central to surrealism and to much of the present cult of the fantastic, is dangerously naïve. Truly dialectical understanding of our cultural predicament can only come out of a cross-questioning of the imaginative and the analytic. Cultivation of the one to deny the other leads only to the production of palimpsests.[17] □

Clark's analysis is, however, somewhat selective, and those who argue against his view of this novel do so by employing a crucial shift in focus. In his brief account of *Heroes and Villains*, as can be seen above, Clark bases his argument on a single incident of *attempted* rape – something which, by the judicious use of ellipses, he rather glosses over. This has the effect of disempowering Marianne twice over. She may indeed be the victim in this scene, but the narrowness of Clark's debate ignores any sense of her as an active protagonist within the text. Critics who disagree with him expand the scope of their analysis to include Carter's depiction of Marianne's own reaction to events, thus formulating a very different view of the role and function of rape in the novel. Paulina Palmer's essay on Carter was published in 1987, the same year as Clark's essay, and therefore she may well not have read it when writing her own analysis of *Heroes and Villains*. Nevertheless, this is a good discussion to set against Clark's, because in it Palmer evokes an echo of his argument. However, she does so only to refute it by placing the violence Marianne suffers in a context which emphasises the power imbalance between her and Jewel – an imbalance which, Palmer argues, is ultimately in Marianne's favour:

■ In *Heroes and Villains* attention is again focused on the social differences between the male and female protagonists. Jewel is a member of a 'barbarian' tribe. He is ill-educated, and prone to irrational fears and fits of violence. Marianne, on the contrary, is the daughter of a professor. She is well-educated, controlled and articulate. However, the social and educational advantages she enjoys are almost entirely cancelled out by the disadvantages of gender. Her relationship with Jewel, whom eventually she marries, is, in terms of power, ambivalent from the start. Finding him lying helpless and wounded after a raid on her home town, she succours him with food. His response is not to show gratitude but to smear her with war-paint and claim her as his hostage. The ideology of male dominance and female submission, Carter implies, is strong enough to obscure the actual facts of the situation. Thus, Marianne discovers, to her surprise, that 'she had wanted to rescue him but found she was accepting his offer to rescue her'.[18] Jewel's treatment of her quickly lapses into physical violence. Having persuaded her to steal a lorry and drive him to freedom, he hits her to make her drive faster. Subsequently, he introduces her into the tribe to which he belongs. When she tries to escape, he follows her to her hiding place in the forest and rapes her.

In making the female heroes of both novels [Palmer is discussing both *The Magic Toyshop* and *Heroes and Villains* here] victims of sexual harassment or rape, Carter encounters certain obvious problems. She runs the risk of depriving the hero of sexual and intellectual autonomy, and reducing her to the state of helpless victim. She also runs the risk of tainting her fiction with the attitudes associated with popular genres which exploit the topic of sex and violence for the purpose of titillation, reproducing the chauvinistic cliché that female pleasure is dependent on submission and victimisation.[19] Carter succeeds in surmounting both these risks. She achieves this by foregrounding the contradiction between the female hero's intellectual autonomy and independent spirit, and her vulnerability to physical attack, one which the male protagonist exploits. Melanie and Marianne are portrayed as courageous and resourceful individuals. They respond to the 'terrible violation of privacy' (p. 90) which the sexual encounters to which they are subjected involve, not with tears or masochistic pleasure but with anger and indignation.

Just as Carter succeeds in crediting her female protagonists with a strong degree of autonomy, so too she manages to make her male protagonists convincingly drawn human beings, without in any way condoning the acts of violence they commit. Her representation of them, trapped in codes of aggression and competition, comes remarkably close to the memorable definition of masculinity coined by Frankie Rickford. Rickford suggests that:

> masculinity may be a state of frozen terror and the urgency of men's sexual desire, a desperation to bury themselves in a warm body to escape from it for a few seconds.[20]

Jewel's acts of violence, for example, appear to be motivated by a determination to dominate Marianne, which is bred of fear. He gives as his reason for the rape the fact that he is 'very frightened' of her (p. 56). He expresses surprise at the discovery that she does not 'sprout sharp teeth in her private parts' (pp. 49, 59), a piece of propaganda promulgated by the tribe to which he belongs (p. 59). Any sign of her vulnerability fills him with pleasure, since he interprets it as proof of his capacity to subjugate her. His triumphant remark, 'I've nailed you on necessity, you poor bitch', (p. 56) when his act of rape forces her into marriage with him, indicates the urgency of the power struggle in which he feels himself to be engaged. Carter's reference to the picture of Eve tempting Adam with a perfidious smile, which he wears tattooed on his back, has the effect of placing this struggle in the context of misogynistic culture. It lifts it from a narrowly personal plane to a political and ideological one.

An important question raised by Carter's treatment of the interrelation between sex and violence in her fiction is: how does one distinguish between a text which constitutes a serious consideration of the topic and one that is an exercise in pornography? The question is complicated by the fact that, as critics have pointed out, the meaning of a visual image or fictional episode is frequently ambiguous. Even though a text generally carries a 'preferred reading',[21] it is, in part, open to the different interpretations which the observer or reader chooses to impose on it. Thus, an episode which one reader may interpret as a serious investigation into the female victim's response to the experience of violent sex, may strike another as pornographic. The austerely functional style of writing in *Heroes and Villains* allows little room for ambiguity. Few readers would be likely to interpret the account of Marianne's rape, in which Carter emphasises the victim's indignation and anger, as in any way titillating.[22] □

Palmer's argument thus promotes a view of the text which sees it as condemnatory of male sexual violence. There is no voyeuristic pleasure to be gained from Carter's depiction of rape because it is portrayed as an act born out of fear and insecurity rather than a sadistic desire for domination, and because the female protagonist refuses to be cowed by it, ultimately gaining ascendancy over the man who threatens her.

A similar approach can be seen in Elizabeth Mahoney's essay on *Heroes and Villains*. Mahoney's argument resembles Palmer's in that it is based on a very similar initial premise: that this is a novel which, in its examination of 'the relations between gender, power and sexual fantasy, undermines conventional codings of feminine sexuality as silent, dependent, passive or masochistic'.[23] Like Palmer, too, she reads the novel alongside *The Magic Toyshop*, which presents similar scenes of near-rape. However, whereas Palmer sees both texts as successfully avoiding the pornographic trap, Mahoney, as the extract quoted below makes clear, regards *The Magic Toyshop* as ultimately compromised through its adherence to 'the realist framework of the *Bildungsroman* [a narrative whose central focus is on the personal development of its main character]'.[24] Both novels, she argues, aim 'to undermine the structures and conventions of representing feminine desire', but whereas '[i]n *The Magic Toyshop*, such structures are uncovered and critiqued ... in *Heroes and Villains*, gendered positions of subject and object are reversed then jettisoned'.[25]

This difference between these two analyses lies in the fact that even while Palmer defends Carter's work against accusations of pornography, the interrogative mode she adopts – which can be seen in the extracts quoted both here and in the previous chapter – indicates her refusal to occlude the problematic elements in the fiction she discusses. She views the early texts as particularly difficult, arguing that, while they present the reader with 'a brilliantly accurate analysis of the oppressive effects of patriarchal structures', they also run the risk 'of making these structures appear even more closed and impenetrable than, in actual fact, they are'.[26] *Heroes and Villains* and *The Magic Toyshop*, therefore, are discussed together as examples of Carter's early novels, and little distinction is made between them in a debate which examines the majority of Carter's writing up to 1984. Mahoney's debate, however, concentrates wholly on *Heroes and Villains* and *The Magic Toyshop*, a narrowing of focus which allows for much more subtle distinctions to be drawn between the two texts. She argues that Carter's choice of the fantastic mode for *Heroes and Villains* allows her 'to represent ... new articulations of desire',[27] and thus empower the fully sexual female subject – it is, as Mahoney rather neatly puts it, 'a fantastic narrative *about* sexual fantasy'.[28]

■ As in *The Magic Toyshop*, issues of fantasy and sexual identity are brought together in *Heroes and Villains* through a rape scene. The threat of rape or state decriminalisation of sexual violence against women is a recurrent trope in the feminist dystopia. It is used as a sign of the extremity of oppression for women in the imagined future and in most texts is only represented implicitly (through details of changes in legislation, for example).[29] Carter, however, risks using this most frightening dystopian 'reality' to expose the misogynistic fantasy behind the act and suggests that because it is a fantasy – narrative – it can be contested and disrupted.

Marianne experiences the threat of rape twice, employing different strategies of resistance in each case. First, while Jewel laughs 'with apparently pure pleasure', his brothers move towards her *en masse*:

> Marianne discovered she was not in the least frightened, only very angry indeed, and began to struggle and shout; at this the brothers laughed but did not cease to crowd in on her. So she closed her eyes and pretended she did not exist. (p.49)[30]

Marianne knows exactly what's happening here and has a strategy for dealing with the prospect of violation, which is in complete contrast to Melanie, pushed to the point of dissolution of her self. Rather than the reader's attention focusing on the erotic fantasy of the violator, such as Uncle Philip in *The Magic Toyshop*, we see only Marianne's anger, her struggle and [...] her refusal to accept the stereotype of the feminine desire upon which their fantasy depends. Her act of self-effacement, a 'desperate device for protection' (p.49), masquerades as ultimate passivity – feminine sexuality as a 'gap' – but is in fact a subversion of the meaning of their fantasy. If she does not see them, 'does not exist', the ontological status of their fantasy changes. Indeed, this resistance is shown to be effective: 'silent, the men fell away from her' (p.49). A few pages later, however, Jewel *does* rape her. Again, the narrative focuses on the woman:

> 'You're nothing but a murderer,' she said, determined to maintain her superior status at all costs.
>
> 'You'll find me the gentlest of assassins,' he replied with too much irony for she did not find him gentle at all.
>
> Feeling between her legs to ascertain the entrance, he thrust his fingers into the wet hold so roughly she knew what the pain would be like; it was scalding, she felt split to the core but she did

not make a single sound for her only strength was her impassivity and she never closed her cold eyes. (p. 55)

The reference here to her cold eyes reminds us of both the power orchestrated by her gaze and that this is *how we see* the narrative. Thus her 'superior status' in the narrative is not questioned: we get her reaction to Jewel's comment and both a physical and emotional response to the violation: 'she felt split to the core'. This representation of the rape of Marianne is obviously quite different from *The Magic Toyshop*, in which any response is either filtered through Melanie's bodily terror [...] or, in fact, *is* the voyeuristic, erotic response of the onlooker [...]. Here Marianne employs a different strategy; she keeps her eyes open and, despite the ritualistic rape taking place, she *is* able to retain 'her strength':

'It was the very worst thing that happened to me since I came away with you,' she said. 'It hurt far worse than the snakebite, because it was intentional. Why did you do it to me?'

He appeared to consider this question seriously.

'There's the matter of our traditional hatred. And, besides, I'm very frightened of you.'

'I have the advantage of you there,' said Marianne, pushing him away and endeavouring to cover herself. (pp. 55–6)

This rape fantasy is disrupted by Marianne's 'superior status', which allows her a questioning and insistent voice ('Why did you do it?') – a voice which uncovers *his* fear.

This voice also allows repressed feminine desire (as in *The Magic Toyshop*) to be articulated:

She pulled the night-dress over her head and threw it away, so she could be still closer to him or, rather, to the magic source of attraction constituted by his brown flesh. And, if anything else but this existed, then she was sure it was not real.

... There was no pain this time. The mysterious glide of planes of flesh within her bore no relation to anything she had heard, read or experienced. She never expected such extreme intimations of pleasure or despair. (p. 83)

Marianne translates fantasy into the real – from what she has 'read' to what she experiences. This is the same process as Uncle Philip watching the 'play', but here the pleasure is not appropriated or assimilated by a controlling spectator. Rather, it is a 'mysterious' and paradoxical experience (the 'magic source of attraction' of her violator) but one which Marianne can take pleasure in all the same: 'Night came; that confusion between need and desire against which she had been warned consumed her' (p. 134).

When Jewel dies, Marianne takes control of the Barbarians and thus of the fantasy narrative: 'I'll be the tiger lady and rule them with a rod of iron' (p. 150). Central to the process of empowerment is a rejection of her fantasy of Jewel:

> She thought: 'I have destroyed him' and felt a warm sense of self-satisfaction, for quite dissolved was the marvellous, defiant construction of textures and colours she first glimpsed marauding her tranquil village; it had vanished as if an illusion which could not sustain itself … She got up and threw the pots of paint he left behind him into the weedy cleft between the station platforms. She threw the mirror after them, in case she saw his face in it, his former extraordinary face left behind there, for it must remain somewhere; she watched the mirror break with pleasure. (p. 147)

By foregrounding the female subject's 'warm sense of self-satisfaction' as she dissolves the fantasy that has kept her in thrall, Carter goes beyond a reversal of conventional representations of feminine desire. The 'female spectator' is able to articulate her own fantasies and, in so doing, to objectify the masculine object of desire ('the furious invention of my virgin nights'). But here, as Marianne breaks the mirror, even that new way of looking is rejected, the construction is 'dissolved'. In its place Carter sketches a fantasy of a new narrative, and it is this that renders the novel more complex than a re-presentation of conventional sexual images of women. The end of *Heroes and Villains* suggests that, once empowered ('She felt the beginnings of a sense of power', p. 144), his new feminine spectator might be able to see her way to an innovative form of fantasy, which incorporates a multiplicity of desires […].[31] □

Mahoney goes on to argue that the novel's perception of time is a particularly important element in its envisaging of such a space of female empowerment:

■ Although it is a condition of the fantasy, and particularly the post-apocalyptic narrative, that time should be disrupted, [Marianne's father] obsessively clings to a sense of the 'real', through time and heirlooms. Time, Marianne realizes, is 'frozen … and the busy clock carved the hours into sculptures of ice', and she is 'not impressed' by the clock (p. 1). By the end of the novel, the clock is, however, in different hands:

Prominent among the minarets, spires and helmets of wrought iron which protruded from the waters was an enormous clock whose hands stood still at the hour of ten though, it was, of course, no longer possible to tell whether this signified ten in the morning or ten at night. This clock was held in the arms and supported on the forward-jutting stomach of a monstrous figure in some kind of plasterwork ... It was the figure of a luxuriously endowed woman scantily clad in a one-piece bathing costume which, at the top, scarcely contained the rising swell of mountainous breasts in the shadowy cleft of which sea birds nested ... The head, equipped with exuberant, shoulder-length curls, was thrown back in erotic ecstasy and, though partially worn away by the salty winds, the face clearly displayed a gigantic pair of lips twisted in a wide, joyous smile ... (p. 138).

I have quoted this passage at length as it brings together the various problematics and possibilities of representing feminine desire that Carter's novel suggests. Thus we have another 'construction', a fantasy in sculpture of an eroticised, feminine figure, 'luxuriously endowed' with 'mountainous breasts' and 'exuberant' hair. This is not, however, passive, 'unspeakable' sexuality or the construction of the feminine sexual self by others that we see in *The Magic Toyshop*. Rather, it is an aggressive ('forward-jutting'), powerful, 'joyous' feminine sexuality, a sexuality which flaunts itself. That it should be this figure left holding the clock, holding 'time', suggests a displacement which is crucial both in Carter's narrative and in any progression towards a new representation of desire.[32] We have moved on from the Father/Professor obsessively 'holding time' and clinging to an outmoded version of the 'real', to a new construction of a feminine subject, taking pleasure in a new textual space. Marianne's mother dies early in the narrative ('... when she ate some poison fruit she took sick almost gladly and made no resistance to death', p. 7) and forms an absence which is only countered at the moment Marianne sees the statue. For this figure is the maternal body signifying a subversive, 'monstrous' version of feminine desire.[33] This space is symbolized by the sea, out of which the statue rises and which Marianne sees for the first time when she sees the statue ('Marianne had never seen the sea', p. 2).[34] □

In her discussion, Mahoney references the work of Gerardine Meaney, who, in her book *(Un)Like Subjects: Women, Theory, Fiction* (1993), analyses the temporal structure of *Heroes and Villains* through reference to the work of the French feminist theorist Julia Kristeva. In an essay published in 1979 entitled 'Women's Time', Kristeva discusses women's relationship to time, arguing that pregnancy and maternity has the effect of removing women from a linear temporal structure into a different form of time, which she defines as both 'cyclical' and 'monumental'. While Meaney identifies Doris Lessing's novel *The Marriages Between Zones Three, Four and Five* as capable of being read as an example of 'monumental' time, it is to *Heroes and Villains* that she turns for her discussion of cyclical time. Having argued that 'what Kristeva calls "monumental" time, "all encompassing and infinite like imaginary space",[35] confounds linear time' in Lessing's novel, she continues:

■ Conventional temporality fares no better in *Heroes and Villains*. Marianne tells Jewel he is an anachronism: '"What's an anachronism," he said darkly. "Teach me what an anachronism is." "A pun in time," she replied cunningly, so that he would not understand her' (p. 56).[36] The sorcerer-priest Donally comments, 'Time is going backwards and coiling up; who let the spring go, I wonder, so that history wound back on itself?' (p. 93).

Cyclical time takes over here. That is precisely what renders the novel so problematic. Cyclical time can be associated with stultifying 'immanence'[37] or with the danger of petrification [...]. It could be described as the space to which women are banished when they are exiled from history. Kristeva describes it spectacularly differently, reclaiming it as a space dizzying in its vastness rather than as 'confinement or restriction to a narrow round of uncreative or repetitive duties'.[38] In 'Women's Time':

There are cycles, gestation, the eternal recurrence of a biological rhythm which conforms to that of nature and imposes a temporality whose stereotyping may shock but whose regularity and unison with what is experienced as extra-subjective time, cosmic time, occasion vertiginous visions and unnameable *jouissance*.[39]

Vertigo often precipitates a fall and the logic of this 'time' in *Heroes and Villains* is the eternal recurrence of a vicious circle, a shocking, stereotyping victory of maternity over the woman as protagonist, as thinker, as producer of her own story. Carter's text directly addresses the issue which disrupts any comfortable conclusions in the work of [Hélène] Cixous and Lessing and which sometimes threatens to overwhelm that of Kristeva: 'I think therefore I am, but if I take time off from thinking, what then?' (p. 98). This question is posed by Donally, the sinister architect of the symbolic in *Heroes and Villains*. He repeatedly scrawls epigrams, ciphers and questions on the crumbling walls of the shelters where Marianne takes refuge with the Barbarians. The question of the self's fate without consciousness or when consciousness is no longer in control is his greatest challenge to this girl who 'keeps on utilizing her perceptions until the very end' (p.81). It is also, of course, the greatest challenge which the concept of a decentred self poses for feminism. Women have sought independence, autonomy, historical and political agency, all of those things which have traditionally defined 'human' subjectivity. That definition has collapsed under the onslaught of contemporary critical theory, perhaps primarily under the onslaught of feminism's claims that women will no longer guarantee the subject's autonomy and agency, but will instead exercise it. If the self is no more than a fragile illusion, sustained by a dualism inimical to women, prey to unconscious drives and produced by language, what is left to resist hegemony and seek change? Towards the end of *Heroes and Villains*, Marianne, pregnant, trapped, finds 'she was not able to think' (p.149) and 'then' the age-old pattern recurs. Jewel dies, becomes a hero, and so fulfils the destiny which Donally insisted would be his, that of the new Arthur, 'the Messiah of the Yahoos'. Marianne survives, becomes a mother and the 'Tiger Lady' (p.150), 'Eve at the end of the world' (p.124). Through Marianne and her child will be completed the process begun by Donally and, reluctantly, Jewel. The novel ends poised for the transformation of the tribe from a loose family grouping to a structured society. If a woman takes time off from thinking, it seems, she is in danger of becoming a mother goddess.[40] □

According to Meaney, therefore, *Heroes and Villains* exposes the most problematic aspect of the Kristevan concept of cyclical time; that the notion of an escape from linear time leaves women excluded from the historical process, and thus vulnerable to mythological stereotyping. Meaney refers to Carter's later work *The Sadeian Woman* (1979) in order to demonstrate Carter's intractable opposition to the mythologizing of women – in particular, the myth of the mother-goddess, which 'culminates in the collapse of sexuality into reproduction, an equation which Carter posits as the most insidious enemy of women'.[41] Meaney detects a 'recurrent conflict emerg[ing] in the writings of Carter and Kristeva between resistance to history as the agent of determinism and desire for access to history as the arena of change'.[42] *Heroes and Villains* thus constitutes an ironic counterpoint to Kristevan theory in that it invokes the concept of cyclical time only to deconstruct it.

■ Eternal goddess, dying and (possibly) reviving god/hero; these are the elements to which the narrative structure of *Heroes and Villains* consistently alludes. Marianne finds the tribe's 'sign' against the evil eye is the sign of the cross, Jewel is to be the 'Messiah of the Yahoos', or the new Arthur (p.124). These 'archetypes' and their myth are subject to the alienating interrogation of a post-nuclear setting, however. In such a setting any renewal is inevitably warped, the concept of eternal continuity has become ironic. Carter engages in that mythologizing of myth which [Roland] Barthes advocates as the most effective method of revealing the signifying structure which myth must conceal if it is to operate as purveyor of universal unchangeability.[43] Indeed, one of Donally's aphorisms neatly summarizes much of Barthes's argument, 'MISTRUST APPEARANCES; THEY NEVER CONCEAL ANYTHING' (p. 60). Donally's imperative is typical of this novel's 'negations'. The mythologist is also the literary and sexual terrorist: 'Juliette [...] embodies "intellectual pleasure in regression" [history wound back on itself]. She attacks civilization with its own systems; she exhibits an iron self-control'.[44] There is much of the Marianne of *Heroes and Villains* in this, particularly Marianne as artist/dreamer, whose 'furious invention' this is. She never completes her work of destruction, however, and the renewal promised in the conclusion may be the establishment, not the removal, of 'a repressive and authoritarian superstructure'.[45, 46] □

Mother-goddesses, therefore, are no solution to women's search for historical agency because they stand outside history. To realise this, however, negates one of the most pervasive cultural myths of all – the quest for an origin. Meaney concludes this strand of her argument by stressing that, although the relinquishing of the myth of the mother is a daunting prospect, it is also full of risky potential.

■ Not only is homecoming impossible, it is no longer possible to postulate home or origin as the premiss for an 'us' or an exclusion of the other. Nothing is stranger than where we come from. Interrogation of her own relation to origin by a female protagonist subverts the metaphors and ideology of social, ethnic and national belonging. This is the consequence of 'the final secularisation of mankind'. This is the source of the pervasive sense of loss in modernism and postmodernism, of their characteristic alienation.

The new and fragile basis it offers for the social contract may yet mark the point at which western culture ceases to mourn the illusion of one's 'own and proper' place and acknowledges 'the difference within us in its most bewildering state and presents it as the ultimate condition of our being with others'.[47, 48] □

An interesting addendum to Meaney's argument, however, can be found in an interview that Carter gave in 1988 to Anna Katsavos. As the above discussion has shown, Gerardine Meaney interprets *Heroes and Villains* as ironically deconstructing ahistorical, mythological conceptions of women, and she uses Carter's argument against myth in *The Sadeian Woman*, published in 1979, to make this point. In Katsavos's interview, however, Carter implies that her references to myth in *Heroes and Villains* were *not* originally intended to be deconstructive, since at that point in her career she did indeed regard myth as potentially liberating.

■ *AK:* [… I]n *Heroes and Villains* myths are not seen as extraordinary lies designed to make people unfree but rather as something necessary and useful. Donally promises to make Jewel a politician, king of all the Yahoos and all the Professors, saying, 'they need a myth as passionately as anyone else; they need a hero'.

AC: When most people are writing over a period of years, what they think they are writing about and what they believe in is a continuum; it's not 'specktic' [*sic*]. I've been publishing fiction since 1966, and I've changed a lot in the way I approach the world and in the way that I organize the world.

Heroes and Villains was quite an important book for me. One of the quotations in the front is from the script of a film called *Alphaville*, made by Jean-Luc Godard. It was a favorite film of mine of the late sixties; there's a computer in *Alphaville* that says the thing that's quoted in the front. ['There are times when reality becomes too complex for Oral Communication. But Legend gives it a form by which it pervades the whole world.'] In these times myth gives history shape. When I wrote that novel in 1968, this was a very resonant theme that I am not so sure of now.

I think that Godard was using the word myth in the same way that Barthes is as well. The film *Alphaville* uses one of the greatest gangster heroes of French cinema, but it projects a sort of trench-coat, Philip Marlowe character into some sort of antiseptic city of the future, and I really think that he was meaning myth in the terms of somebody like Bogart or Philip Marlowe. You know, you try things out and you try things out, and you figure out after a while when they're not working or they stop working or maybe you no longer think it's true. I just became uninterested in these sort of semisacrilized ways of looking at the world. They didn't seem to me to be any help.[49] □

One of the events which was to contribute to this shift in attitude was Carter's move, not just to a new country, but to a completely different culture. Living in Japan, a country in which she was outlandishly foreign, also caused her to look back at her own European ancestry from the perspective of a foreigner. This experience of alienation was to shape her subsequent fiction.

CHAPTER FOUR

The Infernal Desire Machines of Doctor Hoffman (1972) and *Fireworks* (1974)

A FTER THE completion of *Love*, the final book in what was to become known as her 'Bristol Trilogy', Angela Carter left Bristol and her marriage in one fell swoop. With the proceeds of the Somerset Maugham Award won for *Several Perceptions*, Carter went to Japan, where she lived from 1969 to 1972. During her stay there, she produced a novel, *The Infernal Desire Machines of Doctor Hoffman* (1972), and a number of short stories and articles, which were compiled in her first collection of short pieces, *Fireworks* (1974).

Although little criticism has been published on *Fireworks* itself, it not infrequently enters into studies of Carter's work as a means of exploring the effect of Carter's stay in Japan upon her writing. Linden Peach is somewhat unusual in using *Fireworks* as a vantage point from which to look back at the novels which Carter wrote in the 1960s, reading it as 'provid[ing] a gloss on the early fiction'.[1] He is 'reluctant to see the period ... which she spent in Japan ... solely in terms of a watershed',[2] arguing that 'Japan did not simply provide ... [Carter] with new ideas, but confirmed her in the way in which she was developing'.[3] However, although other critics are as unwilling as Peach to ignore the clear thread of continuity that runs between what Carter wrote before and after her stay in Japan, they nevertheless tend to approach the collection from the opposite direction. Instead of regarding *Fireworks* as providing a 'gloss' on the novels she had already written, an aid to their interpretation, they view it as charting subtle shifts in thematic focus and literary technique which were unavoidably to shape the subsequent fiction. As I, for example, have argued, *Fireworks*

■ provides excellent introductory examples of the way in which

Carter's narrative technique, never straightforward to begin with, became more intricately self-referential in terms of both form and content. In these short stories, she challenges her readers with portrayals of violence and desire which shock and disturb, and which intensify their effects by pushing against the boundaries of conventional narrative representation. The collection consists of first-person narratives set in Japan interspersed with surreal fantasies, in which Carter's response to the 'lyrically bizarre holocausts'[4] of Japanese pornography is dramatically displayed in evocative depictions of incest, sadism and sexual domination. Taken as a whole, this is an entire collection of traveller's tales, records of a journey not just into another culture, but also into the dark and dangerous landscape of taboo.[5] □

Lorna Sage, too, regards *Fireworks* as demonstrating that Carter's Japanese experience left its mark on her writing; Sage sees this manifested in an increased sense of artifice and also an increased fascination with pornographic forms.

■ At the time, in Tokyo, whatever she was looking for, she found out the truthfulness *and finality* of appearances, images emptied of their usual freight of recognition and guilt. This was not, in other words, old-fashioned orientalism, but the new-fangled sort that denied you access to any *essence* of otherness. I have already invoked Roland Barthes once, and he comes in again here too. His 1970 book on Japan, *Empire of Signs*, demonstrates the sort of thing that smart semioticians secretly wanted at the time – to discover a culture that despised depth, where 'the inside no longer commands the outside'.[6] The strange tongue

> constitutes a delicious protection ... an auditory film which halts at his ears all the alienations of the mother tongue: the regional and social origins of whoever is speaking, his degree of culture, of intelligence, of taste ... . The unknown language ... forms around me, as I move, a faint vertigo, sweeping me into its artificial emptiness, which is consummated only for me: I live in the interstice, delivered from any fulfilled meaning.[7]

In other words (Barthes doesn't exactly say this, of course) you can escape your culture's sexual norms, and feel free to sleep with strangers: 'in Japan the body exists, acts, shows itself, gives itself, without hysteria, without narcissism, but according to a pure – though subtly discontinuous – erotic project'.[8] Tokyo is a cruel, delightful mirror to the occidental. The coincidence between Barthes's Japan and Carter's is striking: they visited the same country of the skin, no question, and its topography derives from their very Western wants.

Witness Angela's *Fireworks* story called 'Flesh and the Mirror', about sex minus words, class, character, with a wandering stranger, in 'an unambiguous hotel with mirror on the ceiling' (pp. 63–4).[9] 'I was the subject of the sentence written on the mirror ... . Nothing kept me from the fact, the act; I had been precipitated into knowledge of the real conditions of living' (p. 65). Like Barthes, she treasures the new sense she has of the resistance of surfaces. In the Western world 'Women and mirrors are in complicity with one another, to evade the action I/she performs that she/I cannot watch, the action with which I break out of the mirror, with which I assume my appearance. But *this* mirror refused to conspire with me; it was like the first mirror I'd ever seen' (p. 65). This I/she is purely impersonal, has for a moment no bio-logical destiny at all. She discards her inner life and her act delivers her back to herself, her own author. With this vertiginous experience, Carter seems to have exorcised her fear of freakishness and made it writable. The whole episode may of course have been a fantasy bred out of the city. But I think it probably did happen: we expect auto-biographical writing to belong to the confiding, realist mode, and this does not; it looks like an 'exercise' in literary gymnastics. That, though, does not make it out of character for Carter, who was becom-ing more and more openly obsessed with the notion that what we accept as natural is the product of a particular history. Art's purpose on this view is to help us recognise our own artificiality – compare the way toys and people intermingle in her fiction – and to estrange us from our home-selves.[10] □

The first edition of *Fireworks* included an Afterword, in which Carter (although only mock-seriously, one suspects) attributed her interest in the short-story form to the stimulus of her time in Japan. Here, she describes the attraction the short story held for her in terms which recall my own and Lorna Sage's view that this period marked an intensification in her authorial self-consciousness:

■ I started to write short pieces when I was living in a room too small to write a novel in. So the size of my room modified what I did inside it and it was the same with the pieces themselves. The limited trajec-tory of the short narrative concentrates its meaning. Sign and sense can fuse to an extent impossible to achieve among the multiplying ambi-guities of an extended narrative. I found that, although the play of surfaces never ceased to fascinate me, I was not so much exploring them as making abstractions from them. I was writing, therefore, tales.

Though it took me a long time to realise why I liked them, I'd always been fond of Poe, and Hoffmann – Gothic tales, cruel tales, tales of wonder, tales of terror, fabulous narratives that deal directly with the imagery of the unconscious – mirrors; the externalised self; forsaken castles; haunted forests; forbidden sexual objects. Formally the tale differs from the short story in that it makes few pretences at the imitation of life. The tale does not log everyday experience, as the short story does; it interprets everyday experience through a system of imagery derived from subterranean areas behind everyday experience, and therefore the tale cannot betray its readers into a false knowledge of everyday experience.[11] □

What Carter perceived herself as writing at this time, therefore, are short narratives which do not masquerade as naturalism, but are wholly artificial. However, this description is not only applicable to her short fiction, but also functions as an apt summary of the novel she wrote during this period, *The Infernal Desire Machines of Doctor Hoffman*, a novel which, as Susan Rubin Suleiman reports, was written 'in three months, in a Japanese fishing village on an island where she seems to have been the only European'.[12]

However, *The Infernal Desire Machines of Doctor Hoffman* did not attain the success of Carter's previous novels, and it continues to be one of her less popular works. An indication of its initial reception can be gleaned from an interview with Carter published in the *Guardian* in 1972. The ostensible intention of this piece was to publicise her latest novel, but it gets any mention of it out of the way in one sentence which is so vaguely phrased that one wonders whether the interviewer had actually bothered to read it: 'This erotic, surrealist epic, as the publishers have chosen to describe her novel, has taken Mrs Carter a stage further, a whole stratum deeper into darker regions of the imagination which explores with a sometimes blinding intensity'.[13]

Although, as this chapter will demonstrate, criticism on *The Infernal Desire Machines of Doctor Hoffman* has been published, it is surprising how often the novel continues to be glossed over in interviews and surveys of Carter's writing. This ambivalence was, however, echoed by the author herself, who persistently linked it with the lull in popularity she experienced in the early seventies. Interviewed by the *Guardian* once again in 1979, she described it as a 'magnificently commercially unviable' book,[14] an opinion which did not change. Less than a year before her death she reiterated her point, calling it 'the novel which marked the beginning of my obscurity. I went from being a very promising young writer to being completely ignored in two novels'.[15]

In an interview conducted in 1977, Lorna Sage quotes Carter's description of *The Infernal Desire Machines of Doctor Hoffman* as the first book in a trilogy of 'speculative novels',[16] the second volume of which was *The Passion of New Eve*. However, as Elaine Jordan points out, the third volume of this supposed 'trilogy' was either never written, or remained purposely ambiguous: 'I have learnt not to ask what is the third volume: choose your own, or acknowledge that Angela Carter evades conclusion'.[17] This idea that *Hoffman* was part of a larger project, however, reinforces both Jordan's and Sage's view that it marks yet another shift in Carter's narrative focus. Sage, in particular, argues for this book's importance in demonstrating Carter's increasing interest in translating ideas into fiction. In her 1977 interview with Carter she remarks that: 'With *Hoffman*, she became more self-conscious, having been excessively so to start with',[18] an observation she followed up in more detail in *Angela Carter*:

■ *Dr [sic] Hoffman* is very much an intellectual's book, for all its seeming simplicity of structure, and its obsessive, erotic, and kinetic images. Its themes would recur as arguments in the Sade study [*The Sadeian Woman*, published in 1979]. She needed to *theorize* in order to feel in charge, and to cheer herself up, and that has left its mark marvellously on this 1970s fiction, which is full of ideas, *armed* with them. Desiderio avoids being eaten by the river Indians, who are hoping that way magically to absorb his literacy, because he is a good enough anthropologist to tumble to their plans. Like Angela Carter, he has read his Lévi-Strauss, and though he very much wants to be absorbed in this womb-like family, and luxuriates in 'that slight feeling of warm claustrophobia I had learned to identify with the notion "home"', he proves his separateness by reading their intentions so cleverly. [...]

Another reason for her deepening interest in theory was that 'coming out' as a feminist was hard, even though she had been one in a sense all along.[19] □

The link Sage makes here between Carter's growing narrative self-consciousness and her adoption of feminism is echoed by Elaine Jordan. One of the hallmarks of Carter's earlier novels is their fascination with dangerous and seductive maleness – Honeybuzzard in *Shadow Dance*, Finn in *The Magic Toyshop*, Jewel in *Heroes and Villains* – but in *Hoffman*, Jordan says, the author's attention is transferred from male to female characters, which she identifies as a crucial change of allegiance:

■ The dedication of *Hoffman* waves goodbye, I think, to the barbaric, anarchic or revolutionary band of brothers whose opinions have hitherto haunted Angela Carter's fictions, in *Love*, for example [...] and in *Heroes and Villains*. They had served their purpose as objects of desire or as transgressive identifications, stepping-stones to writing radically as a woman.[20] □

The implications of such arguments, however, are potentially contradictory. To say, as Jordan does, that Carter is moving towards 'writing radically as a woman' suggests that her writing is motivated by political concerns. However, Sage's argument that at this point in her career Carter was moving more deeply into the realms of the theoretical and experimental implies that, in the pursuit of the idea, the 'real' could potentially be left behind. Yet a passage drawn from the Jordan essay from which the previous quotation came maintains that the dauntingly wide range of references woven into *Hoffman* actually leads Carter towards a critique of material reality rather than away from it:

■ In *Hoffman*, Angela Carter traces the history of Reason and Desire in literary and philosophic representation, from the Enlightenment through to psychoanalysis and its post-romantic consciousness of the unconscious – Enlightenment seen from its dark side, its blind spot. *Hoffman*'s serial episodes explore our conventions and classificatory myths. To classify, to include and exclude, is human, all too human – for example, as Maxine Hong Kingston's *The Woman Warrior* [1976] suggests, to the traditional Chinese those who are not Chinese may be ghosts, horrible, but not all that real. It is only of the Centaurs, in Section 7 of *Hoffman*, that it can truly be said 'nothing human was alien to them because they were alien to everything human' (p. 175).[21] *Hoffman* explores pornography, the Gothic, fairy tales, horror films, boys' imperial adventure stories, anthropological idylls according to Rousseau or Lévi-Strauss, and the fantasies of philosophy, the world as Will and Idea. The grotesque Count represents Sade and Nietzsche, dressed up as Dracula, but he is also like Marianne in *Heroes and Villains*, in so far as he embodies the solitary will inspired by an idea of itself, seeking perverse gratification no matter what. This option of individual assertion and transgression is acknowledged as one mode of resisting Hoffman's control of desire – it can be aligned also with Norman Mailer's 'Bring out the psychopath in yourself' – but it is rejected here [...] as sado-masochistic, in thrall to what it defies, and as antipathetic to any social ideal. The narrative position – that is, 'Angela Carter' – remains committed to socialism and to feminism. What conclusion to such a desire can there be, in present conditions, but continuing struggle, intelligent resistance along with kindred spirits?[22] □

This view of Carter as a writer who uses literary experimentation actively to critique an extra-textual reality is one which I reiterate in *Angela Carter: Writing From the Front Line*. In my opinion, *Hoffman* can be related to Carter's nostalgia for the political upheavals of the 1960s, expressed in such essays as 'Notes for a Theory of Sixties Style' and 'Fin de Siècle', and thus, for all its narrative self-consciousness, it is ultimately motivated by political concerns.

■ In her introduction added to 'Notes for a Theory of Sixties Style' in its republication in *Nothing Sacred* in 1982, Carter retrospectively describes the sixties as a period in which 'The pleasure principle met the reality principle like an irresistible force encountering an immovable object, and the reverberations of that collision are still echoing about us'.[23] *Hoffman* takes this idea and builds it into an elaborate and surreal fantasy which, while it echoes the disillusion voiced by Carter in such pieces as 'Fin de Siècle', also uses it as a starting point for radical deconstruction of the cultural status quo. [... ...]

Like the short stories in *Fireworks*, this is a narrative about narrative, locked into the kind of metafictional dialect described by Patricia Waugh as 'the construction of a fictional illusion (as in traditional realism) and the laying bare of that illusion'.[24] Waugh's summary of the intentions of metafiction could function equally well as a description of Desiderio's role in the text, *in* the fictional illusion, but not *of* it, and thus, in the final analysis, committed to its deconstruction.

But it would be inaccurate to thus conclude that *Hoffman*'s attention is focused totally inwards upon the issue of its own formation. On the contrary, it engages with the world of the 'real' more radically than any of Carter's novels have so far done. In this sense, it particularly corresponds to Linda Hutcheon's definition of historiographic metafiction which, she says,

> refutes the natural or common-sense methods of distinguishing between historical fact and fiction. It refuses the view that only history has a truth claim, both by questioning the ground of that claim in historiography and by asserting that both history and fiction are discourses, human constructs, signifying systems, and both derive their major claim to truth from that identity.[25]

Such master narratives as time, truth, identity and historical causation are systematically, deliberately, mangled in *Hoffman*, and although the ending apparently sees them restored, it is not to their former state. They may only have been dismantled once, but once is enough to see that they are not incontrovertible, but chosen. Again, it is Desiderio who functions as an excellent example of this intent, his claims to a rational, independent subjectivity growing increasingly desperate as that narrative proceeds. Although he begins the narrative as an exemplary example of the Baudelairean *flâneur*,[26] in whom 'the joy of watching is triumphant',[27] by the end he is a shaken shadow of his former self, having been very nearly seduced into active participation within a world of seductive illusions and complex desires.

It is not accidental, as Lorna Sage also observes, that the setting of this novel is South America, which is 'very much the right setting for this vertiginous frontier-crossing – in literary terms, that is'.[28] This is the territory of magical realism, a form described by Mario Vargas Llosa as 'fantastic literature [which] ... has its roots in objective reality and is a vehicle for exposing social and political evils'.[29] While it may be straining a point to place Carter, the white, Anglo-Saxon product of a white, Anglo-Saxon culture, alongside Latin American authors who write out of a history of political oppression and cultural domination, there is nevertheless a clear parallel. The label 'magical realist' was freely applied to Carter throughout her later career, and it was one she was happy to accept, citing Gabriel García Márquez and Alejo Carpentier, for example, as major influences on her own work.

What her adoption of the magical realist mode essentially offers Carter is a way of engaging with the world outside the text in a critical way [...]. For all its fantastic content, this novel is an extremely politicised analysis of power and colonisation.[30] □

In his study of Carter's fiction, Aidan Day makes a similar point, maintaining that Desiderio represents rejection of the ultimate implications of a postmodern world-view. Doctor Hoffman is, therefore, a species of arch-postmodernist; a point Day reinforces in his discussion through reference to John Fowles's *The French Lieutenant's Woman* (1969):

■ In *Dr Hoffman* it is unreality that Desiderio describes as overwhelming the inhabitants of the city once Hoffman starts his siege, an unreality that the Minister [of Determination] tries to distinguish from reality but which Hoffman refuses to allow to be so distinguished. Desiderio learns many of the details of Hoffman's view of the world from the proprietor of a peep-show whom he encounters in his travels in search of the Doctor. The proprietor is an old tutor of Hoffman's and he still acts as a mouthpiece for Hoffman's ideas. He keeps changing the pictures that he exhibits in his show. The principle underlying the changes he makes is random: the peep-show proprietor is himself blind and has never seen the pictures. The peep-show and the travelling fair that, in chapter four, it is displayed in, are metaphors for the world once Hoffman has started the war. It is a world, paralleling that endorsed by Fowles in *The French Lieutenant's Woman*, which is governed by no single, transcendent authority and which does not proceed in a progressive line. In fact, it is not a world, but a series of worlds. Desiderio describes the metaphoric fair and recounts the peep-show proprietor's metaphoric reflections as follows:

I often watched the roundabouts circulate upon their static journeys. 'Nothing,' said the peep-show proprietor, 'is ever completed; it only changes.' As he pleased, he altered the displays he had

never seen, murmuring: 'No hidden unity.' ... The fairground was a
moving toy-shop, an ambulant raree-show coming to life in con-
vulsive fits and starts whenever the procession stopped, regulated
only by the implicit awareness of a lack of rules. (p.99)[31]

The lack of rules in peep-show and fair means that they run according
to a dynamic that stands contrary to the Minister's belief in rules for
distinguishing reality from unreality. The distinction is not meaning-
ful to Hoffman, because the human imagination is so involved in constituting reality that it is invalid to separate the authentically real from
the constructed. In Hoffman's world-view we are inside the postmodern 'awareness', as Hans Bertens puts it, 'that representations
create rather than reflect reality'.[32] Through the peep-show proprietor,
Desiderio learns of the ideas of another of Hoffman's teachers,
Mendoza. The peep-show proprietor reports that:

> Mendoza ... claimed that if a thing were sufficiently artificial, it
> became absolutely equivalent to the genuine ... Hoffman refined
> Mendoza's initially crude hypotheses of fissile time and synthetic
> authenticity and wove them together to form another mode of con-
> sciousness altogether. (pp.102–3)

This dissolving of boundaries between the synthetic and the authentic
aligns Hoffman's world-view with postmodern ideas about representation and reality. For one of his main principles, as summarised by
Desiderio in the fourth chapter, is that 'everything it is possible to
imagine can also exist' (p.97). The principle is elaborated by Hoffman
himself in the last chapter of the book, when he says to Desiderio: 'I can
make you perceive ideas with your senses because I do not acknowledge any essential difference in the phenomenological bases of the
two modes of thought' (p.206). Hoffman's vision of the possibility of
actualising any of the imagination's imaginings threatens Desiderio's
city, where empirical reality is usurped by the manifold, unstable and
ever-changing concretisations of fantasy. And, just as in the peep-show
and travelling fair, there is no single authority directing these manifestations in the city along a single line. Hoffman lets the peep-show proprietor keep a set of 'magic samples' (p.105): these are something like
paradigms of everything that may exist in the universe, everything
mental or corporeal, except that in Hoffman's universe, of course, the
'or' has no meaning since all mental things can be actualised. [... ...]

The samples are the source of energy which enables the manifold
and changing substantial mirages, the concretisations of fantasies, to
appear in the city. And the absence of any coherence in the appearance
of these substantial mirages is captured when Desiderio describes the

peep-show proprietor turning up a 'handful of magic samples in the air' and letting them fall randomly. [...]

The world according to the peep-show proprietor is – not unlike the world of chance rather than of single, authoritative direction in *The French Lieutenant's Woman* – subject only to the principles of infinity, randomness and change. Desiderio notes the peep-show proprietor's observations that '"Things cannot be exhausted"; or "In the imagina- tion, nothing is past, nothing can be forgotten". Or: "Change is the only valid response to phenomena"' (p.104). Fowles [...] sees the idea of the endlessness and openness of creativity, natural or human, as a liberating idea. In a comparable vein, Hoffman and his aide the peep- show proprietor see what has been unleashed on the city as a stage in the liberation of humanity. The proprietor looks forward to when the Doctor will bring about a state of 'Nebulous Time', which will be 'a period of absolute mutability' (p.99). As he describes this stage to Desiderio, the proprietor sounds like a postmodernist theorist going on about the depthlessness of the signs, the depthlessness of the repre- sentations that constitute the world and which make untenable any idea of autonomous, objective reality:

> you must never forget that the Doctor's philosophy is not so much transcendental as incidental. It utilizes all the incidents that ripple the depthless surfaces of, you understand, the sensual world ... we will live on as many layers of consciousness as we can, all at the same time. After the Doctor liberates us, that is (pp.99–100).[33] □

It is David Punter, however, who has written one of the most detailed analyses of the status of reality in *Hoffman*. He, too, sees the peep-show as an important episode in this respect, and although his interpretation of it is rather more complex than Day's, he is ultimately making a very similar point. Punter's interest here is in the way in which the text dramatises the free play of the unconscious, in a psychoanalytical sense, thus foregrounding subjectivity as 'constructed' rather than 'natural'. For Punter, narrative plays a crucial role in this formation of conscious- ness, which is incarnated in a linguistic system which gives it an illusion of unity and structure.

His debate also provides an interesting point of departure from the views of Elaine Jordan and Lorna Sage regarding this novel, which have already been quoted in this chapter. Whereas, as we have seen, both Jordan and Sage regard *Hoffman* as marking the beginning of a more obvious engagement with feminism on Carter's part, Punter identifies this shift as occurring one book further on, arguing that *Hoffman* is the last of Carter's novels to examine subjectivity without foregrounding gender as an essential 'structuring principle' in its formation.

■ 'You could effectively evolve a persona from your predicament, if you tried' (p. 190),[34] Desiderio is admonished in *Doctor Hoffman* at one point, although Carter does not here go for easy answers. Indeed, the 'answers' with which she presents us are exceedingly difficult, rather in the manner of the metaphysical speculations of Flann O'Brien:[35] and thus the question of the reality status – or, perhaps, varying reality statuses – of the 'phantoms' which Hoffman unleashes on the city remains to the end a matter for conjecture. That conjecture is simultaneously a metaphysical one, about the concept of the symbol; what we might term a semiotic one, about the relation between the sign and its referent; and a sociosexual one, for it raises the questions of the ontological location of desire and of the arbitrariness of change.

Imagistically, the 'question of reality' – and to give it this formulation is already to underestimate the powerful web of ironies through which Carter mediates this metaphysicalisation of the political – is represented in terms of opacity and transparency, vision and shadow. A key term, cropping up throughout Desiderio's wanderings like a talisman but never subjected to the indignity of abstract 'explanation', is 'persistence of vision', which carries two different but related meanings. First, it is this ambiguous persistence, manifested chiefly in the emaciated and academic shape of the Doctor himself, which achieves the alchemical transmutations of desire into material manifestation and thus threatens those limits of the conceivable which Desiderio ends up by defending. But second, it is persistence of vision which maintains our illusion of continuity in the world, which moulds our discrete presents into a coherent narrative. It is the proprietor of the peep-show, which perhaps causes these transformational phenomena, who points out that there is 'no hidden unity' (p. 126); thus, that his demonstrations of carnality and violence become coherent and intelligible only through a 'persistent' trick of the eye and psyche, through a refraction of the perennial Oedipal search for origins.[36] Sexual energy is the key to the manifestation of desire; but to subdue this perpetual slow explosion to the logistics of orgasm and climax is to submit ourselves to a teleology which merely demonstrates our obsessional inability to escape from the family which gave us birth. The ultimate acrobats of desire, down in the technological hub of the Doctor's replacement universe, embody postponement, or perhaps a hidden fear of premature ejaculation; certainly it is premature ejaculation which occurs in terms of the narrative itself, as Desiderio knows: both in that, within the mutual fiction of the later course of the world which Desiderio weaves around himself and the reader, we are supposed already to know the outcome of the story through history books, and also, more concretely, in that he gives us the conclusion of the story ahead of its 'natural' place, and himself bemoans the fact: 'but there I go again – running ahead of myself! See, I have ruined all the suspense. I have quite spoiled my climax' (p. 268).

The Doctor's system, for system it is (the unconscious here is very deliberately structured like a language), operates on the basis of continuing possibility, and it is this which strikes the hard resistant material of the universe in the shape of the Minister of Determination and his Kafkaesque police force. The early stages of the conflict, of which Desiderio, the 'desired one', is going to become the solution, involve the Minister's attempts to prevent the Doctor's illusions from swamping the real by the use of various technological devices, none of which prove particularly effective in a world where objects may change their names, shapes and functions from moment to moment. One of these weapons requires for its efficacy the construction of a model of the Doctor's 'unreality atom', which turns out to be bristling with 'projections' (p. 27); but these projections, of course, are not literal bumps, but the material form of the psychological projections which colour and shape our apprehension of the Other. The universe Carter portrays, however, cannot be simply predicated on the limitless power of these projections as far as the individual is concerned, for here ignorant projections clash by night; that is, projections ignorant of their own and others' origin, so that a battle of psychic power is enacted reminiscent, especially in the shape of the vampire Count, of the psychological power-struggles which lie at the root of sword-and-sorcery fiction.

Besides, since the projections teem from the unconscious, they can be *known* neither in their aetiology (the lost box of 'samples') nor in their manifestation; and we remain uncertain, in particular, about the nature of Desiderio's own unconscious. He is at once an allegorical figure for the object of desire, and thus undergoes a transmutation with each book of the novel; and a representation of a historically specific type of alienated consciousness, which means that despite these transmutations he possesses a residual consistency felt as boredom and disaffection. It is precisely the survival of this root of tedium which provides him with the vacant strength to quash the Doctor's schemes, and at this level we can read the text as a series of figures for the defeat of the political aspirations of the 1960s and in particular of the father-figures of liberation, [Wilhelm] Reich and [Herbert] Marcuse.[37]

But we can nonetheless plot the shapes of desire as the text envisages them by entering the kaleidoscope of what Desiderio variously becomes, even if he pulls back from the brink of immersion in these internal fictions and, indeed, never fully understands his own role in them. There is the faithful operative given a heroic mission; the visitant lover whose congress with the enervated Mary Anne precipitates her death; the compliant member of family which he becomes on the boat of the River People; the peep-show proprietor's nephew who, in a world of transitory freaks, possesses 'the unique allure of the norm' (p. 128); the half-willing companion of the 'erotic traveller'; the again heroic killer of the black chieftain of cannibals; and, of course, over all the potential lover of the elusive Albertina. But the structure which is woven from these tales remains ambivalent. It might be that the Boys' Own quality of Desiderio's incarnations reflects a paucity of imagination, perhaps specifically of male imagination, on Desiderio's part; or it might equally well be that in these largely adjuvant [auxiliary] shapes is reflected a specific historical role for the 'British' consciousness within international conflict, that the unconscious of the text, split as it is between New World and Old, has an even more precise bearing on cultural attitudes than would appear from the examination of Desiderio's attenuated psyche.[38]

It is only with the River People that he claims to feel 'at home', and this feeling is made the site for an appalling summary of familial claustrophobia. His putative child-bride appears at first to carry everywhere with her a doll, but this is next revealed to be a fish in doll's clothing, symbol indeed for desire and for the phallus but neatly bound up in conventional wrappings, slippery and to be toyed with as Desiderio is himself toyed with by her family. But this representation of captured 'difference' finally yields its secret, and is replaced in turn by a knife, the knife which will effect the real desire which the family has invested in Desiderio and will ensure that his knowledge, severed and offered with the hunks of his meat, will pass for ever safely back to the family and ensure a closed circle of deprivation and incest. From the doll to the fish to the knife, we move from pure representation through the shadowy realm of the symbolic into the ghastly manifestation of the real. It is the ambiguous realm of the fish which Doctor Hoffman's enemies suppose him, Nemo-like, to inhabit, although in the end it seems doubtful that this is the correct interpretation. Albertina, his daughter, describes the Minister's assaults on her father's efforts, and in particular that functionary's decision to 'keep a strict control of his actualities by adjusting their names to agree with them perfectly':

> So, you understand, that no shadow would fall between the word and the thing described. For the Minister hypothesised my father worked in that shadowy land between the thinkable and the thing thought of, and, if he destroyed this difference, he would destroy my father. (pp. 249–50)

The Minister employs a team of logical positivists to embark on this great work of classification, on the construction of a philosophy of identity and, indeed, through the agency of Desiderio he is in the end successful and the forces of order inflict another crushing defeat on the uprising of the imagination; but then Desiderio is the 'new youth', has himself been formed by the Minister's society, but the society of apparent institutional order and totalitarian conformism. How, then, could it be otherwise? To Desiderio, even the form of the Doctor himself, which we may presume to be as malleable for the perceiving subject as that of his daughter, appears only as another grey-suited seeker after power, and Desiderio's cynicism brooks no culmination but a restoration of the 'absence' which bred him.

Doctor Hoffman, then, attempts a subversion of narrative, on the grounds that narrative is itself ideological in form, even before we begin to consider its content; in other words, that narrative attempts to bind together and naturalise the disunited subject and that this attempt is made at the service of specific societal interests. But this places us, of course, again in the hall of mirrors: 'Desiderio', the desired one, is also anagrammatically ambivalent: the name contains the 'desired I', but also the 'desired O', and this encapsulates the problems of subjectivity which the text explores. Desiderio reverses the tradition of the search, or rather he displays the ambivalence of that search. Alongside the seeking for self lies always the hunt for the zero, for the still point, the thanatic [death-driven] impulse which requires him to set all things at nought and thus to represent the 'limits' of consciousness in their most extreme form, as a closing in and closing down. What gives him privilege is his apparent lack of interest in the unification of the self; but this is associated throughout with a negation of value, and thus the final consummation with Albertina is turned almost accidentally into a series of deaths as Desiderio makes real the point of resistance which brings all the efforts of fantasy to emerge into the world down to dust.[39] □

Punter, therefore, emphasises Carter's ultimate adherence to materialism as much as any of the other critics cited in this chapter. As can be seen in the above extract, he links the battle between the Minister of Determination and Doctor Hoffman to the activist politics of the 1960s. By relating Hoffman, in particular, to Herbert Marcuse, a social theorist who influenced the politics of the revolutionary New Left, Punter makes the novel an allegory for the defeat of an optimism prevalent in the 1960s that grass-roots political activism could overthrow repressive regimes. As another critic of the novel, Susan Rubin Suleiman, observes, '[i]t is difficult to resist an allegorical reading' of *Hoffman*.[40] She, however, problematises Punter's conclusion, arguing that 'he seems to find Desiderio's choice itself a kind of failure'.[41]

DOCTOR HOFFMAN AND FIREWORKS

■ What Punter fails to mention is that the kind of pleasure offered to Desiderio by Doctor Hoffman is extremely drab; the Doctor, scientifically literalising the Surrealist dictum that desire makes the world go round, succeeds in channelling sexual energy to fuel the huge machines that bombard the city with mirages. To this end, he employs lovers who voluntarily spend all their time copulating in 'love pens', the energy they release being immediately collected and transformed into fuel. (As I have said, *Doctor Hoffman* is a novel 'of' as well as 'about' the Surrealist imagination!) Desiderio, desire itself, would be the prize energy producer if he consented to enter the love pen that awaits him and Albertina. Instead, appalled at the contradiction within a 'liberation philosophy' that depends on slavery (even if the slaves are willing love slaves), he turns and runs, killing both father and daughter.

Ricarda Smith, reading this ending, criticises Punter for what she considers his celebratory view of Marcuse (for she too sees Doctor Hoffman as an allegory of the 1960s philosopher). According to Smith, Carter is quite critical of Marcuse – indeed: 'contradicts Marcuse's optimistic view that ... highly advanced productivity makes a "non-repressive civilization" possible'.[42] As for me, I find both Punter's and Smith's readings plausible. I am surprised, however, that neither mentions Surrealism, even though the character of Doctor Hoffman is, both textually and representationally, much more of a Surrealist than a Marcuse. Marcuse himself, in a crucial passage in *Eros and Civilization* [1955] where he argues for the social and liberating value of fantasy, can think of no better support for his argument than to quote a passage from the first Surrealist Manifesto, in French, ending with the sentence I have chosen as an epigraph: 'La seule imagination me rend compte de ce qui *peut être*' ['Imagination alone offers me some intimation of what *can be*'].[43]

To say that Carter 'contradicts Marcuse's optimism' – more exactly, the optimism Marcuse shared with the Surrealists about the liberating potential of fantasy and desire – is, I think, to miss an important point. For if it is indeed true that Doctor Hoffman is no hero, and that his method of liberation mocks its own proclaimed aims, it is not at all certain that he is an allegory of either Marcuse's philosophy or the Surrealists'. I would suggest that if he is an allegory of anything, it is of the technological appropriation (but I prefer the Gallicism *récupération*) of Surrealism and liberation philosophy – precisely that *récupération* which Marcuse himself, not at all optimistically, analysed as early as the 1961 preface to the second edition of *Eros and Civilization*. Marcuse called this mode of *récupération* 'repressive desublimation' and saw in it, with something close to despair, the latest ruse of capitalism. He himself had hoped for something quite different: 'non-repressive sublimation', or the diffusion of the erotic impulse to all aspects of life, with an attendant decrease in aggression and release of the creative faculties. In his terms (but also in Surrealist terms), this would be the triumph of the Pleasure Principle over the Reality Principle: work itself would become a form of play. Instead, repressive desublimation turned this project on its head, and made even play – or love – into a form of work.[44] □

Suleiman proceeds to move from references to Marcuse to a discussion of Guy Debord's book *La Société du spectacle*, which was published in 1967, seven years after Marcuse's *Eros and Civilization*. She argues that these works can be linked on the grounds that both critique the impact of technology on society, and regard it as operating to distance people from each other and their environment. Suleiman quotes Debord's opening lines: 'All the life of societies in which modern conditions of production dominate presents itself as an immense accumulation of *spectacles*. Everything that was directly lived has distanced itself in a representation.'[45] In this context, *Hoffman* becomes, not a nostalgic allegory of 1960s politics, but an ironic parody of 'the nightmarish synthesis of repressive desublimation and the society of the spectacle'.[46] In these terms, Desiderio's murder of Doctor Hoffman preserves the society of the spectacle, and the Surrealist imagination Hoffman attempts to both channel and master 'becomes a private passion, not a means to change the world'.[47]

In Suleiman's analysis, therefore, Desiderio still fails, but his failure is both inevitable and necessary. It is inevitable because Suleiman, like Punter, regards Desiderio as incapable of endorsing Hoffman's world-view. But whereas Punter stresses the nostalgia which imbues the final scenes of the novel, Suleiman interrogates the validity of such an emotion through reference to an aspect of the novel which Punter ignores. In the final section of her essay, she introduces the issue of the text's portrayal of sexual politics, and draws attention to the myriad examples of female abuse with which the reader is presented. In a world dominated by the dialectics of desire, she argues, Carter's intention is to stress that women are always victims – therefore, however seductive it might be (for the male subject at least), such a world is not ultimately tenable. Although its destruction condemns Desiderio to a lifetime of loss, he nevertheless cannot escape accusations of complicity in the numerous acts of exploitation he has witnessed in his journey through Nebulous Time.

■ If the 'Surrealist imagination' founders on the shoals of the society of the spectacle, then one of the reasons for this foundering is related not to technology or postmodern capitalism, but to sexual politics. Technology and capitalism change with the times. [...] Sexual politics, by contrast, is timeless, transcultural, international – or so Carter

implies, in my reading of her novel. Here is one place where the gap
between technology and ideology becomes apparent: even the most
revolutionary technological advances do not necessarily change the
relations between men and women. Desiderio, in his various travels,
observes a number of societies: the society of the Amerindian River
People, that of the African tribe, and that of the Centaurs. In all these,
especially in the last two, women are in a horrifying subordinate position. In the African tribe, women are raised to be soulless soldiers by
having all feeling, including maternal feeling, literally excised out of
them. Among the Centaurs, women do all the work while the men
pray – and women are 'tattooed all over, even in their faces, in order to
cause them more suffering, for [the Centaurs] believed women were
born only to suffer' (p. 172).[48]

This sexual politics of inequality does not characterise only the
primitive or fantastic societies, it also characterises every other world
that Desiderio visits or inhabits. The city he lived in, before the
onslaught of Doctor Hoffman's images, was 'thickly, obtusely masculine' (p. 15), as is the Minister of Determination. But so, in its own
way, is the insubstantial dream-world of Doctor Hoffman. The peep-
show displays that Desiderio describes at several points are like
Surrealist paintings, to be sure; but they are also unmistakably male
voyeuristic fantasies (as Surrealist paintings often are), representing
female orifices and body parts, and scenes of extreme sexual violence
perpetrated on the bodies of women. One of them, bearing the suggestive title 'Everyone knows what the night is for', shows a three-
dimensional model of a mutilated woman with a knife in her belly
(p. 45). [...] Continuing the voyeur theme, the 'Erotic Traveller' chapter (Chapter 5) has Desiderio and the Count visit a Sadeian brothel,
the 'House of Anonymity', which features live prostitutes staged in the
most degraded and violated poses. In a sense, the violation spills over
to the two men, who are dressed for the occasion in special costumes
which mask their faces while leaving their genitals fully exposed: 'the
garb grossly emphasized our manhoods while utterly denying our
humanity' (p. 130).

Desiderio's own position in the novel is ambiguous. As a man, he
generally enjoys the male privileges. (This is most emphasised in the
episode with the Centaurs: Albertina is raped by every male in the
group, and when she heals she is sent into the fields to work with the
women; Desiderio, as befits a man, is allowed to study and roam,
learning the Centaur's customs and mythology.) At the same time, he
clearly has an unusually sharp view of and sympathy for women's
roles, and on at least one occasion he is made to find out 'what it is to
be a woman' in a more violent way, when he is gang-raped by nine
Moroccan acrobats in the travelling circus he accompanies disguised

as the peepshow proprietor's nephew. This experience, he later tells us, allows him to understand what Albertina goes through when she is raped by the Centaurs, and to 'suffer with her' in the process. Finally, Desiderio is physically a mirror-image of Albertina, who herself takes the shape of a young man on several occasions. They are 'exactly the same height' (p. 136), and by the end of their adventures they look like twins [...].

Here, in the sexual ambiguities of the lovers, may lie the most politically radical aspect of *The Infernal Desire Machines of Doctor Hoffman* [...], however, the ending is quite dark, if ironic: the social status quo is maintained and, despite the son's heroisation, the Father wins. It doesn't matter which Father, the Minister or Doctor Hoffman, for they both want to lay down the law – and even if it is not the same law, women's place remains identical in both. Albertina, like countless other daughters in literature (and life), loves her daddy above all other men, even to the point of self-sacrifice. Desiderio, like countless other males in Western literature and life, 'kills the thing he loves', and spends the rest of his days dreaming about her.

From all of which one may conclude that if the world is really to change, it will have to start by imagining 'what it is to be a woman' – and man – differently. Differently from the Minister, differently from Doctor Hoffman, differently even from the Surrealists, whose imaginative faculties faltered on the threshold of sexual roles.[49] □

Previous chapters of this study have indicated that Carter exhibited interest in the spectacle of female victimisation from her earliest work. However, the early part of this chapter has already cited examples of critics who assert that her experience of Japanese society intensified this interest, providing Carter with plenty of examples of that culture's tendency to associate pain with pleasure. In her essay 'Once More into the Mangle', for example, Carter reflects on the role allocated to the female heroine in Japanese comic strips, in which '[f]ormed only to suffer, she is subjected to every indignity'.[50] The disturbing tableaux provided by the peep-show in *Hoffman* bear an obvious relationship to the 'freeze-frames' of the comic-books, which feature the heroine's violated body 'emphatically stuck through with a sword, or her decapitated but still weeping head'.[51]

However, during this period, Carter encountered another piece of work which was enormously to influence her depiction of sexual violence in her fiction, but which owed nothing to oriental culture. Carter first encountered the work of the Marquis de Sade whilst in Japan, and Linden Peach, in his study of Carter's novels, argues that *Hoffman* is the first book in which she is not merely employing subject-matter that could be construed as pornographic, but is consciously representing a pornographic *style* – a difference he attributes directly to her new interest in de Sade.

■ Here [...] Carter parodies the principal tradition of pornographic writing. As she explains in *The Sadeian Woman* (1979), since pornography is 'produced in the main by men for an all-male clientele' it has 'certain analogies with a male brothel'.[52] Desiderio is the author of a fantasy which, as Sally Robinson [...] says, 'enlists an array of misogynistic sentiment and fantasy'.[53] However, here Carter as a female author is appropriating a male consciousness to expose how women are trapped, like the woman reader of this novel, in a male imaginary. Moreover, the narrative technique of ventriloquism – a female author speaking in a male voice – is employed to create not just pornography but an especially sadistic version of it. Hence as a parody of pornography, Desiderio's account positions the (male) reader as voyeur but does not necessarily guarantee a voyeuristic, pleasure position for him.[54] □

Peach, therefore, does not read Carter's adoption of pornographic tropes as problematic, since her ultimate intent is deconstructive. Other commentators on her work, however, are rather more critical; not necessarily of Carter's intentions, but of the degree of success with which she realises them. In her essay 'In Despair of the Old Adams: Angela Carter's *The Infernal Desire Machines of Dr.* [sic] *Hoffman*', Cornel Bonca echoes Day and Suleiman in her claim that the realm of desire rests on the perpetuation of the image of woman as the object of desire. She also resembles Peach in her argument that Carter emphasises the *un*desirability of this situation for women through the adoption of the styles and conventions of pornographic writing. For Bonca, however, this attempt to use pornography against itself fails because Carter is unable successfully to formulate a positive conception of female sexuality with which to replace the familiar scenes of oppression: hence the novel freezes in the pornographic frame, unable to escape its own conceptualisations of woman as victim or whore.

■ The liberation of imagination and desire [...] creates its own power vacuum, which authoritative impulses rush to fill. So it's not just Reason that suppresses, as the liberal tradition insists; the images of Dr. Hoffman's desire machines, when totally unrestrained, create their own inexorable logic of domination that, at [its] extremes, [leads] to bondage, cruelty, even murder. (Carter is very close to [Georges] Bataille: 'In essence, the domain of eroticism is the domain of violence, of violation'; and perhaps with Camille Paglia: 'whenever sexual freedom is sought or achieved, sadomasochism will not be far behind'.)[55] The novel offers no middle position where the powers of eros and the powers of reason can negotiate, but this is an apocalyptic book, written at the tail end of an era that failed to bring to fruition the promise of Norman O. Brown's *Life against Death* [1959] and so is as furiously pessimistic as that other apocalyptic wonder of the early 1970s, *Gravity's Rainbow* [1973].

Desiderio's style, much like Carter's in her books of the sixties and seventies, is an unsettling combination of English empirical exactitude – the book is full of elaborately described tableaux which feel 'objective', static, and often cruelly distant – and a fevered-brow Gothic decadence whirling with emotional tumult. This makes sense because Desiderio is a man caught between two fathers, the Reason-freak Minister and a mad Dionysian genius. However, the style creates some strange and striking verbal effects, much in the line of Sade, [Edgar Allan] Poe and [Charles] Baudelaire (and Bataille and [Michel] Foucault as well), all of whom train the surgical lights and steely instruments of cold reason on the dark chthonic [underground] recesses of sexual desire. For example, Desiderio describes what he sees inside a peep show:

> Here, a wax figure of the headless body of a mutilated woman lay in a pool of painted blood. She wore only the remains of a pair of black mesh stockings and a ripped suspender belt of shiny black rubber. Her arms stuck out stiffly on either side of her and once again I noticed the loving care with which the craftsmen who manufactured her had simulated the growth of underarm hair. The right breast had been partially segmented and hung open to reveal two surfaces of meat as bright and false as the plaster sirloins which hang in toy butcher's shops while her belly was covered with some kind of paint that always contrived to look wet and, from the paint, emerged the handle of an enormous knife which was kept always a-quiver by the action (probably) of a spring. (pp. 56–7)[56]

The exhibit is mordantly titled EVERYONE KNOWS WHAT THE NIGHT IS FOR, but it's hard to tell what we're supposed to 'know' from it, ironically or otherwise. That this representation of a mutilated woman contains 'simulated' growth of underarm hair, that the spliced breast looks like meat from a 'toy' butcher's shop, and that the blood on this woman's belly is 'contrived to look wet' set up a gap in knowledge, a gaping wound, really, between horror and its representation. And this gap makes the tableau more horrible, not less. We might call this a semiotic horror: what incites a reader's revulsion and fear is precisely the opening that the description calls up between signifier and signified. The reality of mutilation, while calling up deep and ancient anxieties, is presented as unpresentable: and the viewer (or reader) experiences the fear of mutilation in deep solitude precisely because language and image can't seem to get at it.

This sort of style is essentially pornographic. Anyone who has ever watched a cheap porno video, where pink bodies writhe under the blinding glare of a two-hundred-fifty-watt bulb, knows what I mean. The scene of people having sex is made ob-scene: impossible to see, because the garish white light, however much it does expose, cloaks the secret essences of sex that people come to pornography to discover. Carter's language works like this harsh white light: it deliberately shows language in cruel relation to its subjects, allowing it to perform, in dark satiric fashion, the objectivizing function it usually performs in social discourse. In her polemical study *The Sadeian Woman* Carter calls the Marquis de Sade a 'moral pornographer' – one who turns pornography's conventions on their head for morally and ideologically instructive purposes, and Carter evidently had her own ambitions in this line.[57]

But what the instructive moral pornography of *Desire Machines* lacks is a vision that transcends the gap, that heals the wound. The novel rages against the cruelty of sexuality but can no more offer an image of sane sexuality than it can render an interesting Minister of Determination. Like one of its forerunners, *Gulliver's Travels* [1726], the book's rage simply overwhelms the possibilities of a positive vision. Seven years later, in *The Sadeian Woman*, Carter touted Sade as the man who put 'pornography in the service of women', who declared 'himself unequivocally for the right of women to fuck'; but she also realized that 'For Sade, all tenderness is false, a deceit, a trap; all pleasure contains within itself the seeds of atrocities', and that 'His misanthropy bred a hatred of the mothering function' (pp. 37, 27, 25, 36). In that study, Carter seemed to declare herself a Sadeian woman with an affirmative vision: she wanted to make tenderness possible amid the exploration of the outer reaches of sexuality. That she could succeed is clear from the quirky but gentle sex comedy of *Wise Children* and in such stories as 'The Company of Wolves', where a fearless and sexually very healthy Little Red Riding Hood soothes the ravenous wolf by bedding him down. [...] However, in *Desire Machines* Carter isn't so sanguine. There is no cheerful, healthy sex here, where the agonistic demands for power and control are resolved in consensual pleasure. There is only the dead end of sexual domination.[58] □

As Bonca implies, Carter was to attempt to negotiate herself out of 'the dead end of sexual domination' in later texts, none of which quite reproduces the bleakness of *Hoffman*'s vision. In her next novel, *The Passion of New Eve*, the surreal landscapes of Nebulous Time metamorphose into the cities and deserts of America, and the male narrator is estranged from his own body – a move which enables Carter to engage in a radical and disturbing exploration of gender identity.

CHAPTER FIVE

The Passion of New Eve (1977)

THE PASSION of New Eve is coming to occupy a belated position of
prominence in Carter's *oeuvre*. Its radical portrayals of femininity and
masculinity, its evocation of lurid, surreal landscapes, and its persistent
undermining of narrative perspective and causality link it to many cur-
rently fashionable theories to do with gender, transgender, technology
and the postmodern. As we shall see, many discussions of this novel
acknowledge that the readings they propose have been constructed
retrospectively, as it were, out of ideas that post-date the publication of
the novel itself.

When *The Passion of New Eve* appeared in 1977, however, it received a
mixed, and somewhat baffled, reception. Peter Ackroyd's review in the
Spectator was typical:

■ Now that the conventional realistic novel has been embalmed with
the sneer still on its face, certain 'modern' writers are veering wildly
towards the grotesque, the fantastic and the merely silly. Surrealism is,
after all, only realism with the ends cut off. Angela Carter's new novel
doesn't quite resolve the dilemma which lurks here somewhere. Hers is
a simple story of rape, castration and apocalypse. Novels of future shock
are actually the easiest to write since they require only limited powers
of observation and description – and, at this level, imagination is the
cheapest commodity of all. Angela Carter's vision of New York must
be the most lurid yet, surpassing even Doris Lessing in its horror: gangs
of women's-libbers blow up 'wedding shops', and send gift-parcels of
'well-honed razors' to new brides. That uneasy tone, perched somewhere between high seriousness and farce, unsettles the narrative as it
leaps from one improbability to the next. And Angela Carter isn't
quite sure where to land or, even, whether to land at all.[1] □

Ackroyd goes on to dismiss Carter's style ('languorous, sickly and poly-
syllabic'), the plot ('culled from any number of B-films'), and the novel's

ultimate intent ('[t]o say as the blurb does that she is investigating "the nature of the mythology of sexuality" is like acclaiming Ken Russell as "the musicologist and literary critic"'). In fact, in an interview with Olga Kenyon, Carter later remarked that 'Only *Gay News* gave me a really sympathetic review'.[2]

Like its predecessor, *The Infernal Desire Machines of Doctor Hoffman*, *The Passion of New Eve* is a difficult novel, and has been described by Lorna Sage – in a generally very complimentary study – as 'a raw and savage book' which is too busy working through ideas to be bothered with entertaining an audience.[3] Bearing out Sage's opinion to a certain extent, Carter was always very explicit about the fact that this was intended as a novel of ideas. She described it to Olga Kenyon as 'my most heavily plotted book, an imitation of a generically foreign novel';[4] although she went on to describe its genesis in terms which suggest she actually had the reader very much in mind when she was writing:

■ The novel was sparked off by a visit to the USA in 1969. It was the height of the Vietnam war, with violent public demos and piles of garbage in New York streets. If you remember, it was the year of gay riots in Greenwich village, when they even chucked rocks; so my scenario of uprisings isn't all that far-fetched. But I wanted to make it as pleasurable as possible, I put the film stars in a real art deco house. I loved writing that glass castle, it's partly inspired by Celtic mythology, partly by the idea of a sterile Fisher King. I give the hero and heroine a fabulous liebestod [love-suicide], they deserve it, and so does the reader.[5] □

Carter was also very clear concerning her authorial intentions and, when interviewed by John Haffenden in 1984, she expressed disappointment that readers of the novel hadn't always fully understood the book's central message:

■ In *The Passion of New Eve* the central character is a transvestite movie star, and I created this person in order to say some quite specific things about the cultural production of femininity. The promotion slogan for the film *Gilda* [1946], starring Rita Hayworth, was 'There was never a woman like Gilda', and that may have been one of the reasons why I would make this Hollywood star a transvestite, a man, because only a man could think of femininity in terms of that slogan. Quite a number of people read *The Passion of New Eve* as a feminist tract and recoiled with suitable horror and dread, but in fact there is quite a careful and elaborate discussion of femininity as a commodity, of Hollywood producing illusions as tangible commodities – yet most of that was completely by-passed. I don't mind that, because you can't dictate how a book should be read. But I spent a long time on that novel, which meant so much to me for various reasons, and obviously I was disappointed that it should be treated as just another riotous extravaganza.

It was intended as a piece of black comedy. One reviewer, a great gay spokesperson and writer, said he found Mother 'such a cosy person' because of all those tits! One of the snags is that I do put everything in a novel to be *read* [...] on as many levels as you can comfortably cope with at the time. In *The Passion of New Eve* the transvestite character Tristessa has a glass house – the kind of place in which you shouldn't live if you throw stones – which is an image of a certain kind of psychic vulnerability. Tristessa has set up in the house a waxworks called The Hall of the Immortals, which contains the dead martyrs of Hollywood including Jean Harlow and Judy Garland, and that was supposed to be indicating something quite specific about the nature of illusion and of personality which Hollywood did and does invent.[6] □

Carter is at pains here to stress that *The Passion of New Eve* is no unthinking 'tract', but a thoughtful and precise anatomisation of the way in which cinema perpetuates its illusions. It is interesting, however, to contrast Carter's disclaimer here with an essay published in 1983, in which she refers to *The Passion of New Eve* using the very terminology she dismissed in her conversation with Haffenden a year later. In 'Notes from the Front Line', she describes it as an 'anti-mythic novel [...] conceived [...] as a feminist tract about the social creation of femininity, among other things'.[7]

Typically, however, the term 'feminist tract' takes on different shades of meaning in Carter's hands. Certainly, 'Notes from the Front Line' links the novel's interest in 'the social creation of femininity' to an explicitly feminist standpoint. She began to define herself as a feminist, Carter said, when she began to 'question ... the nature of my reality as a woman. How that social fiction of my "femininity" was created, by means outside my control, and palmed off on me as the real thing'.[8] *The Passion of New Eve*, so centrally concerned with the cultural production of femininity, can be viewed from this perspective as the most developed 'feminist' novel she had as yet written. However, the elaborate games that Carter plays with gender identity in this text means that the nature of both femininity and masculinity is subjected to critique, with the result that the novel is therefore resistant to simplistic analyses which seek to interpret it as a female wish-fulfilment fantasy.

In her essay 'The Dangers of Angela Carter', Elaine Jordan asserts that to assume that the narrator of *The Passion of New Eve* is 'a role model for a new woman' is fundamentally to misread the text, and to underestimate the real complexity of Carter's narrative project.

■ The title's analogy with the passion of Christ the Messiah might suggest such a reading – but this is blasphemous not authoritative; Carter is playing with alternative theologies of the power of virginity and the androgyny of God's son. Rather, Eve/Evelyn, like Desiderio in *Hoffman*, is akin to the passive hero of [Walter] Scott's novels, who is put through certain phases of action for the instruction of the reader. It is the action and the commentary on it which signify. In *The Passion of New Eve* these phases are modelled on those of the alchemical search: first *nigredo*, the melting of the metals, as in the chaos of New York where blackness actually holds a promise for the future as yet unseen; then the whitening phase in which elements separate out, as in the fragments of American lifestyles Eve encounters; and finally *rubedo*, the red fire of revolution which may produce pure gold. The Czech alchemist in New York is one pointer to such a reading; and given this story's concern with cinema, one model could have been Sergei Eisenstein's notion of combining alchemy with dialectical materialism, in montage.[9] So all this demands special knowledge? Yes, why not? Curiosity, as Charles Perrault said, is a charming passion. It is not essential for a feminist writer to assume naïve readers, or for every reader to see all possible readings. In my mother's tenement there are many apartments, and that's not the only house there is. This may mislead readers who are not already politically aware, as [Robert] Clark fears? Get away – I'm not as daft as you think, my mother always says.[10] □

Jordan's view of *The Passion of New Eve* as a multi-layered text which, in its efforts to address a multiplicity of ideas and a wide variety of readers, is open to a range of possible interpretations, is reiterated in David Punter's analysis in *The Hidden Script: Writing and the Unconscious* (1985). Along with other critics of the novel, Punter examines how it seeks to explode the universal archetypes through which 'Woman' is codified as the passive object of masculine desire. He stresses how the recurring trope of mirroring, which estranges gender from the body and the image from the self, attains its apotheosis in the moment when the male narrator Evelyn sees himself in the mirror for the first time after his transformation into the female Eve. In the viewing of an image which is both himself and a stranger, Eve(lyn) experiences

■ the wrench and dislocation which is at the heart of woman's relationship with herself in a world riddled with masculine power-structures: inner self forced apart from the subject of self-presentation, an awareness of hollowness, a disbelief that this self-on-view can be taken as a full representation of the person alongside the bitter knowledge that it will be, that at every point the woman is locked into the metaphysical insult of the masculine gaze.[11] □

Unusually, however, Punter goes on to examine how his interpretation of
the narrative is unavoidably influenced by his gender: 'My own experience
of the reading relations of the text, as a male reader, is bizarre, and makes
me doubt – as it is designed to – the gendered structure of narrative.'[12]

■ As a male reader, I find myself the victim of illusions. Although I
am aware that Carter is a woman, and although that extra-textual consciousness is incarnated within the text in her obvious proximity to
Leilah/Lilith, I nonetheless find that the first-person narrative of
Evelyn/Eve appears to me throughout, no matter what the overt sex of
the new Messiah at the time, as a masculine narrative. When Evelyn
becomes Eve, my experience is of viewing a masquerade; I read Eve
still through the male consciousness (Evelyn's) of what he has
become. It is as though Evelyn forms a barrier, a thin film which
stretches between 'Carter' and Eve at all points; and thus I too am
forced to tread that line, to respond as a male to the residual male in
Eve. Perhaps this is a recourse against humiliation, a refusal of the
childed quality of masculinity which is postulated both in Evelyn's
encounter with Mother and also, earlier on, in his fear when he is
returned to the artificial womb of Beulah:

> I was utterly helpless, in a strange land, in the strangest of places –
> buried deep in a blind room seamless as an egg deep in a nameless
> desert a long way from home. I broke down and I think I must have
> called for my mother because, when I did so, there was an explosion
> of soft, ironic laughter from the concealed loudspeakers so I knew
> that, however silent they were, they were always listening to me. At
> that, my shame became too much to bear and I buried my tear-
> stained face in my cold bed. Oh, that low, bubbling laughter! 'Cry
> baby. Cry baby.' No humiliation like a child's humiliation. (p.26)[13]

And yet, of course, the real humiliation is not quite that; rather, it is
the re-emergence of the child at the inappropriate moment, the discovery that this solitude does not excite the enactment of male myths of
heroism but is, instead, insupportable.[14] □

In thus drawing attention to the complications inherent in his relationship to the text as a male reader, Punter is not implying that it is therefore addressed only to women. In fact, he is saying quite the opposite.
Men and women might well understand the text in different ways, but
both will be drawn into a critique of gender-based determinism – the
notion that one's identity is inescapably dependent on one's sex – since
masculinity and femininity are placed under equally searching scrutiny
in Carter's novel.

The reader's relationship to the narrative forms only part of Punter's debate, but Alison Lee addresses the same issue in far more detail in her essay 'Angela Carter's New Eve(lyn): De/Engendering Narrative', published in 1996. Her view that 'the reader, even with the whole story in front of her or him, is in a ... perplexing position if she or he tries to pin down whether the narrative voice or the focalization is male or female',[15] recalls the sense of confusion expressed by Punter.

■ The most interesting aspect of this section of the novel is the complication of the narrative level and extent of participation. To some degree the novel imitates the narrative structure of one of its intertexts – *Great Expectations* – in that Eve is narrating in retrospect, yet she is both the I and the not-I narrator. Determining narrative level in the section of the novel that tells Evelyn's story depends entirely on whether the reader sees Eve as a man in a woman's body or as a woman [...]. To use [Shlomith] Rimmon-Kenan's terms, Eve is extra-heterodiegetic if she has indeed become a woman separate from Evelyn, but intrahomodiegetic if Evelyn is still part of Eve. Given that hetero- and homodiegesis are determined by a narrator's participation in the story either not at all or 'at least in some manifestation of his "self"',[16] it is worth noting that 'self', here, is a liminal concept of which neither Evelyn nor Eve is very sure. Indeed, the issue is complicated because there are 'feminine' qualities in Evelyn even before his metamorphosis and 'masculine' qualities in Eve after it: 'As I have told you, I was slender and delicately made; now I was dressed like this girl, I looked like this girl's sister, except that I was far prettier than she' (p. 55).[17] Evelyn recognises in himself 'a fatal lack' (p. 34), one that he thinks is reflected by Leilah. Eve, who is 'literally in two minds' after her operation (p. 77), comments, 'I would often make a gesture with my hands that was out of Eve's character or exclaim with a subtly male inflection ... Although I was a woman, I was now passing for a woman, but, then, many women born spend their whole lives in just such *imitations*' (p. 101) [Lee's emphasis]. And as Eve becomes 'almost the thing I was' (p. 107), she comments that remembering her life as Evelyn 'was like remembering a film I'd seen once whose performances did not concern me. Even my memories no longer fitted me, they were old clothes belonging to somebody else no longer living' (p. 92).

There is no marked change of 'voice' between the parts of the novel that concern Eve and Evelyn, although in both sections comments are made about women's speech being incomprehensible. Leilah's speech is reported indirectly, and the narrator comments that 'her argot or patois was infinitely strange to me, I could hardly understand a word she said' (p. 26). The women in Zero's harem are forced to utter animal noises because 'Zero believed women were made from a different soul substance from men, a more primitive, animal stuff', and so 'our first words every morning were spoken in a language we ourselves could not understand' (p. 97). And yet this too is reported speech which the reader does not read. However, even the direct discourse cannot be easily assigned either to male or female. The first sentence, for example, appears to be spoken by Evelyn: 'The last night I spent in London, I took some girl or other to the movies and, through her mediation, I paid you a little tribute of spermatozoa, Tristessa' (p. 5). Logically, the speaker is Evelyn, since only Evelyn could pay such a tribute. Yet it could also be argued that the speaker is an Evelyn who has been temporarily remembered by Eve, whose distance from an 'actual' Evelyn is made clear in the formality, almost parody, of the phrase 'tribute of spermatozoa'. At this point of retrospective telling, neither Tristessa nor Evelyn 'exists' except in Eve's memory; each is re-created by Eve, who soon makes her presence known. The way in which she does so imitates Leilah's erotic journey through the labyrinthine New York streets. As Evelyn, consumed with desire, follows Leilah, she leaves behind an Ariadne's thread of clothing dropped on the street for Evelyn to pick up: her dress, crotchless knickers, fur coat, and stockings. When Eve narrates the opening chapters, her narration becomes itself a kind of striptease, when she drops clues about her voice and plot: 'Tristessa. Enigma. Illusion. Woman? Ah!' (p. 6). Eve continues, 'The black Lady never advised me on those techniques when she fitted me up with a uterus of my own' (p. 9), and 'There was a seventeenth-century print, tinted by hand, of a hermaphrodite carrying a golden egg that exercised a curious fascination upon me, the dual form with its breasts and its cock, its calm, comprehensive face. (Coming events? ...)' (p. 13). Although these clues, Tiresias-like, prophesy something of the future, they complicate the narrative. Like the discarded articles of clothing, Eve's snippets of information dropped along the way for the reader to pick up make it clear that the narrator is, and is not, Evelyn. However, while tempting the reader to pursue the erotic game, Eve's discarded clues do not lead the reader to a fulfilment of desire. The clues are clues about how not to read the various labyrinths appearing in the novel, and this includes the narrative itself. At the heart of each labyrinth is something that seems to be a center or a culmination but is in fact a dual, if not multiple, being: Leilah, Mother, and Tristessa. But centers fluctuate: Leilah becomes Lilith, Mother goes mad, Tristessa is revealed to be male and female. [... ...]

When, as a member of Zero's harem, Eve is subjected to Zero's violent coupling, she says:

And more than my body, some other equally essential part of my being was ravaged by him for, when he mounted me with his single eye blazing like the mouth of an automatic, his little body imperfectly stripped, I felt myself to be, not myself but he; and the experience of this crucial lack of self, which always brought with it a shock of introspection, forced me to know myself as a former violator at the moment of my own violation (pp. 101–2).

The phrase 'not myself but he' points back to Eve's life as Evelyn, suggesting that she recognizes herself as both self and other. Indeed, the fluidity of gender in the novel in both the transsexual Eve and the transvestite Tristessa accounts for some of the difficulties in ascribing levels of narrative and focalization. Gender does not determine narrative; it makes narrative identity as complex as gender identity.[18] ☐

For Lee, it is this very sense of narrative confusion which makes *The Passion of New Eve* a text which exemplifies 'a feminist writing practice' as defined by Rachael Blau DuPlessis. To support this point, she quotes directly from DuPlessis's book *Writing Beyond the Ending: Narrative Strategies of Twentieth-Century Women Writers*:

■ One may assert that any female cultural practice that makes the 'meaning production process' itself 'the site of struggle' may be considered feminist. These authors are 'feminist' because they construct a variety of oppositional strategies to the depiction of gender institutions in narrative. A writer expresses dissent from an ideological formation by attacking elements of narrative that repeat, sustain or embody the values and attitudes in question. So after breaking the sentence, a rupture with the internalization of the authorities and voices of dominance, the woman writer will create that further rupture … breaking the sequence – the expected order.[19] ☐

Continues Lee: 'Indeterminacy in *The Passion of New Eve* is a challenge to the reader to recognize where the ruptures occur, where centers cannot hold, and where ideological formations are undermined in the narrative.'[20] The fluidity of gender identity which so disturbs the stability of the narrative voice is not an endorsement of androgyny – the state in which male and female co-exist in perfect balance – but instead lays stress on gender as a performance which is being continuously generated and (often imperfectly) sustained. Lee's understanding of gender as performance is indebted to the work of Judith Butler, an influential gender theorist, whose book *Gender Trouble* was published in 1990. Lee draws on Butler's views towards the end of her debate in order to argue that the text's feminist message hinges on this sense of performativity.

■ Judith Butler, in *Gender Trouble*, makes the point that gender 'is the repeated stylisation of the body, a set of repeated acts within a highly rigid regulatory frame that congeal over time to produce the appearance of substance, of a natural source of being'.[21] Mother's fondest wish – to kill time and live forever – is perhaps an effort to eliminate precisely those frames that regulate gender. But it is also clear that her project will fail, because although Mother, like Eve, is a technological construction, she believes in the essence of what her appearance conveys. For both Tristessa and Eve, gender is 'an ongoing discursive practice';[22] for Mother, it is a 'concrete fact' (p. 58). [... ...]

What is clear about both Tristessa and Eve, however, is the lack of an 'original' gender. Butler argues that gender parody, as in transvestism, 'is *of* the very notion of an original ... so gender parody reveals that the original identity after which gender fashions itself is an imitation without an origin'. In such 'fluidity of identities', she sees an openness to 'resignification and recontextualisation; parodic proliferation deprives hegemonic culture and its critics of the claim to naturalized or essentialist gender identities'.[23] Zero and Mother are characters who, despite their self-construction as male and female incarnate, do see an essential identity. Each has eliminated, or wishes to eliminate, the 'other'. For Eve and Tristessa, though, gender cannot help being performative because its liminality provides multiple possibilities.

In Carter's novel, this multiplicity is reflected in the narrative and in the shifting voice and look of the narrator. It seems to me that the ideological possibilities of 'Who speaks?' and 'Who sees?' give narratology a critical potential, to use Bal's term,[24] one that can combine the semiotic and referential. Susan Lanser's intriguing arguments for a feminist narratology include the suggestion that narratology might provide a model for determining whether there is a 'woman's writing'.[25] She makes the point that the 'precision and abstraction of narratological systems offers [*sic*] the safety for investigation that more impressionistic theories of difference do not. In a novel such as *The Passion of New Eve*, however [...] the narrative system can be shown to be neither abstract nor precise, depending on the questions one asks of it, and it is this that makes it most fruitful for feminist study. I do not mean to suggest that the opposite of 'abstract and precise' in itself makes anything feminist or typical of women's writing [...] but it is the heteroglossia, the multiplicity, the undermining of binaries that make a text like Carter's feminist in both its narrative structure and its story.[26] □

In a detailed and highly interesting essay, 'Unexpected Geometries: Transgressive Symbolism and the Transsexual Subject in Angela Carter's

The Passion of New Eve', Heather L. Johnson takes Lee's discussion of the performative nature of gender one step further. Whereas Lee's theoretical touchstone in this regard is Judith Butler, Johnson draws on the work of transsexual theorist Sandy Stone, whose influential essay 'The Empire Strikes Back: A Posttranssexual Manifesto' was published in 1991. Johnson explores *The Passion of New Eve* as a work which anticipates the vogue for transsexual autobiography, in which the speaking subject, like the fictional Eve(lyn), is dislocated from an 'original' or 'authentic' gender identity.

■ Carter's text reveals some intriguing similarities to these concurrent non-fictional accounts of gender experience, addressing the problematic relation of fantasy and history in autobiography – a relation which, for the transsexual, involves the disclosure or denial of an 'other' gendered past. Comparison with this non-fiction reveals, for instance, that in contrast to the absence in transsexual self-presentations, as Stone notes, of an 'erotic sense of their own bodies', the configurations of desire recounted in Eve(lyn)'s narrative become all the more conspicuous.[27]

To historicize *The Passion of New Eve* in this way is indeed to underline the avant-garde nature of Carter's writing. Her novel seems to pre-empt, by nearly two decades, recent developments in the discipline of gender studies such as the intersection of gender theory and transsexual autobiography in the work of Stone, Kate Bornstein and others.[28] More specifically, I would argue that in her protagonist's declaration of his/her complex history of gender identification, Carter prefigures the provocative notion of a 'post-transsexual' identity.[29] □

Like Elaine Jordan in the essay quoted earlier in this chapter, Johnson examines the extent to which *The Passion of New Eve* draws on alchemical references, and finds them highly significant to her study of the narrative's portrayal of gender. As a practice centrally concerned with transmutation and metamorphosis, she argues, alchemy functions as an apt metaphor for the ever-changing configurations of gender within the novel.

■ It is within this arena of metaphors – this site of play, possibility and exchange – that Carter introduces the gender-transgressive figure. Initially, Evelyn and Tristessa embody fixed and polarized positions of gender in relation to one another. Soon, however, they experience that same dynamic across their own individual bodies. For instance, the classic relation of male gaze and female object is present in the opening scene when Evelyn is aroused by the projection of Tristessa's image on the cinema screen. Similarly, when he later describes Leilah as 'a visitor in her own flesh' (p.27),[30] Evelyn seems to sense the discrepancy between an inferred, elusive subjectivity (invisible and therefore threatening to him) and her body as defined by a conventionally heterosexual paradigm of desire. His physical relationship with Leilah ends in feelings of disgust – a response to her differences from him as she comes to embody maternity, blackness and the feminine. These categories of alterity are all seen as disruptive, and necessary, to the world of the 'disembodied consciousness', where the domination of the rational depends, as Jane Gallop argues, 'on other sexes, classes, and races to embody the body', and it is in a world grounded on this cultural premise that Evelyn centres himself.[31]

Accordingly, he dreams of 'meeting Tristessa, she stark naked, tied, perhaps to a tree in a midnight forest' (p. 7). This image is soon explicitly allied to the experience of suffering, when Baroslav tells the story of the Gestapo murder of his wife during which 'he, tied to a tree, watched all and could do nothing' (p. 14). While the two images have distinctive contexts, this repetition noticeably replaces the fetishized female of the first scene with a male subject, and it is he who gives voice to the agony of the experience. Here the fantasized woman is silent and passive, while the historical man in speaking is active. Evelyn's male narrative certainly endorses this stereotypical and hierarchical view of gender relations.

Once he has been surgically provided with a replicated female body, Eve(lyn) transfers this dichotomous relation onto himself, thereby reproducing a perception of the self that is recognizably transvestite in character. He feels a discrepancy between outward female appearance and a sense of himself as essentially or internally male. Again, the interior/exterior model of subjectivity supports an identification of the body with the female and the mind with the male. Invoking the metaphor of the New World, Carter describes Eve(lyn) in a narcissistic pose: 'I delighted me ... I drew my discoverer's hand along the taut line of my shin and my thigh' (p. 146). In fact, he reacts to his body as if it were the body of a woman he desires: 'the cock in my head, still, twitched at the sight of myself' (p. 75). Here we encounter the first sign of the intriguing shape assumed by desire in Carter's novel.

It is this distinctive configuration of desire that prompts a shift in the focus of our present attention from the allegorical to the historical, as Carter's portrayal invites comparison to non-fictional accounts of transgender experience. For Eve(lyn)'s perception of his body in this case is strikingly similar to the transsexual Renée Richards's autobiographical account of her own post-operative moment when shown her newly-constructed genitals: 'What I saw was essentially what I had seen so many times between the legs of the women with whom I'd been intimate'.[32] Surely we have to question the gender status of the 'I' in this passage, for although Richards presents this as his first thought as a 'woman', it certainly seems to speak from his pre-operative subject position as a man. In Evelyn's case, since he is determined to reverse the surgery that Mother performed, he first reacts to the new female body as a garment he will wear only temporarily. So, while Evelyn does eventually approximate the subjecthood of the transsexual, this shift originates in the initial reaction of the transvestite.

Tristessa is complicit in a similar projection of this dynamic onto his own body in his identity as transvestite. Enacting the trajectory of male desire across the feminine body which is his own, Tristessa reproduces the relation of a male artist to an objectified female subject. He fetishizes parts of his body in a way accurately characteristic of the male transvestite. The psychologist Robert Stoller, one of the principal theorists of transvestism in the 1960s, gives an example of this in an account provided by one of his subjects: 'Sometimes in my mind I could mostly imagine the legs [his own] as being girls' legs.'[33] The desiring viewer and the desired object, usually distinct figures, are here confined within the one body. [... ...]

With her exaggerated femininity and her association with the theatre and performance, Tristessa is clearly the embodiment of camp in *The Passion of New Eve*. Tristessa's elusive identity seems to reside somewhere in the many fictional roles she dramatizes and in the wardrobe of variously gendered costumes from old Hollywood films. In assuming the exaggerated shape of the drag queen, her own subjectivity is triply mediated by the role of starlet, the fictional heroines she plays, and the cinema screen itself. Consequently, the multiply coded figure acts as a 'screen' onto which definitions of femininity and male desire are projected. Appearing to Eve(lyn) 'in seven veils of celluloid', Tristessa demonstrates 'every kitsch excess of the mode of femininity' (p. 71). Nevertheless, both modes of gender flicker across the transvestite's face. As they escape together in the abandoned helicopter, Eve(lyn) observes Tristessa looking back at the shattered house: 'he, she was lifted as on a wire, the mimic flight of the theatre, from the tomb she'd made for herself: he looked about him with the curiosity of Lazarus' (p. 143). The interchange of pronouns, signifying the simultaneous presence of both genders at this moment, is expressed in terms of mimetic performance and the trickery of ghostly resurrection.

The drag queen's metaphoric role is further highlighted when we consider the differences between her gender performance and that of Eve(lyn). As cross-dressers, both Tristessa, and in certain circumstances, Eve(lyn) are concerned with the act of 'passing'. To pass is to conform to a set of culturally determined signs, and by this means cross-dressers and non-cross-dressers alike attempt to project a 'pure', uncomplicated gender identity. [...]

Eve(lyn) [...] is described in the act of passing while she is not yet fully reconciled to her new body. During the consummation with Tristessa (in the male role), she is careful to mimic a woman's pleasure,

'heretofore, seen but never experienced' (p. 147), and so emits a calcu-
lated sigh at a strategic moment. Yet perhaps the most cunning act of
passing which Eve(lyn) performs is the act of narration itself. The
reader catches a glimpse of this performance when his/her narration
slips during a sexual attack by Zero which makes the victim cry. At
first the tears are explained as an altruistic and heroic measure to
ensure that the distraught and envious wives of Zero are not heard by
him. 'No. I'm lying', the narrator then confesses, 'I cried because of the
pain' (p. 107). In the terms of the novel, this admission of pretence
may be read as gender-based. The initial impulse is to deny the physical
intrusion and relate the incident in his accustomed voice of male
bravado, before shifting into a 'feminine' register (that is, like Tristessa).
In the narrator's abrupt change of story, Carter makes explicit both the
gendered nature of fiction and the fictive nature of gender.[34] □

As the discussions drawn from the work of Alison Lee and Heather L.
Johnson indicate, *The Passion of New Eve* is surrounded by debates which
investigate the text's portrayal of gender, and the extent to which that
influences the speaking position assumed within the narrative. Another
way of looking at this issue, however, is to place Carter's representation
of the ambiguously gendered body in the context of the backdrop against
which it is located. Heather L. Johnson, indeed, includes this approach in
her analysis, which considers the metaphorical significance of the novel's
American setting. A more comprehensive debate, however, is provided
by Lucie Armitt in her book *Theorising the Fantastic* (1996), in which she
aligns the ruptures in gender and narrative perspective in the text with
what she terms its 'conflicting geographies':

■ In tension with the solidly factual landscape of the known (but
foreign) continent of North America reside the futurist, dystopian
speculations of cybernetic experimentation. Alongside the decentring
of the fully gendered subject is a parallel decentring of spatial territory,
where the desert becomes a place of rebirth and the city becomes a
desert of death. Switching places with the fully developed body, the
fully developed city of/after postmodernism becomes, in itself, a
cybernetic structure within which [as Baudrillard puts it] 'the only
tissue ... is that of the freeways ... an incessant transurbanistic tissue'
and the corpuscles within this tapestry of veins and arteries comprise
'thousands of cars ... coming from nowhere, going nowhere: an
immense collective act ... without objectives'.[35] Of course, as Carter's
earlier novel *The Magic Toyshop* (1967) tells us, woman herself is an
'America ... [a] new found land', where received and enclosing
mythologies of the body can be reconceptualized in new and fantastic
forms.[36] In this sense, Carter's relocation of the historical past as

dystopian future transforms itself into a topographical landscape upon which the power-games of virtual maternal omnipotence play out their sadistic fantasies in a defamiliarized gangland state. Iain Chambers, in his postmodern reading of cultural identity, refers to the act of journeying to the United States as 'life lived in the third person, as myth, as dream, as cinema'.[37] And, in *The Passion of New Eve*, mythology does indeed combine with the cinematic and the fantastic, but here it produces a first-person narrator split into a singular third person within him/herself. In this respect, like so many others, Eve/lyn is not dissimilar to Tristessa him/herself: 'She had been the dream itself made flesh though the flesh I knew her in was not flesh itself but only a moving picture of flesh, real but not substantial' (pp. 7–8).[38, 39] □

The work of the theorist Jean Baudrillard, which is quoted in the above extract although Armitt gives his name only in a footnote, is of central importance to this section of her argument. She draws convincing parallels between Baudrillard and Carter in order to propose that *The Passion of New Eve* is an anticipation of simulation theory: a postmodern state of existence in which the 'simulation', or the copy, has obliterated reality. Armitt does not underplay the bleakness of the scenario Carter creates in this novel. She argues that Carter transforms America into a surreal landscape; a random assemblage of objects and events among which any sense of moral obligation or political engagement has been lost.

■ Baudrillard's *America*, first published in 1986, could almost have been based upon Carter's fictional narrative. As a novel intrinsically concerned with theoretically eclectic explorations, *The Passion of New Eve* brilliantly prefigures the work that Baudrillard and [Donna] Haraway have subsequently accomplished in the related areas of philosophy of simulation and cyborgian politics. For Baudrillard, America (more specifically the United States of America) epitomizes and embodies the postmodern preoccupation with the processes and order of the simulacra: 'The Americans ... have no sense of simulation. They are themselves simulation in its most developed state'. Like Carter, Baudrillard also juxtaposes city and desert, structuring his text around the motif of travel – a travelling that seeks a geography of time, space and cultural essence. But there is another important characteristic that they share, and this is their refusal to situate themselves safely within an 'acceptable' political framework. Solipsistically drawn into the pleasures of the game, Baudrillard calmly asserts that 'Politics frees itself in the spectacle, in the all-out advertising effect' of society.[40] In many ways this is written into the spectacular topography of *The Passion of New Eve*, its endlessly cinematic preoccupations tending to aestheticize the horrific violence they portray:

> The first thing I saw ... was, in a shop window, an obese plaster
> gnome squatly perched on a plaster toadstool ... The next thing I
> saw were rats, black as buboes, gnawing at a heap of garbage. And
> the third thing I saw was a black man running down the middle of
> the road as fast as he could go, screaming and clutching his throat,
> an unstoppable cravat, red in colour and sticky, mortal, flowed out
> from between his fingers. (p. 10)

As if the third of these images is not horrific enough in itself, Carter
transforms it into something inhumanly chilling through this precise
collocation of visual fragments. What is so profoundly disturbing is
the way in which it contextualizes racial violence as both kitsch (the
presiding art-work of the postmodern), through its association with
the squat gnome, and then as 'ethnic cleansing', through the implied
paralleling of the man with the rats which are as 'black as buboes'. Of
course Carter, like Baudrillard, is pointing out the horror of this, but
she does so in a manner that remains highly unresolved. For these
images are only very slightly defamiliarized by situating their
dystopian application within a televisual realism that is far too close
for comfort to the world of today. This also returns us to the postmodern. While such scenes clearly come under Carter's own definition
of the surreal – 'looking at the world as though it were strange' – they
fit Baudrillard's definition of the hyperreal even better. In these terms,
such images can *only* be understood as being '"obscenely" on display,
moving endlessly ... across a surface where there is no control or
stabilising depth'.[41] Undoubtedly, then, this novel shares Baudrillard's
desperate cynicism. And yet at times it is only through such cynicism
that we find genuinely illuminating insights into twentieth-century
life: 'Driving is a spectacular form of amnesia. Everything is to be
discovered, everything to be obliterated'. For our purposes the most
significant aspect of this derives from the effect it has upon our understanding of the fantastic. In a landscape that has *become* a science-
fiction backdrop, where is the place in which fantasy is to be found?
What role might wish-fulfilment play in a country in which 'among
that ... monotony of the human species, lies the tragedy of a utopian
dream made reality'? Here, even the very notion of the dream, that
very basis of our inner phantasy, has been supplanted by its technological simulacrum, the hologram: 'Everything [being] destined to
reappear as simulation. Landscape as photography, women as the sexual scenario ... terrorism as fashion'.[42] Without its wish-fulfilment
context, the dream structure is simply a cultural bombardment of
clashing motifs, its inheritance a mere set of anarchic displacements.
This is the culture that Carter takes on.[43] □

Armitt then turns to a discussion of America's relationship with its own history. Drawing on Baudrillard once again, she argues that America 'is ... obsessed with the nature of origins, even as it tries to render them absent',[44] and that this forms another point of connection with *The Passion of New Eve*, whose central characters are beings who, lacking a past, nevertheless are compelled to formulate their own autobiographies. Eve's voyage into the cave at the end of the novel represents the ultimate attempt to return 'home', since it is also a figurative voyage into the body of the Mother who made her. However, Armitt is careful to warn her readers that Carter is 'resistant to simple utopianism ... this scene poses far more questions than it answers'.[45] It is at this point in her discussion that Armitt enlarges on her other main theoretical reference – the work of the technotheorist Donna Haraway. For the journey to the mother is not, of course, a journey towards a 'natural' point of origin, but leads to the 'technological womb'[46] which brought Eve into being. For Armitt, this evokes the half-organic, half-synthetic figure of the cyborg, to whom Haraway ascribes a central symbolic importance. In its fusion of opposites the cyborg is a contradictory image; a characteristic upon which Armitt draws in order to make her point that *The Passion of New Eve* is a highly postmodern text which evades synthesis and closure.

■ [W]hat better motif than Haraway's cyborg to explore the nature (and culture) of gender relations and their textual exploration through fantasy fiction? That 'All of New Eve's experience came through two channels of sensation, her own fleshly ones and his mental ones' (pp.77–8) demonstrates that Eve/lyn's androgyny renders him/her a cyborg. But in addition (and again in the true spirit of Haraway's creation) s/he is also a typical manifestation of the postmodern subject and his/her problematic position regarding the so-called 'natural' world. As Haraway tells us, organisms are not born; they are made in world-changing techno-scientific practices by particular collective actors in particular times and places. 'In the belly of the local/global monster ... often called the postmodern world, global technology appears to denature everything, to make everything a malleable matter of strategic decisions and mobile production and reproductive processes'.[47] This is clearly the case surrounding New Eve's (re-)creation. In similar vein, Haraway's cyborg is a 'monstrous and illegitimate' creature whose anatomy is 'a hybrid of machine and organism'. And yet the victim status often inflicted on such 'monsters' conceals the fact that their contemporary cyborg double (which Haraway embraces as a prototype for new readings of female identity) is a creature who takes '*pleasure* in the confusion of boundaries' and *demands* the type of 'pleasurably tight coupling' denied its nineteenth-century counterpart in particular.[48] At first sight *The Passion of New Eve* seems centrally preoccupied with finding a role for precisely the type of cybernetic 'hopeful monsters' that Haraway and others seem to advocate. But questions remain as to whether existence as cyborg is genuinely liberatory. As is made clear, his/her femininity is fleshly while his/her masculinity remains cerebral. This reinforces, rather than invalidates, standard gender assumptions. In addition, though Evelyn becomes biologically female, his gender orientation remains masculine throughout, as his/her reference to Leilah as a 'gorgeous piece of flesh and acquiescence' (p.172) towards the end of the text illustrates. Indeed Carter requires this inbuilt cultural tension, using it to play with (although certainly not along with) such binary oppositions.

According to many feminist theorists, society's phallocentrism derives from a foundational binary power structure within which the prioritisation of masculine traits is privileged at the expense of the feminine. In their appropriately named *The Newly Born Woman* [1975], Hélène Cixous and Catherine Clément illustrate this by listing several actual or metaphorical manifestations of this polarity under the heading 'Where is she?'.[49] A number of these binary couplings are directly applicable to *The Passion of New Eve*, but the most important is the pairing of the sun (masculine) with the moon (feminine). William Blake explicitly foregrounds this in his own poem about Beulah,[50] and Carter metaphoricalizes it in her architectural creation of Beulah as a subterranean shrine. In addition, just as Cixous and Clément set these principles up in an ongoing struggle for dominance whereby one must succeed at the expense of the other, so Beulah (literally and in its architectural symbolism) permits entry to its depths only at the expense of the castrated phallus. And yet a closer look challenges such binary divides, for Beulah is a place of fusion, not one of separation. Or, as P.H. Butter explains, Beulah is:

a state of being in which the contraries (male and female etc.) are in harmony, 'married'. For the eternals entry into Beulah is a descent, into a 'land of shadows' ... a realm where shines only the moon, a reflection of the sun of eternity ... the divine voice is heard in the songs of Beulah ... So the daughters are muses, channels of inspiration'.[51]

[... I]t is not at Tristessa's palace, with Zero's wives looking on, that Eve/lyn is married, but here at Beulah with Mother as high priestess and her daughters in attendance. In this narrative integration of the sacred and the secular, Eve/lyn embodies the ultimate marriage whereby 'a man will ... be united to his own wife, and they will become one flesh'.[52] This 'one flesh' is Carter's own cyborg: a complex combination of masculine and feminine, goddess and whore, secular and sacred and spirit and flesh.

Carter's usage of the mythological and the futurist also allows her to situate the cybernetic as a complex interaction between the temporal and the spatial. As David Howarth argues, 'temporality is equated with dislocation or event, whereas space, or better spatialization, is the moment of the representation or inscription of dislocation'.[53] This complicated reversal takes on meaning when placed in the context of *The Passion of New Eve*. Set against a backdrop of Judeo-Christian tradition, Eve's sacrilegious birth dislocates the established temporal sequencing of the biblical narrative and redefines him/her as space/hole by attributing him with that orifice out of which humanity emerges over and over again. This space functions to denounce the power of chronology and, in the process, symbolises precisely that 'moment of the ... inscription of dislocation'. This is a birthing which, like Haraway and Baudrillard's treatment of the body, invokes the mother's power only ultimately to denounce her potency. In this sense, far from being irrelevant, the mother exists as a central site of loss or, as Mother herself puts it, 'the wound that does not heal' (p. 64). No wonder, then, that Eve/lyn becomes a 'perfect stranger' to him/herself (p. 38), for s/he is not only, as is frequently emphasized, perfection through artifice, but also perfect-*ed*, finished and complete without genealogy.

In conclusion, one can imagine few novels more clearly encapsulating Baudrillard's belief that 'the soul is over with and now it is an ideally naturalized body which absorbs its energy'.[54] As Carter herself argues, 'Mother goddesses are just as silly a notion as father gods' and, in that sense, it is perhaps important to avoid the inevitable over-simplifications of ideological consolation.[55] A goddess of the flesh is far too close for comfort to received patriarchal associations of women's bodies with the passive status of the sacred vessel or temple. *The Passion of New Eve* remains a dark, sinister, even dangerous book in terms of the nihilistic (anti-)ideologies with which it plays. In that regard, Carter, like Haraway, leaves us with intriguing but worrying deconstructions of gender.[56] □

I personally agree with Armitt's conclusion that *The Passion of New Eve* is an unsettling book which does not completely work through the issues it raises. In *Angela Carter: Writing From the Front Line*, I argue that, although the reader is encouraged to read Eve's final progress through the cave of the Mother at the end of the novel as a journey towards resolution, the novel ends with a 'freeze-frame' effect which allows no way out of the contradictions set up within the text.

■ The hope that Carter is holding out at the end of *The Passion of New Eve* is, therefore, the hope of escape from the dream factory, in which performance is the condition for existence, and where 'male' and 'female' are not so much biological categories as roles people play. The continually recurring trope of dualism within this text, however, indicates its awareness that the notion of the performative subject itself conveys a dual, contradictory, significance. On the one hand, it can be seen as a liberatory concept, indicative of the multiple, malleable subject capable of an infinite degree of self-creation. On the other, though, the actual number and character of the roles accessible to the subject may well be limited by the ideological structure within which it finds itself placed. The ambiguous Tristessa, embodiment of an absolutely unambiguous socially conditioned femininity, is a figure whose very reason for existence is to act as a vehicle for this paradox.

I don't think the text ever escapes from such contradictions, or even that it wishes to. Indeed, the confusion surrounding its ending is an effective narrative underscoring of the thematic points Carter is trying to make within the narrative. During her time in the sea-cave, Eve gets the impression that time itself is running in reverse, so that the world into which she re-emerges is one free of myths, symbols and stereotypes. It is apt in the context of this generally film-conscious novel that this action is evocatively conveyed through the use of cinematic metaphor:

> Rivers neatly roll up on themselves like spools of film and turn in on their own sources. The final drops of the Mississippi, the Ohio, the Hudson, tremble on a blade of grass; the sun dries them up, the grass sinks back into the earth. (p. 185)[57]

But this carries with it the inevitable question of whether this is a genuinely new start, or merely the beginning of the second showing. As the first sentence of the final chapter states, we 'start from our conclusions', but it remains debatable whether the direction of our trajectory is 'away from' or 'back to'. If it is the latter, we have become bound up ever more tightly in the 'entangled orders of simulation'.[58] If it is the former, the novel's lack of a definite conclusion indicates that it is unimaginable and unrepresentable.[59] □

Not all critics, however, have read the ending of *The Passion of New Eve* quite as pessimistically. Elaine Jordan, for example, makes it sound positively hopeful. Whereas Armitt argued that Eve ends the novel inescapably enmeshed in the contradictory discourses of technology and biology, for Jordan, Eve ends up running 'from both science and myth'. She regards *The Passion of New Eve* as 'an exploratory fiction, a sort of allegory of options, which evokes recognitions of past, present and future possibilities':

■ As a writer with a revolutionary socialist will [... Carter] cannot *describe* what has not happened, only give some space to hopes. The future lies open at the end of *The Passion of New Eve*, as at the end of most of Carter's other fictions. 'Mother' withers away [...] a necessary phase but one that has to be superseded. Mother ends up as the cheery but decrepit old woman on the beach (p. 177): this is the end of myths of the Mother. Eve will be a mother to someone not yet representable, whom she may love but who will go on to live beyond her imagination and will: though prehistory, Evelyn's own and that of humanity, can be replayed like a reel of old film [...], that film can be remade. The end of *The Passion of New Eve* looks to an unknown future, one which inevitably includes the possibility of new films, more myth-making. 'Woman' enters history, rewrites it with herself in it, and tells more stories, as she's always done.[60] □

Jordan's conclusion regarding *The Passion of New Eve* draws heavily on the concept of Carter as a 'demythologiser', and the belief that an escape from mythic stereotypes and structures thus opens the way for new possibilities. Aidan Day's reading of the text's ending is similarly dependent on this idea, arguing that Carter's ultimate adherence to a 'rationalist' ideology is indicated in the text's final 'jettisoning of old myths'.[61] In Day's analysis, Carter resists the relativism which he believes lies at the basis of postmodernist writing practice because she retains an adherence to a moral stance from which certain views of the world can be clearly perceived as wrong.

■ At the outset of Evelyn's/Eve's journeying through the realms of myth Baroslav the alchemist had said, 'The age of reason is over' (p. 13).[62] Now that myth has been exorcised, reason may return. Eve is carrying a child conceived in her love-making in the desert with Tristessa. Eve and her child may set out in the boat on the ocean of life firmly orientated within the rational possibilities of history rather than the irrational prejudices of myth. [...]

In John Fowles's *The French Lieutenant's Woman*, evolution understood as a random process is taken as paradigm for a post-modernism which stresses the human and cultural contingency of interpretations of the world. This is not entirely unlike Carter's view in *The Passion of New Eve* of evolution as something which does not sanction mythic essentialism. But there is a very important difference. Carter's vision of the mutability and interchangeableness of things in evolution is not the same as an argument for the pure relativity of all human versions of reality. Carter uses the rational scientific conception of evolution in a rationalistic manner: to argue against those interpretations of gender – myths of Mother, Zero's myths of the male as against the female, Tristessa's 'irrational and absurd' (p. 144) construction of womanhood – that make essentialist claims which contradict scientific, evolutionary evidence that there is nothing essential. The evidence that there is nothing essential is not taken, as in some extreme postmodernisms, to authorise versions of reality – specifically versions of gender – which claim that there *is* something essential. An author like Fowles may have made the point that no *one* interpretation of reality is essential or founded in the Absolute. But Carter introduces an additional manoeuvre into the anti-essentialist argument when she distinguishes between myth and irrationalism, on the one hand, and history and rationalism, on the other; when she comes out against mythic, irrational interpretations of reality that indeed claim absolute grounds. Carter's rational understanding that nothing is essential rules out of court any views, particularly of gender, which claim that certain things are essential. The rational understanding of non-essentialism does not lead here to relativism but to a ground from which judgement between views of the world can be made. The politics of gender are not relativised in *The Passion of New Eve* any more than Carter relativises herself as the author of her fictions. To this extent, Carter resists postmodernism. Evelyn's or Zero's or Tristessa's or Mother's projections of what is are clearly seen as wrong. The book sustains a commitment to reason as the ground from which such wrongness may be discovered and as the ground upon which further debates and conflicts, but also the genuine possibility of growth, may be based. That things are *made* rather than *determined* is a rational perception that itself is not relativised by Carter.

The new Eve, constructed along the patriarchal lines which constructed the old Eve, has yet to become genuinely new. But that is what, now free of old myths, she can become. [... T]he demythologising sympathies of the book are with the rational disquisitions and conflicts of history. Only on the basis of those disquisitions and conflicts can a new condition be imagined.[63] □

Neither Jordan nor Day argues for an unequivocally positive conclusion to *The Passion of New Eve*, as indicated in their use of qualifications: Carter can 'only give space to *some* hopes' (Jordan); new Eve '*has yet to become* genuinely new' (Day). However, their views of the text stand in obvious contrast to my own and Armitt's claims that the text remains enmeshed in the contradictions with which it has played throughout, and that in it Carter raises far more questions than she answers.

Many critics, however, regard *The Passion of New Eve* as marking the end of another stage in Carter's writing career, noting that her authorial voice and her relationship with her audience were to change in subsequent publications. Lorna Sage, for example, argues that 'Nineteen seventy-nine was Angela Carter's *annus mirabilis* as a writer, the hinge-moment or turning point when she invented for herself a new authorial persona, and began for the first time to be read widely and *collusively*, by readers who identified with her as a reader and re-writer'.[64] Nevertheless, the amount of critical controversy her subsequent publications generated shows that, although her writing of the late 1970s onwards won her popularity with a wider reading public, its aura of accessibility is really only a veneer. Beneath the entertaining surface of these texts, which draw more frequently on burlesque, fairy tale and pantomime than post-modernism and cultural theory, Carter remained as enquiring, contentious and fascinated by narrative risk as ever.

CHAPTER SIX

The Sadeian Woman (1979) and *The Bloody Chamber* (1979)

I F THIS book were dealing with criticism on Carter's work in the chronological order of its publication, it would begin with a chapter on *The Bloody Chamber*, a collection of revised fairy tales which was the book that finally brought Carter to wider public attention. This is Lorna Sage's description of the subsequent upswing in Carter's career:

■ The fairy tale idea enabled her to *read* in public with a new appropriateness and panache, as though she was *telling* these stories. She took to teaching creative writing, too. [...] Bit by bit her earlier work would be republished (in Picador and King Penguin, as well as Virago); she would acquire a solid relation with Chatto & Windus, when Carmen Callil moved there; she would become a delighting globe-trotter, a visiting writer/teacher/performer; and her work would be translated into all the major European languages.[1] □

Carter had already translated Charles Perrault's fairy tales into English in 1977, and went on to edit two collections of fairy tales for Virago Press – *The Virago Book of Fairy Tales* (1990), and *The Second Virago Book of Fairy Tales* (1992). Indeed, so pervasive did her association with the form become, argues Merja Makinen in her essay 'Angela Carter's *The Bloody Chamber* and the Decolonization of Feminine Sexuality', that it came to mould the way in which Carter herself was regarded in the popular imagination. To support this point, Makinen quotes from obituaries published following Carter's death in 1992:

■ Margaret Atwood's memorial in the *Observer* opens with Carter's 'intelligence and kindness' and goes on to construct her as a mythical fairy-tale figure: 'The amazing thing about her, for me, was that someone who looked so much like the Fairy Godmother ... should actually *be* so much like the Fairy Godmother. She seemed, always, on the verge of bestowing something – some talisman, some magic token ...'. Lorna Sage's obituary in the *Guardian* talked of her 'powers of enchantment and hilarity, her generous inventiveness' while the Late Show's memorial on BBC2 had the presenter calling her the 'white witch of English literature', J. G. Ballard a 'friendly witch', and Salman Rushdie claimed 'English literature has lost its high sorceress, its benevolent witch queen ... deprived of the fairy queen we cannot find the magic that will heal us' and finished by describing her as 'a very good wizard, perhaps the first wizard de-luxe'.[2] But this concurrence of white witch/fairy godmother mythologising needs watching; it is always the dangerously problematic that are mythologised in order to make them less dangerous. As Carter herself argued strongly in *Sadeian Woman*, 'if women allow themselves to be consoled for their culturally determined lack of access to the modes of intellectual debate by the invocation of hypothetical great goddesses, they are simply flattering themselves into submission (a technique often used on them by men).'[3, 4] □

Makinen goes on to argue that such an image does not do Carter any justice, for:

■ The books are not by some benign magician. The strengths and the dangers of her texts lie in a much more aggressive subversiveness and a much more active eroticism than perhaps the decorum around death can allow. For me, the problematics of Carter's writing was [*sic*] captured with more frankness when *New Society* dubbed her – wrongly, I think, but wittily – the 'high-priestess of post-graduate porn' in 1987. For Carter's work has consistently dealt with representations of the physical abuse of women in phallocentric cultures, of women alienated from themselves within the male gaze, and conversely of women who grab their own sexuality and fight back, of women troubled by and even powered by their own violence.[5] □

Although Makinen is referring to Carter's body of work as a whole here, this is an excellent description of *The Bloody Chamber*, and one which not only indicates the reason why this text is the point at which sustained academic criticism on Carter's work begins, but also explains why it continues to be one of her most widely-debated works. For although the short stories in *The Bloody Chamber* exploit a familiar narrative form, and hence might be considered rather more accessible than her earlier work, they are nevertheless equally unsettling in their apparent eroticising of sexual violence and victimisation. It is clear from Carter's responses to questions in interviews regarding this collection of short stories that such subversion was entirely intentional, because she wanted to draw the reader's attention to the often unpalatable realities that underpinned the familiar nursery stories. As she said to Helen Cagney Watts in 1985:

■ The tales in my volume *The Bloody Chamber* are part of the oral history of Europe, but what has happened is that these stories have gone into the bourgeois nursery and therefore lost their origins. It's important to remember that many folk tales were never written down, but passed from generation to generation by people who were mostly illiterate. These tales, especially many of the French fairy tales, actually recorded instances of everyday peasant life in the seventeenth century. Many people are horrified by the fairy tales of the Grimm Brothers, because of the hideous events which occur in some of these stories. But in 'Hop o' my thumb', for example, the mother sends her children out into the forest to starve, not because she is intrinsically evil, but because she does not want to watch them die of hunger in front of her eyes. These sort of things did happen! So I suppose that what interests me is the way in which these fairy tales and folklore are methods of making sense of events and certain occurrences in a particular imaginative way.[6] □

The origins of *The Bloody Chamber*, then, lie in Carter's materialism; her desire to bring fairy tale back down to earth in order to demonstrate how it could be used to explore the real conditions of everyday life. However, these short stories alone were not enough to earn Carter the sobriquet from *New Society* quoted above by Makinen. Although, as previous chapters in this study have discussed, Carter's interest in pornography was evident from at least 1972 onwards, in the same year in which *The Bloody Chamber* appeared that interest was to become explicit, when she published a critical analysis of the work of the infamous eighteenth-century French pornographer, the Marquis de Sade.

The extent to which de Sade was an influence on her work can be gauged by a remark made by Carter in her interview with Helen Cagney Watts. When asked whether her portrayal of sexuality was influenced by the ideas of Michel Foucault, Carter's response was that, while 'my reading of Foucault has possibly influenced me to some extent [...] really, though, it has been my reading of the Marquis de Sade that has probably had more impact; it is *the* text on sexuality and power'.[7] *The Sadeian Woman* was the outcome of this fascination with de Sade, which began when Carter came across his work in a second-hand bookshop in Japan. Such an association between a self-proclaimed feminist and one of the world's most notorious pornographers was always guaranteed to be a controversial coupling, and many critical responses to the text have duly registered appropriate shock and disgust. Although *The Sadeian Woman* is not, strictly speaking, fiction, it is a hotly-debated text within Carter's *oeuvre*, and thus deserves inclusion here.

Indeed, most critical analyses of *The Sadeian Woman* either look back-wards to link it to *The Passion of New Eve*, or (more commonly) forwards to its association with the short stories published in *The Bloody Chamber*. For Lorna Sage, for example, '*The Sadeian Woman* strips off the ideas enacted as fiction in *New Eve*, and presents them nakedly as arguments';[8] whereas Margaret Atwood asserts that '*The Bloody Chamber* may be read as a "writing against" de Sade, a talking-back to him'.[9] *The Sadeian Woman* has rarely been examined on its own merits, although this chap-ter will refer to two examples: Nanette Altevers' 'Gender Matters in *The Sadeian Woman*', published in *The Review of Contemporary Fiction* in 1994, and Sally Keenan's highly recommended essay '*The Sadeian Woman*: Feminism as Treason', which appeared in Bristow and Broughton's 1997 anthology *The Infernal Desires of Angela Carter*. The book has also, as we shall see, become something of a *cause célèbre* in the feminist debate over pornography and censorship. The rest of the chapter will go on to examine the critical debate surrounding *The Bloody Chamber*, in which *The Sadeian Woman* occupies an important position.

Given its controversial status, it is distinctly ironic that *The Sadeian Woman* was originally commissioned by the feminist press Virago to be one of its inaugural titles of 1977. However, it took Carter two years longer to write and, judging by comments made to Les Bedford in 1977, she found the task rather a chore:

■ *Les Bedford:* What about Sade? You're writing a book on Sade, aren't you?

Angela Carter: I am. I mean, I must have done something awful in a pre-vious life to have embarked on this impossible task. It's like emptying the sea with a cup with a hole in it.

LB: I think from Sade you seem to get a lot of your ideas about oppo-sites, good and evil and so on being one.

AC: I don't know, I think perhaps we operate in the same area. Yes, we operate in the same area of European obsessions, like sex and death and politics, and religion. I mean, Sade's dichotomies are Calvinist, really. They are ... well, his idea of good and evil are absolutely distinct states, they can never change from one to the other, there's no possible mediation in his world. It's a very frightening and distressing one.

LB: And that's the book you've not finished?

AC: I haven't finished. I have two drawers of material for it. I've been working on it for three years. [... ...]

I have to finish the book for my own peace of mind. It's very diffi-cult, and I keep doing lots of other things in the interval. I have a novel that I have been meaning to write during this year, and I have been trying to finish off de Sade. He's like Rasputin, I mean, he won't die [...].[10] □

Carter's equivocations here are indicative that her relationship with de Sade was not an entirely easy one, and that she did not necessarily regard his ideas as meshing with her own. Sally Keenan argues that, for Carter, wrestling with de Sade became the means by which she could work through her relationship to feminism. However, Keenan also examines the critical reception accorded to *The Sadeian Woman* which shows that even feminist reviewers found the book difficult to come to terms with, and were uncertain as to Carter's exact intentions.

■ Although I do not read Carter's *oeuvre* as a neat chronological progression towards a more utopian feminist perspective, it is possible to see *The Sadeian Woman* as a watershed moment in her thinking about feminism, a moment when her fictional narratives became increasingly bound up with theoretical considerations. Returning to examine *The Sadeian Woman* in the light of the later fiction and its reception, one is brought face to face with the radical nature of Carter's work: its complex paradoxes, its theoretical seriousness, and that characteristic refusal to settle in one fixed place. Perhaps, above all, what a retrospective examination of the text highlights is its almost heretical disagreement with certain aspects of feminist thinking current in the 1970s. First, her suggestion that women too readily identify with images of themselves as victims of patriarchal oppression, was a distinctly unfashionable notion in the mid-1970s. Her savage indictment of the figure of Sade's Justine as an extreme embodiment of this complicity made her argument the more treasonable since she was using the arch misogynist in support of it. Second, there was the attack she launched on the idealisation of motherhood in its various forms. The wide spectrum of that idealisation manifested in much 1970s feminist theorising is rejected in *The Sadeian Woman*, either explicitly or implicitly: the recreation of mother goddesses or the eco-feminists' reassertion of Nature as Mother, for instance. Third, there is her challenge, albeit an oblique one, to the revisionary psychoanalytic theories of the French feminists, especially Hélène Cixous and Julia Kristeva, in whose work during the 1970s, motherhood and the maternal body assume crucial significance in a whole variety of ways.[11]

If *The Sadeian Woman* was a response to certain assumptions current in feminist thinking in the 1970s, what was the critical reaction to the book? How was Carter's provocative intervention into debates about female sexuality received in 1979? What is most striking is the wide range of the media giving it review space – both tabloids and broadsheet papers in the mainstream press as well as the alternative press. That diversity of coverage is matched by a diversity of critical responses: the anticipation of sexual titillation (from a clearly disappointed reviewer in the *Birmingham Sun*); an interesting failure with little relevance to modern women (the *Financial Times*); a serious contribution to contemporary cultural politics (*Gay News*). The book was clearly controversial, and with some notable exceptions, many of the reviewers expressed puzzlement as to the main thrust of its argument. Several feminist reviewers, while conceding Carter's claim that Sade may be useful for women in that he separates women's sexuality from their reproductive function, nevertheless expressed qualms about 'the ethics of the connection' (Ann Oakley) between Sade and feminism, an imaginative leap they could not make. A repeated point was that Carter failed to sustain her argument in support of Sade and was forced to throw him over in an abrupt and unsatisfactory conclusion (Sara Maitland, Julia O'Faolain, *Women's Report*), and that she had led her readers on a 'wild goose chase', as Maitland called it.[12] The implicit desire for a clear conclusion that could be slotted into a feminist agenda fails to acknowledge certain characteristic features of Carter's writing: an intention to provoke questions rather than to provide answers, to engage with contradictions without seeking necessarily to resolve them. In the 'Polemical Preface' where Carter sets out her thesis, it is clear that the use of Sade is paradoxical. This is the point and challenge of the book: an attempt to jolt the reader out of customary associations and habits of thought. Carter was not looking to Sade for a model, but rather to provide a speculative starting point. The most positive reactions to the book in 1979 came from those who acknowledged Carter's understanding of Sade's work as a founding moment for our modern sensibility regarding sexual matters. Marsaili Cameron, writing in *Gay News*, made the valid point that:

> This book is not primarily a study of de Sade himself either as a writer or as an historical figure ... . Ranging from pornography and mythology to psychoanalysis to points west, it is mainly concerned with the elucidation of our own tortured ideas of sexuality inherited from the past.

In thinking of Carter's work as a complete body of work, as we now must, I am interested in the location of this text in that body of writing, and even more perhaps in the place I sense that it has occupied in many women's reading of Carter, and in the formation of their feminist politics. In thinking about this chapter, I asked Carter readers of my acquaintance about their responses on first encountering *The Sadeian Woman*, and also crucially at what point in time they had read it. I was interested to learn that for several it had not only been the book of Carter's that had first engendered their interest in her work, but that it had played a significant role in forming or reformulating their feminism. For some, it presented a puzzling mix of the fascinating and disturbing which prompted them to think through questions about their own sexuality and their attitudes to pornography in new ways. Yet for others, it provided a turning point that caused them to dispel previously unchallenged assumptions about being on the side of 'innocence'. One woman described her first reading as a shock of recognition, of how Carter had crystallised her own not fully formulated ideas about the issue of women's complicity with their sexual oppression.[13] □

One aspect of Carter's argument that her readers found particularly troublesome was her coinage of the term 'moral pornographer', which she applied to a theoretical figure 'who might use pornography as a critique of current relationships between the sexes'.[14] As she wryly remarked in 1988, it 'was a phrase that got me into a lot of trouble with [...] some of the sisters'.[15] Nanette Altevers, however, in a short but vehemently argued essay, maintains that those who find her use of this term offensive 'miss completely the significance of *The Sadeian Woman*'.[16] Altevers' essay is a robust defence of Carter's arguments, taking as its main object of criticism Robert Clark's critique of Carter's representation of sex in 'Angela Carter's Desire Machines'. Altevers quotes Clark's view that '[s]uch a commitment precludes an affirmative feminism founded in referential commitment to women's historical and organic being',[17] but argues that this is a misreading of Carter's intentions. Instead, Altevers proposes a view of Carter as a writer whose primary allegiance is a materialist feminist practice which is concerned with locating women within their historical context. 'Contrary to Clark's assertion', she argues, 'Carter's "primary allegiance" is to no theoretical position; it is to a feminist politics that would rectify the material oppression that women experience daily'. The main body of Altevers' discussion, in fact, circumvents the idea of the 'moral pornographer' in order to analyse *The Sadeian Woman* as not primarily concerned with pornography *per se*, but with pornography's role in perpetuating stereotypical, static, definitions of women.

■ Carter's critique of the ideology of pornography is intricately and inevitably bound up with her critique of myth 'Since all pornography derives directly from myth' (p.6).[18] And it is the very fact that myth derives from theory rather than from experience that irritates her: 'mythology' presents us 'with ideas about ourselves which don't come out of practice; they come out of theory. They come out of pure theory'. Indeed, by the time she wrote *The Sadeian Woman*, Carter was 'getting really ratty with the whole idea of myth'. She was 'getting quite ratty with the sort of appeals by some of the women's movements to have these sort of [primitive] "Ur-religions" because it didn't seem to me at all to the point. The point seemed to be the here and now, what we should do now.'[19] Her attack on myth – according to Carter, all myths are 'consolatory nonsenses' (p. 5) – is peculiarly timely, given the overwhelming success of the recent best-seller, *Women Who Run with the Wolves*, which celebrates precisely what Carter in 1978 referred to as the 'most insulting mythic redefinition of myself, that of occult priestess' (p. 5).[20] □

Altevers' point here is reiterated in Keenan's argument that '[t]he provocation in Carter's use of Sade is not her supposed validation of pornography, but her employment of his work to expose her female readers to their own complicity with the fictional representations of themselves as mythic archetypes'.[21]

As Keenan goes on to note, however, many mainstream feminists have refused to find this sufficient justification for Carter's referencing of de Sade, and their attacks on *The Sadeian Woman* have frequently been vociferous. Andrea Dworkin, for example, has condemned it as a 'pseudo-feminist literary essay' which ignores the real suffering of de Sade's victims in order to confer heroic status upon the pornographer.[22] Dworkin's opinion is echoed by Susanne Kappeler in *The Pornography of Representation* (1986), in which she argues that Carter, in reading de Sade from the point of view of a literary critic rather than as a feminist, ends up betraying women:

■ The conception of art and literature as aesthetic domains, disconnected from reality through a boundary between fiction and fact, has also led to the arbitrary cutting off of the author from reality. The scriptural attitude towards works of art sees in the artist not a member of the human community, but the ideal of the Subject: incarnated in the word, finding full expression in the medium. 'Writing is that neutral, composite, oblique space where our subject slips away, the negative where all identity is lost,' writes Roland Barthes.[23] The 'subject' which slips away is the subject of social identity: writing is the space of the Subject, of living subjectivity, where subjectivity is liberated from social, economic, gender, class and all other intersubjective constraints and the subject constitutes and loses itself in language, in signification, in the infinity of meaning. This aesthetic stance towards this metaphysical space has become so naturalized that we see nothing wrong with it. The critic accepts the boundaries, leaps within, and continues to show up and lay bare what the artist has shown up and laid bare before him, for him. What they lay bare is, if not 'reflected reality', the attainment of full subjectivity, of fulfilment in expression, of the play with meaning and the consummation of the feeling of delight by the privileged cultural subject.

Thus Angela Carter as literary critic can claim Sade as a virtual 'forerunner' of feminist critics: he has said, shown, enumerated and laid bare the mechanisms and mechanics of the pornographic scenario, of the degradation of women, before them and for them. They need only enumerate after him. Carter writes:

> Sade remains a monstrous and daunting cultural edifice; yet I would like to think that he put pornography in the service of women, or, perhaps, allowed it to be invaded by an ideology not inimical to women. And give the old monster his due: let us introduce him with an exhilarating burst of rhetoric: 'Charming sex, you will be free: just as men do, you shall enjoy all the pleasures that Nature makes your duty, do not withhold yourselves from one. Must the more divine half of mankind be kept in chains by the other? Ah, break those bonds: nature wills it.' (p. 37)[24]

Here Carter, the potential feminist critic, has withdrawn into the literary sanctuary, has become literary critic: 'Sade' is no longer the man she so carefully researched, the multiple rapist and murderer, but as writer, as pornographer, deserves a literary critical response that treats him as artist and writing subject. Like good modern literary critics, we move from the author/writer to the *oeuvre*/text which by literary convention bears his name: Sade is a Cultural Edifice (a rock of culture). A literary artefact, removed by convention of the literary beyond the reach of political, of feminist critique. Sade's pornographic assault on one particular patriarchal representation of woman – the Mother – renders him, in the eyes of Carter, a provider of a service to women. His murderous 'misanthropy' (sic), she argues, 'has bred a hatred of the mothering function that led him to demystify the most sanctified aspects of women and if he invented women who suffered, he also invented women who caused suffering' (p. 36). Women, of course, neither produced nor sanctified the mothering aspect of their patriarchal representation, but it is doubtful whether they would thank Sade for replacing the myth of the Mother with that of the victim or the inverted pornographic sadist. Besides falling into the trap of the literary sanctuary, Carter here lapses into the fallacy of equal opportunities: following her provider, she seems eager to take up the opportunity he invents for her: to cause suffering 'just as men do'.

But Sade is more subtle than Carter gives him credit for. He does not rattle her chains in order for her to escape them, and she should suspect his 'liberating' spirit bred from hatred. But dazzled by the offer of equal opportunities, she misreads him. While his options are strictly binary – to suffer or to cause suffering, to belong to one half of 'mankind' or the other – these are not for her to choose from: they are gender specific. What he offers her – as Barthes is to offer later on – is to choose an attitude to her preordained role: 'break those bonds', 'be free' – embrace your chains with ecstasy. 'You shall enjoy ... your duty'. Freedom and enjoyment are ordered with the authority of a direct imperative, they are a strict duty. Sade, with the flourish of his magician's hat, emerges from this extraordinary edifice of rhetoric to bow with a smile: Nature Himself! For, these pleasures of women (chains, rape and murder), Nature makes their duty, Nature wills. Carter, still lolling in the literary sanctuary, applauds this creation and sees an 'ideology not inimical to women' in this 'exhilarating burst of rhetoric'. Since it all happens in the realm of the literary, it cannot possibly be 'inimical' to women in the real world, and the literary in turn is far beyond the reach of feminist or moral terms such as 'inimical'.[25] □

Patricia Duncker's essay 'Re-Imagining the Fairy Tales: Angela Carter's Bloody Chambers' was published two years before Kappeler's critique, but attacks her work on very much the same grounds: that Carter becomes trapped in the very reactionary discourses she is attempting to criticise, and thus ends up perpetuating rather than deconstructing them.

■ Carter's extraordinary fascination with De Sade simmers at the root of what is both disturbing reactionary [sic] and sadly unoriginal in her work. She knows that 'the tale has relations with the subliterary forms of pornography, ballad and dream'.[26] In *The Sadeian Woman* she suggests that the Devil is best slain with his own weapons and argues the case for the moral pornographer, who is, curiously, envisaged as male.

> The moral pornographer would be an artist who uses pornographic material as part of the acceptance of the logic of a world of absolute sexual licence for all the genders, and projects a model of the way such a world might work. A moral pornographer might use pornography as a critique of current relations between the sexes. His business would be the total demystification of the flesh and the subsequent revelation, through the infinite modulations of the sexual act, of the real relations between man and his kind. Such a pornographer would not be the enemy of women, perhaps because he might begin to penetrate to the heart of the contempt for women that distorts our culture even as he entered the realms of true obscenity as he describes it. (pp. 19–20)[27]

This is, I would suggest, utter nonsense. Pornography, indeed, the representation of all sexual relations between men and women, will necessarily 'render explicit the nature of social relations in the society in which they take place' (p. 20). That is why most bourgeois fiction concentrates upon the choices surrounding courtship and marriage, for it is there that the values and realities upon which a society is based will be most sharply revealed. The realities of power, perhaps, but not the imagined experience of desire. Pornography, heightened, stylised, remote, mirrors precisely these socially-constructed realities. The realities of male desire, aggression, force; the reality of women, compliant and submissive. Where then shall imagined desire, the expression of feminist eroticism, be found, apprehended, expressed? Andrea Dworkin argues that this can only emerge when the division of sexual polarity is destroyed, when male and female sexual identities are reborn.[28, 29] □

As the title of her essay indicates, Duncker links her condemnation of *The Sadeian Woman* to a critique of *The Bloody Chamber*, a project which she regards as equally problematic. Just as Carter fails in her endeavour to make pornography serve the interests of women, so her attempt to rewrite fairy tales from a feminist point of view leads to her entanglement in the misogynistic attitudes they encode.

■ Apart from 'The Erl-King', which she presumably adapts from Goethe's ballad, Carter chooses a sequence of classic tales most of which are to be found in Perrault; the story of Bluebeard and his wives in 'The Bloody Chamber', two versions of 'Beauty and the Beast' in 'The Courtship of Mr Lyon' and 'The Tiger's Bride', an operatic Puss-in-Boots which deliberately suggests the Baroque ornamentation of Rossini's music, Snow-White in 'The Snow Child', Sleeping Beauty as a Gothic vampire in 'The Lady of the House of Love', two versions of Red Riding Hood and a tale that combines motifs from several of these, 'Wolf-Alice'. The animal aspects of human sexuality are her particular concern; thus the wolf and the lion roam through the tales seeking whom they may erotically devour [...]. But the infernal trap inherent in the fairy tale, which fits the form to its purpose, to be the carrier of ideology, proves too complex and pervasive to avoid. Carter is rewriting the tales within the strait-jacket of their original structures. The characters she re-creates must to some extent, continue to exist as abstractions. Identity continues to be defined by role, so that shifting the perspective from the impersonal voice to the inner confessional narrative as she does in several of the tales, merely explains, amplifies and re-produces rather than alters the original, deeply, rigidly sexist psychology of the erotic. The disarming of aggressive male sexuality by the virtuous bride is at the root of The Frog Prince and Beauty and the Beast. Carter transposes this moral into the narrative 'The

Company of Wolves'. So that the erotic confrontation and reversal at the end becomes a meeting of sexual aggression and the cliché of female erotic ingenuity. Red Riding Hood sees that rape is inevitable [...] and decides to strip off, lie back and enjoy it. She wants it really. They all do. The message is spelt out. 'The Tiger's Bride' argues a variation on the original bargain; the heroine is sold to the highest bidder in the marriage pact, but she too strips off all artifice, the lies inherent in borrowed garments, and reveals herself as she is, the mirror image of his feline predatory sexuality. [...] I would suggest that all we are watching, beautifully packaged and unveiled, is the ritual disrobing of the willing victim of pornography.

Carter's tales are, supposedly, celebrations of erotic desire. But male sexuality has too long, too tenaciously been linked with power and possession, the capture, breaking and ownership of women. The explicitly erotic currents in her tales mirror these realities. Pornography, that is, the representation of overtly sexual material with the intention to arouse prurient, vicarious desire, uses the language of male sexuality. Even the women's equivalent of soft porn, romance novels and 'bodice-rippers', all conform to recognisably male fantasies of domination, submission and possession. Heterosexual feminists have not yet invented an alternative, anti-sexist language of the erotic. Carter envisages women's sensuality simply as a response to male arousal. She has no conception of women's sexuality as autonomous desire.[30] □

Duncker's essay has its mirror-image in Margaret Atwood's essay 'Running with the Tigers', which comes to the opposite conclusion via the same route. Like Duncker, Atwood examines the relationship between *The Bloody Chamber* and *The Sadeian Woman*, but while Duncker decides that neither offers anything more than unreconstructed portrayals of female victimisation, thus proving that Carter is incapable of surmounting the limitations inherent in either pornography or fairy tale, Atwood argues that the books are linked through their exploration of the relationship between victim and aggressor: a dynamic in which gender is not always the determining factor: 'In both books, the distinctions drawn are not so much between male and female as between "tigers" and "lambs", carnivores and herbivores, those who are preyed upon and those who do the preying.'[31] Carter uncovers this conundrum in the work of de Sade, where it is represented by 'a sort of Siamese twin, both halves entirely constructed by men: the traditional-role female victim, Justine, and de Sade's "new woman", Juliette, who is instead a victimiser'.[32] However, Atwood argues, those who regard Carter as endorsing either of these polarities are reading her incorrectly: what she is in fact searching for is a fusion of the two – and this is where *The Bloody Chamber* comes in:

■ *The Bloody Chamber* may be read as a 'writing against' de Sade, a talking-back to him; and, above all, as an exploration of the possibilities for the kind of synthesis de Sade himself could never find because he wasn't even looking for it. Predator and prey, master and slave, are the only two categories – or roles, because in his world one person may play both, although alternately – that he can acknowledge; above all, for him sex between unequals cannot be mutually pleasurable, because pleasure belongs to the eater, not to the eaten. What Carter seems to be doing in *The Bloody Chamber* – among other things – is looking for ways in which the tiger and the lamb, or the tiger and lamb parts of the psyche, can reach some sort of accommodation.

The Bloody Chamber can be understood much better as an exploration of the narrative possibilities of de Sade's lamb-and-tiger dichotomy than as a 'standard' work of early-seventies to-the-barricades feminism. There have, historically, been two main strands of feminist theory – that which maintained that women were fundamentally no different from men, and should therefore be allowed to do the same jobs and have the same rights as men; and that which postulated women as essentially other, but better: group-minded, sensitive and caring consensus-builders rather than aggressive, egotistical despoilers; birth-giving rather than death-dealing; gardeners rather than warriors; sufferers rather than inflicters of suffering; lambs rather than tigers. This latter strand of thinking has claimed special privileges for women on the grounds of their moral superiority, but it has been played several ways: women are more deserving than men, but because of the lamb-like nature of their superiority they also need more protection. This can be used to keep women isolated on their Victorian pedestals just as easily as it can be used to grant them special status and head-of-the-queue position in, say, job equity battles. (Women, being lambs, can't *seize* the head of the queue; they have to have it conferred upon them.)

It is Carter's contention that a certain amount of tigerishness may be necessary if women are to achieve an independent as opposed to a dependent existence; if they are to avoid – at the extreme end of passivity – becoming meat. They need, in their own self-interest, to assimilate at least some of Juliette's will-to-power. But their change from lamb to tiger need not be a divesting of all 'feminine' qualities, as it is for de Sade; also, although society may slant things so that women appear to be better candidates for meat-eating, the nature of men is not fixed by Carter as inevitably predatory, with females as their 'natural' prey. Lambhood and tigerishness may be found in either gender, and in the same individual at different times. In this respect, Carter's arrangements are much more subject to mutability than are de Sade's. He postulates the permanence and 'decreed' nature of virtue and vice:

Juliette is born evil, Justine good, and so they remain. Carter, however, celebrates relativity and metamorphosis and 'the complexity of human relations'. 'The notion of a universality of human experience', she says, 'is a confidence trick and the notion of a universality of female experience is a clever confidence trick' (p. 12).[33] She sees all myths, including those of pornography and also recent feminist mother-goddess myths, as 'consolatory nonsenses' (p. 5). But in *The Bloody Chamber* she proceeds to provide us with consolations of another kind, and she does so through the folk tale form, which is about as close to myth as you can get. In other words, to combat traditional myths about the nature of woman, she constructs other, more subversive ones.[34] □

Regarding them as being 'arranged according to categories of meat-eater',[35] Atwood proceeds to analyse each of the short stories collected in *The Bloody Chamber* in turn. In their different ways all, she argues, strive for a balance between the two opposing polarities of 'tiger' and 'lamb' in order to escape from the limitations of the roles de Sade allocated to the players in his pornographic fantasies: '*You see* – [Carter] appears to be saying to the Marquis [...] – *you didn't have to confine yourself to those mechanistic stage sets, those mechanical rituals. It wasn't just eat or be eaten. You could have been human!*'[36] Much hinges for Atwood on this word 'human', for she regards Carter's work as exemplifying the principle that to be human is to be neither 'tiger' nor 'lamb', but a fully-functional subject, 'part of that complexity, that mixed blessing, which Carter valued above the "consolatory nonsense" of absolutist, reductionist myth, of "spurious archetype"'.[37] This conclusion demonstrates that Atwood therefore finds precisely the synthesis in *The Bloody Chamber* that Duncker is left still searching for at the end of her discussion:

■ Carter chooses to inhabit a tiny room of her own in the house of fiction. For women, that space has always been paralysingly, cripplingly small. I think we need the 'multiplying ambiguities of an extended narrative'. To imagine ourselves whole. We cannot fit neatly into patterns or models as Cinderellas, ugly sisters, wicked step-mothers, fairy God-mothers, and still acknowledge our several existences, experienced or imagined. We need the space to carve out our own erotic identities, as free women. And then to rewrite the fairy tales – with a bolder hand.[38] □

It is worthwhile, however, to place these two conflicting views of *The Bloody Chamber* in their historical context. Patricia Duncker's essay was published in 1984, and was the first in a series of pieces published throughout the eighties which found much to criticise in Carter's revision of fairy tale, being followed, in 1987 and 1988 respectively, by Robert Clark's 'Angela Carter's Desire Machine' and by Avis Lewallen's 'Wayward Girls but Wicked Women?'[39] All three critics concluded that Carter's stories reinforced misogynistic stereotypes, confining their female protagonists to the limited choice – in Lewallen's memorable words – of whether to 'fuck or be fucked'. And according to Clark's analysis, if they don't like either of the two alternatives on offer, they get raped anyway. As he says of Carter's 'Little Red Riding Hood' story, 'The Company of Wolves':

■ The point of view is that of the male voyeur; the implication may be that the girl has her own sexual power, but this meaning lies perilously close to the idea that all women want it really and only need forcing to overcome their scruples [...]. The revision of the story trades on the appearance of offering an improved image of female sexuality, but in effect it reinscribes men and women in positions not foreign to the works of Ian Fleming or Norman Mailer.[40] □

In their defence, it could be said that critics such as Duncker, Clark and Lewallen were reacting as much against other critical analyses of *The Bloody Chamber* as they were against the tales themselves. *The Bloody Chamber* was one of the first of Carter's books to receive widespread academic attention, and it anticipated a trend amongst feminists in the late seventies onwards to appropriate and rework fairy-tale narratives, mostly by employing a process of simple reversal which foregrounded the role of the heroine in order to make her the active figure in the text. According to this criterion, the more dominant the female protagonist, the more 'feminist' the story. Several feminist academics analysed *The Bloody Chamber* from this perspective in the eighties, and Ellen Cronan Rose's discussion, published in 1984, is typical. Cronan Rose examines three collections of feminist fairy tales – Anne Sexton's *Transformations* (1971) and Olga Broumas's *Beginning with O* (1977), as well as *The Bloody Chamber* – in order to analyse 'what happens when a woman writer turns to the male cultural myths embedded in fairy tales'.[41] In her argument she draws heavily on Bruno Bettelheim's Freudian study of fairy tale, *The Uses of Enchantment* (1976), and on Sandra M. Gilbert and Susan Gubar's *The Madwoman in the Attic* (1979), which reads the fairy tale as a vehicle for the perpetuation of female oppression in culture. Cronan Rose's interpretation of *The Bloody Chamber* as a series of stories which show women breaking free of patriarchal restrictions in order to achieve (re)union with their matriarchal origins appears rather simplistic in the light of subsequent debates:

■ Judging from her fairy tales, Angela Carter's sense of the possibilities for a woman's growth toward healthy adult identity is more optimistic than Sexton's and more complicated than Broumas's. Sexton [...] is a pessimist, angry with the status quo but apparently resigned to it. Broumas is an optimist, but a shortsighted one; if the only option to the status quo is lesbian separatism, not all women will see Broumas's as a viable alternative. In technical terms, Sexton is an analyst of fairy tales and their cultural implications, while Broumas is an improviser, using the tales as a base for imaginative speculation. Carter is both.

The Bloody Chamber contains two versions of 'Beauty and the Beast', the first a fairly straightforward retelling of the original version by Mme. Le Prince de Beaumont, the second a fanciful improvisation on it. Together they constitute a critique of the idea of adult womanhood sanctioned by patriarchy and a suggested alternative to it.

Bettelheim concludes The Uses of Enchantment with a lengthy discussion of 'Beauty and the Beast' because for him it represents the apex of the development to adult womanhood: the successful transfer of a girl's Oedipal attachment to her father to an appropriate partner of the opposite sex.[42] But what seems to Bettelheim 'all gentleness and loving devotion' in 'Beauty and the Beast' – the attachment of Beauty to her father, the Beast's supplication of her love – is perceived differently by Angela Carter. In her first retelling of the tale, 'The Courtship of Mr Lyon', Carter – like Sexton – keeps intact the plot of the original. But again like Sexton, she highlights and subtly modifies certain of its features. Beauty's father, for instance, thinks of his daughter as 'his girl-child, his pet'. Unlike the timid father in the original story, he is not frightened when he discovers an apparently empty mansion in the snow storm; he seems to recognize in its masculine provision for his needs (a decanter of whiskey and a rare roast beef sandwich) something of the comfort of a men's club. And when the beast materializes, he addresses him accordingly – 'My good fellow'.

Beauty remains with the Beast as long as she does 'because her father wanted her to do so'. 'Do not think she had no will of her own', the narrator cautions. And yet one must wonder whether she does. Or if she does, whether the conditions of her life will allow it to have efficacy. She seems a mere pawn, tugged in one direction by her father's call to join him in his recovered prosperity and in another by the Beast's appeal to her pity. Self-sacrifice wins out over hedonism, proving that Beauty is a truly feminine woman. In effect, the Beast blackmails Beauty into marrying him by going on a hunger strike [...]. In retelling 'Beauty and the Beast', Carter has indicated that, in patriarchal cultural myths, women do not grow up. They simply change masters – from a beastly father to a fatherly beast. Having discovered this, she is free to invent a tale in which Beauty breaks free from paternal domination.

The patriarchal bonding implicit in 'The Courtship of Mr Lyon' is made explicit in 'The Tiger's Bride', where Beauty's 'profligate father gambles with the Beast, who beggars him. He is left with nothing. 'Except the girl', the Beast reminds him, and persuades the father to gamble further. 'My father said he loved me yet he staked his daughter on a hand of cards'. He loses. Beauty wins, because in 'The Tiger's Bride', the Beast is not an enchanted prince, a father-in-the-making. He is an animal, 'a great, feline, tawny shape', who wears the mask and clothing of a man awkwardly and with discomfort. Moreover, he does not assume the prerogatives of patriarchy, does not ask Beauty to marry him. He asks only that Beauty strip off her clothes and stand before him naked.

What is naked is the metaphor. Earlier during her stay with the Beast, attended by a clockwork maid, Beauty had discovered her identity, as patriarchy has decreed it:

> I was a young girl, a virgin, and therefore men denied me rationality just as they denied it to all those who were not exactly like themselves … . I meditated on the nature of my own state, how I had been bought and sold, passed from hand to hand. That clockwork girl who powdered my cheeks for me; had I not been allotted only the same kind of imitative life amongst men that the doll-maker had given her?

So, although it is not easy for her to obey the Beast's command, Beauty has nothing to lose and everything to gain by stripping herself of her clothes and her socialized identity. Abandoned by men, she turns to the Beast and discovers herself. The tale ends with the Beast licking Beauty: 'And each stroke of his tongue ripped off skin after successive skin, all the skins of a life in the world, and left behind a nascent patina of shining hairs'.

According to Bettelheim, animals in fairy tales represent our animal nature – in general terms our 'untamed id', more specifically our sexual impulses. The significance, for him, of 'Beauty and the Beast' is that it suggests 'that eventually there comes a time when we must learn what we have not known before – or to put it psycho-analytically, to undo the repression of sex. What we had experienced as dangerous, loathsome, something to be shunned, must change its appearance so that it is experienced as truly beautiful'.[43] Carter's tale is just as much about 'undoing the repression of sex' as is the original. But it is also about undoing the oppression of gender. Beauty discovers the animal in herself – her sexuality – only by stripping herself of the veneer of civilization which has socialized her as a woman.

Carter's retelling of 'Beauty and the Beast' also questions the

Freudian account of female development, in which a woman achieves sexual maturity by shifting her attachment from a father to a male lover. In her two versions of 'Little Red Riding Hood' she offers a (nonlesbian) alternative, suggesting that a woman achieves (hetero-) sexual maturity by affirming her own sexuality through identifying with her (grand) mother. The process, as it unfolds in 'The Werewolf' and 'The Company of Wolves', is complex. First, as the title should suggest, in 'The Werewolf' Little Red Riding Hood discovers that her grandmother and the wolf are one and the same. In so doing, she is making a very important discovery: that to be a mature woman means to be sexual, animal. Understandably, this horrifies the young girl. So she calls out to the neighbours, who drive her werewolf grandmother out of the house and stone her to death. But although the little girl kills her grandmother, she does not then go home to mother and safety. Instead 'the child lived in her grandmother's house; she prospered'. Little Red Riding Hood may have been initially repulsed by the knowledge that becoming an adult woman will involve acknowledging the animal in herself. But the second step in her negotiation of that developmental process is signalled by her decision to remain in her grandmother's house. She is symbolically declaring her readiness to grow up.

That process of growth is completed in 'The Company of Wolves', where little Red Riding Hood ends up 'sweet and sound ... in granny's bed, between the paws of the tender wolf'. Inhabiting not only granny's house but her bed, Red Riding Hood has in a sense become her grandmother. Making love with the wolf, in a 'savage marriage ceremony', she is also embracing her grandmother and thus acknowledging and affirming her adult female sexuality. Bettelheim says that it is love which transforms adult sexuality into something beautiful. Carter seems to be saying that love is not possible until one has come to accept and enjoy her sexuality, an accomplishment she associates in these stories with the mother/daughter relationship.[44] □

Contrast this conclusion with that reached by Lucie Armitt a decade later:

■ In 'The Company of Wolves', the protagonist, desiring to become 'nobody's meat' (p. 118),[45] frees herself from her passive genealogical inheritance by banishing all authority from her parents. ('Her father ... is away in the forest ... and her mother cannot deny her' (p. 114)), and by permitting the wolf to dispense with her grandmother, so giving herself every licence to trespass. Carter does much the same in banishing the formulaic fairy-foremother from her own literary inheritance.[46] □

Whereas Cronan Rose regards the narratives in *The Bloody Chamber* as signalling a properly 'feminist' desire for reintegration with a matriarchal history, Armitt, whose discussion in this essay is informed by the post-modern feminism of the French psychoanalytical theorist Julia Kristeva, is not at all concerned with making the stories fit a clearly defined feminist formula. Indeed, she regards the arguments surrounding the text as inherently limited, so preoccupied with these stories' relationship to the fairy-tale form that they fail to take into account how the separate narratives relate to each other. She does not only attribute this failure to Clark and Duncker, but also to those critics who subsequently argued against them, such as Elaine Jordan and Merja Makinen. Armitt takes her debate beyond issues of gender in order to consider the formal aspects of the text – a trajectory which not only leads her away from the easy, unproblematic readings exemplified by Cronan Rose, but also causes her to question whether these stories are fairy tales at all.

■ [A]lthough Jordan and Makinen present full and intelligent arguments[47] detailing the ways in which Carter's representation of female sexuality 'play[s] with and upon (if not prey[s] upon) the earlier misogynistic version' of the fairy-tale,[48] neither engages with the way in which her chosen narrative *form and structure* contribute to this ideological reorientation. It is not simply the characters themselves (and the transformative potential of their bodily metamorphoses) that free up new and anti-conventional readings of women's pleasure. The stories comprising *The Bloody Chamber* are also (inter)textual metamorphoses of both the fairy-tale *and* each other.

According to Duncker, the fairy-tale itself is so entrenched in patriarchally restrictive kinship systems that no amount of revision can free it up for positive feminist aims. But in firmly situating these texts within a predetermined formulaic inheritance it is actually Duncker, rather than Carter, who remains ensnared. Perhaps we either need to accept that these stories are not fairy-tales at all, or radically rethink what a fairy-tale is. After all, while Carter's two *Virago Book[s] of Fairy Tales* (1991 and 1993) are self-evidently collections of revisionary fairy-stories, can the same so easily be said of a collection called *The Bloody Chamber*? Quite clearly, rather than being fairy-tales which contain a few Gothic elements, these are actually Gothic tales that prey upon the restrictive enclosures of fairy-story formulae in a manner that threatens to become 'masochistically' self-destructive. In order to comprehend this point fully, we need to elaborate upon what characterizes the structural conventions of a fairy-tale, namely the interrelationship between play, space and narrative consolation in the never-never world of the happy ever after.

The conventional fairy-tale operates as a seemingly safe site of play, something it has in common with all formulaic fictions. This is the way Bruno Bettelheim insists not simply on reading, but also defining, the fairy-tale form. Fairy-tales, he argues, playfully enable children to resolve real-life dilemmas through controlled textual means. But just as Clark and Duncker are misguided in their desire to play safe in their reading of Carter on female sexuality, so Bettelheim is wrong to stick so rigidly to consolatory mechanisms in his reading of the fairy-tale. If the fairy-tale *only* exists as the literature of consolation, then what happens to such a tale when it refuses to console? Or, to put it another way, if '"The Three Little Pigs" is a fairy-tale because the wolf gets what he deserves',[49] then what happens in the case of 'The Company of Wolves', where 'what the wolf deserves' is neither here nor there? [...]

Readings such as Bettelheim's condescendingly situate safety within a play-pen environment, where protection is really a disguise for restraint. Such approaches are not unusual. Many critics of fantasy fictions still tend to define genre in terms of rigid spatial demarcations which segregate the inner consensus of the formulaic from the amorphous 'outside world' of general fiction.[50] One simply cannot do this with *The Bloody Chamber*. When Carter's collection is simply viewed as a rereading, reworking or revision of the fairy-tale mode, it inevitably has to function within a generic stranglehold that will always (however reluctantly) reduce its stories to closed dream-texts. Bettelheim's readings are enlightening in many ways, but like his own definition of the fairy-tale they are always constrained by the limitations of a consolation that pushes towards narrative (en)closure. One thing remains clear: if Carter's reading of sexuality is positively problematic, then her usage of the fairy-tale form is even more so. In agreeing that the form of play Carter favours in *The Bloody Chamber* bears precious little relationship to Bettelheim's over-protective play-pen, we must start to loosen our grip on the fairy-tale structures and open this collection up to the vagaries of narrative free play.[51] □

Armitt's formalist reading is grounded in the assumption that *The Bloody Chamber* essentially comprises a single narrative; a 'body' of text whose boundaries are rendered provisional and uncertain. Although, as we have seen, Armitt's views on the feminist intentions of this text are diametrically opposed to the interpretation offered by Cronan Rose, her analysis does not ignore the issue of gender. However, her examination of the structural elements of the text leads her to a very different conclusion from that proposed by those who critique Carter's portrayal of women as reactionary:

■ Herein lies the crux of the debate over female sexuality in these stories: are the women active or passive, erotic or inert? The violence inherent in the word 'bloody' leads us to expect the chamber to be the location for hideous and violent sexual excess. But what if we read the word 'chamber' not as a room, but as a vase or a vessel for carrying liquid? In this case the blood is the liquid with which the vessel is filled (indeed the substance that gives the vase its definition). The associated excesses are those of overspill, not those which threaten containment. In this case it is not the chamber that contains and thus constrains the woman (who then becomes a terrified victim), but the woman herself who takes control of the vessel of excess.[52] □

Armitt enlarges on this point through reference to a passage from the story 'The Erl King':

■ A young girl would go into the wood as trustingly as Red Riding Hood ... [but] she will be trapped in her own illusion because everything in the wood is exactly as it seems.
    The woods enclose and then enclose again, like a system of Chinese boxes opening one into another; the intimate perspectives of the wood changed endlessly around the interloper, the imaginary traveller walking towards an invented distance that perpetually receded towards me. It is easy to lose yourself in these woods. (p.85)

[... I]t is common for Carter's female characters to become victims of their own illusory existence, but just how trusting *is* the girl in this case? If the narrator is drawing a comparison with the conventional Little Red Riding Hood of the child's tale, then we may well infer that Carter's protagonist is equally naïve, obedient and thus a victim. But her own version of Little Red Riding Hood in 'The Company of Wolves' is far more worldly-wise than this. A girl 'as trusting as her' would be wily, adventurous, but never gullible. Further evidence favours the second of these two readings. A strange and rather uncomfortable shift in tense and pronoun midway through the passage signals a shift in narrative voice. The first paragraph is written in the third person, suggestive of somebody else speaking on behalf of the girl. Once we enter the enclosures of the forest, however, that voice is replaced by the girl's own. This shift immediately transforms the otherwise cautionary note of the final sentence into a welcome anticipation of future events. The girl takes on the role of Gothic interloper, whereas the reader becomes the 'imaginary traveller'. And the woods endlessly change around us too, our interaction projecting us into their labyrinth, stirring up the fixity of the frame to find endless vistas of opportunity for this girl. After all, these frames only appear to close off all the options. No sooner have they closed down than they open up 'one into another' again, even if they remain defined by the wood.

Despite her own words here, nothing in Carter's work is ever 'exactly as it seems' – let alone women's relationship with these wooden frames.

[... I]n a Gothic narrative there is always a complex trickery inherent in the representation of the image as revealing and as reveiling. In Carter's case, Duncker effectively charges her with producing revelations which serve to re-encode terrible secrets, locking women away within a closeted existence as hideous corpses, sexless puppets, or those who fall foul of self-destructive excess. Certainly, in the case of the fairy-tale tradition, literary genealogies themselves depend upon passivity in the sense of formulaic conformity, and this is the legacy of *The Bloody Chamber*. But Carter takes issue with this genealogy, she does not simply accept it lying down. In 'The Lady of the House of Love', for example, the portrait's concern with the inheritance of familial characteristics is shown to be the cause of the protagonist's enslavement. Thus we are told that the lady's 'ancestors sometimes peer out of the windows of her eyes' in 'a perpetual repetition of their own passions' (p. 103). She has, so to speak, been 'framed' by her own genealogy, the deliberate choice of the term 'peer' as opposed to 'stare' or 'gaze' reinforcing this awareness. Behind that glassy face, just as the eyes of the apparently inert portrait move, so her eyes encapsulate the conflict which exists on the precarious site of abjection between overspill and containment. The reader must positively engage with this conflict.

Frames do not simply encase portraits in this short story collection. In overall structural terms they also strive to contain the free play of the individual tales in a manner that is highly unusual. Conventionally, the Gothic narrative shackles the night-dream world and situates the narrator safely beyond its limits. 'The Bloody Chamber' itself follows this dynamic, luring us into a false sense of narrative security in which the precise boundaries between the internal (present) and external (retrospective) time sequences remain clear. But as we progress through the tales as a whole, the apparent limitations imposed upon each as discrete spatio-temporal (and even textual) entities are breached by the type of narrative overspill already witnessed between 'The Lady of the House of Love' and 'The Erl-King'. In other words, images, symbols and motifs from one story turn up in another in a way that reiterates and reworks the concerns of a previous vignette. As a whole, this multiplicity of interconnecting frames is [...] only precariously contained within the larger frame of the whole. The motif of the portrait should have prepared us for this dynamic. Just as the word 'form' synonymously refers to the anatomy inscribed on canvas and the mode of representation, so the word 'frame' can likewise define the skeletal content (the human frame) as much as it does the boundary marker.

Undeniably, the central male protagonist of 'The Bloody Chamber' and the vampiric central female protagonist of 'The Lady of the House of Love' are depicted as metamorphic figures oscillating along the boundaries between the human and the bestial, because they are anatomical representations (perhaps even portrait representations) of the transgressive and untamed excess of their own sexual practices. But since *The Bloody Chamber* functions less as a collection of individual short stories and more as a single narrative which uses the short story medium to work and rework compulsive repetitions, it should also come as no surprise that both these narrative metamorphoses and the metamorphic forms they depict work to destabilize each other from within. It is not simply that the eponymous Lady of the House is a metamorphic character within the frame of her own text but that, beyond the limits of that frame, she crops up in the guise of the eponymous Tiger's Bride and/or the wolf's love in 'The Company of Wolves'. Similarly, it seems that there is really only one central male protagonist who, beginning as a lion, passes through a variety of predatory masculine metamorphoses before ending up as a wolf who is simultaneously both man and woman. [...] Throughout the collection, such oscillating figures perpetually appear and disappear before our very eyes, which gives them a disorientingly ephemeral quality. Once we consider how this is mirrored by the narratives within which they are only partially contained, it is unsurprising that, with the exception of perhaps 'The Bloody Chamber', 'The Company of Wolves' and 'The Lady of the House of Love', one of the major problems facing the reader of these ten stories is that they seem always to be dissolving into each other.[53] □

What this discussion of Armitt's essay demonstrates is that the critical debate surrounding *The Bloody Chamber* has become split between those who regard it as a collection of subversively revised fairy stories, and who condemn or praise it on their assessment of how successfully Carter has achieved this revision; and those who regard it as a postmodern narrative whose extreme and overt self-consciousness constitutes its own critique. Although Armitt's analysis shows that a concern with gender issues is not incompatible with a more theoretical interest in *The Bloody Chamber*'s experimentation with form, the issue of sexual politics is removed from the central position it has hitherto occupied in analyses of this text.

An example of an argument which quite deliberately attempts to balance these two critical trajectories is provided by Cristina Bacchilega's book *Postmodern Fairy Tales: Gender and Narrative Strategies*, which was published in 1997. Bacchilega does not focus exclusively on *The Bloody Chamber*, but also examines a number of contemporary re-tellings of such traditional fairy tales as 'Little Red Riding Hood', 'Bluebeard' and

'Beauty and the Beast'. However, as the extract below, drawn from her concluding chapter, demonstrates, Carter's text dominates Bacchilega's thesis:

■ I distinguish 'postmodern' retellings from other contemporary fairy tales on the grounds of narrative strategies (doubling as both decon-structive and reconstructive mimicry) and subject representations (self-contradictory versions of the self in performance). [...]
   Throughout this book [...] Angela Carter's demythologising narra-tives have exemplified the transformative powers of postmodern magic and its interpellation of women. I have focused on selected stories, but her entire 1979 collection can be seen as a sustained re-vision of the fairy tale. *The Bloody Chamber* performs the multiple meanings of its title: Bluebeard's forbidden room, a high-class bed-room, a windowless cell, the grandmother's house, a castle's vault; but also the *legislative assembly* which – as village, family, 'man'kind, or Lacanian mirror – sets developmental and social norms for Carter's heroines to follow; the *body's cavities*, most metaphorically the womb, then the orbit of the eye, the chambers of the heart, the interstices of the brain; and the *space for holding charge* in an explosive book, for hold-ing narrative fire in the destructive war of the sexes. In and out of these lords' and ladies' chambers, women's blood is spilled; at times, Carter arrests its theft, at others, she re-values its flow. The encounter of beast and beauty, human and other, woman and man is enacted in every room: as the masks peeled off in one scenario are refracted dif-ferently in another, suspicion lingers but dynamics shift. In the mirror of such contained intertextuality, the stories I have discussed reflect on each other through the work of repetition against itself. If we read the collection teleologically, almost in linear progression towards some sexual and narrative liberation, the transformation of the mirror in the bloody chamber is positively magic: from inorganic to speculum serv-ing the masculine gaze in 'The Bloody Chamber', to dream-like but porous matter in which to envision our futures, in 'Wolf-Alice'. But these images still hinge on the 'Snow Child', disembodied at the cen-ter of the book. If we read the stories in juxtaposition to one another, talking back at each other, Bluebeard's mirror has transformed but not shattered: the ending of 'Wolf-Alice' could be another 'seeing is believing' trick. The construction of each reading is shaken by the emerging of another tunnel, another underground chamber, another story, another audience.[54] □

According to Bacchilega, therefore, it is through the distinctive tech-niques of the postmodern fairy tale that the female subject can be con-structed in new, potentially utopian, forms. And, as mentioned at the beginning of this chapter, this was a project of Carter's which did not end with the publication of *The Bloody Chamber*. Her task of editing the two Virago Press collections of feminist fairy tales gave her the opportunity of expounding her views on the function of fairy tale, and her two subsequent collections of short stories, *Black Venus* and *American Ghosts and Old World Wonders*, both contained other fairy-tale narratives – another wolf story, 'Peter and the Wolf'; and 'Ashputtle *or* The Mother's Ghost', her own take on the Brothers Grimm story '*Aschenputtel*'.

In her study of fairy tale, *From the Beast to the Blonde: On Fairy Tales and Their Tellers* (1994), Marina Warner argues that Angela Carter's love of masquerade, metamorphoses and fantastic quests is rooted in her fascination with the fairy-tale form. Warner implies that such 'fairy tale' themes became more and more important in Carter's fiction as her career progressed, signalled by her increasing use of a lighter and more humorous tone:

■ The growing presence of humour in Carter's fiction signals her defiant hold on 'heroic optimism', the mood she singled out as characteristic of fairy tales, the principle which sustained the idea of a happy ending, whatever the odds. But heroic optimism shades into gallows humour. Although laughter breaks the silence and jesting can be provocative, disruptive, anarchic and unsettling, some laughter never unburdens itself from knowledge of its own pessimism; it remains intrinsically ironic.[55] □

Carter's interest in fairy tale had nothing to do with the false consolations of 'living happily ever after'. Instead, she regarded the form as essentially pragmatic, 'the most vital connection we have with the imaginations of the ordinary men and women whose labour created our world'.[56] This mixture of pragmatism, ironic humour and elusive happy endings was to be the vital ingredient in what Warner terms Carter's 'last, full-stretch flights'[57] – *Nights at the Circus* and *Wise Children*.

CHAPTER SEVEN

Nights at the Circus (1984) and *Black Venus* (1985)

A NGELA CARTER published her eighth novel in 1984, and, unlike so many of her other books, it received widespread and largely favourable reviews. Robert Nye, writing in the *Guardian*, described it as Carter's 'most ambitious novel to date [which] breaks fresh ground both in content and style, [...] without doubt her finest achievement so far, and a remarkable book by any standards'. Reading the novel's primary concern as the 'education' of its leading male character, Jack Walser, at the hands of the winged heroine Fevvers, Nye concludes:

■ Angela Carter has a useful sense of humour, and she does not spare Walser a single revelation of his own shortcomings. The thing could have degenerated into a feminist tract, though, disfigured by its own savage comedy, were it not for the richness and liveliness of the portrait of Fevvers herself; coarse, uproarious, hectic, inventive, pre-posterous, soaring through the air with the greatest of ease, the daring young woman on the flying trapeze. Fevvers has to be the most outrageous and entertaining revelation of the White Goddess in a blue moon.[1] □

When *Nights at the Circus* was published in America a few months later, it was similarly praised; although, in a piece that appeared in the *New York Times*, Carolyn See's response was slightly more equivocal than Nye's. She criticises the book for labouring its points unnecessarily:

■ [T]he reader begins to feel like a child who's spent all his allowance on 10 pounds of chocolate chip cookies and eaten every one of them down to the last crumb. Page by page, even chapter by chapter, *Nights at the Circus* is delicious, a sweet for the mind, but after a while it's hard not to get a little queasy.

By the last third of the book, Angela Carter has already made her point about the 19th-century woman giving way to the larger, more powerful, altogether enchanting Winged Victory. We understand that by combining the wiles of a con artist with real self-confidence there's nothing she can't do. We're not surprised to find, however, that when Fevvers loses Walser she droops like the proverbial bird in the gilded cage (which persona is also part of her act); that she lets her hair grow in brown at the roots and that she even breaks a wing. You can't fly without love: well, that's a laudable sentiment, but not exactly a new one.

Mrs. Carter, who is the author of seven previous novels and two collections of short stories, might have remembered that at the circus, or in a book, the real trick is to quit while you're ahead, to get off stage with the audience begging for more. *Nights at the Circus* is a class act, drawing as it does on a mad mixture of Mary Poppins, Djuna Barnes's 'Nightwood' [1936], Greek mythology and reruns of 'The Bionic Woman'. It's wonderful to read, but there comes a time when you long for the circus to be over so you can go home to your quiet bed.[2] □

Taken together, however, the opinions expressed by Nye and See typify critical reaction to *Nights at the Circus*, which is, broadly speaking, divided between those who regard Carter's adoption of a more accessible style and approach a roaring success; and those who find its expansiveness and grandiose narrative ambitions a little too much to take. Without doubt, however, it was Carter's most commercially successful book of her career thus far, and protests were raised when it did not appear on the shortlist for the 1984 Booker Prize, although it did win the James Tait Black Memorial Prize for the best novel of that year. Publicity for *Nights at the Circus* was enhanced by the further release in 1984 of Neil Jordan's film adaptation of Carter's short story from *The Bloody Chamber*, 'The Company of Wolves', for which she wrote the screenplay.

In an essay which traces the relationship between Carter's writing and feminism, Merja Makinen has usefully backed up the commonplace observation that Carter experienced a sharp rise in popularity towards the end of her career with facts and figures which place that upswing within a commercial context. Makinen, like Nye, notes that Carter's change in style undoubtedly contributed to this wider success. However, Makinen also connects the success of *Nights at the Circus* with changes taking place within the literary marketplace, particularly as regards the promotion of feminist texts.

■ The last two novels, with their lighter tone and more exuberant construction of interrelationships, probably have the widest readership of all [of Carter's books]. This mellowing of textual aggression is not the only explanation for the increasing popularity of Carter's later texts.

Helen Carr notes that the mid-eighties saw the arrival of South American magic realism on the British scene.[3] From that moment, Carter's readers could assign her anarchic fusion of fantasy and realism to an intelligible genre, and so feel more secure.

However, a fuller explanation of Carter's popularity needs to take account of marketing and distribution: not just accessibility of ideology, but accessibility of purchase. Is the text on the general bookshop shelves? Is it marketed under a feminist imprint, thus signalling to the potential reader, for feminist eyes only? [...] In Britain, Angela Carter [...] has been published by mainstream publishers from the beginning. The publishing history for her hardback fictions runs: Heinemann 1966–70, Hart-Davis 1971–2, Gollancz 1977–84, Chatto & Windus 1984–92. As far as marketing and distribution are concerned, Carter has always been presented directly to mainstream audiences.

Both *Passion of New Eve* (1977) and *Bloody Chamber* (1979) initially came out under Gollancz's 'Fantasy' series, placing them within a specific genre, and the former was the first into paperback – being issued by Arrow in 1978. In 1981 Penguin issued *Bloody Chamber* along with *Heroes and Villains* and *The Infernal Desire Machines of Dr [sic] Hoffman*. In the same year Virago published the paperback of *Magic Toyshop*, followed by *Passion of New Eve* the year after, and *Fireworks* in 1987. The covers of both publishing houses initially focused on the surreal, vaguely sci-fi elements, Penguin doing a nice line in suggestive plants, designed by James Marsh. [...] Virago also published Carter's non-fiction and commissioned her to edit collections of stories.

Nights at the Circus reached a very large audience, in paperback. Picador published it in 1985 and it was taken up as a major lead title for Pan to promote and distribute. [Nicci] Gerrard cites Virago's average fiction print-run as 5,000–7,000 in the second half of the eighties.[4] By the early nineties, *Nights at the Circus* had achieved sales which exceeded this figure ten times over.[5] □

From this perspective, therefore, the increase in public interest in Carter's fiction in the 1980s was not due to *Nights at the Circus* alone, but to the fact that it appeared in the midst of a general remarketing of her work.

One could also argue, however, that it was not just the writing that was being repackaged for more general consumption, and point to the fact that most of the substantial interviews with Carter that are now most frequently referenced in studies of her work date from 1984 onwards. Although quite a bit of what Carter says in these pieces are reiterations of ideas she had already voiced in her own articles and essays, such profiles constitute a promotion of the author as a figure of legitimate public and academic interest. Ian McEwan's profile in the

Sunday Times and John Haffenden's interview in the *Literary Review*, both published hard on the heels of *Nights at the Circus*, serve a double purpose. Not only do they publicise Carter's new novel (and in McEwan's case, the film *The Company of Wolves* as well), they also introduce readers to the author herself, describing her house and baby along with the writing. Moreover, in their recapitulations of Carter's life and career, they alert readers who might have been unaware of them to her previous publications, thus emphasising her status as the writer of an established body of work.

In these pieces, Carter herself presents *Nights at the Circus* as the work of her maturity, and the culmination of ideas she had been working on for a long time. To Ian McEwan, for example, she said that '[s]he wrote the first sketches for *Nights at the Circus* almost 10 years ago. "I had to wait till I was big enough, strong enough, to write about a winged woman"'.[6] To John Haffenden, she talked at length of her desire to use fiction to communicate serious ideas, and *Nights at the Circus* appears as the culmination of that concern:

■ It's almost an accident that I was trained to read books as having many layers. Using the word 'allegory' may make it all too concrete. Certainly I was using straightforward allegorical ideas in parts of *Nights at the Circus*. Mignon, for example, is supposed to be Europe, the unfortunate, bedraggled orphan – Europe after the War – which is why she carries such a weight of literary and musical references on her frail shoulders. But it does seem a bit of an imposition to say to readers that if you read this book you have got to be thinking all the time; so it's there if you want it. From *The Magic Toyshop* onwards I've tried to keep an entertaining surface to the novels, so that you don't have to read them as a system of signification if you don't want to. [...] The idea behind *Nights at the Circus* was very much to entertain and instruct, and I purposely used certain eighteenth-century fictional devices – the picaresque, where people have adventures in order to find themselves in places where they can discuss philosophical concepts. That mingling of adventure and the discussion of what one might loosely call philosophical concepts occurs, for example, when the characters reach Siberia: they can discuss Life and Art as they stride off through the snow.[7] □

This idea of *Nights at the Circus* as representing a climactic moment in Carter's *oeuvre* is reiterated in critical surveys of her work. Paulina Palmer, for example, in an essay which constitutes one of the earliest critical overviews of Carter's writing, presents it as steadily progressing from a preoccupation with oppression to a more celebratory and utopian mode, which *Nights at the Circus* exemplifies.

■ In her 'early' texts (those published prior to 1978), it is the analytic and 'demythologising' impulse which is to the fore. These include *The Magic Toyshop* (1967), *Heroes and Villains* (1969) and *The Passion of New Eve* (1977). The themes which occupy her at this stage are: gender and its construction, the cultural production of femininity, male power under patriarchy, and the myths and institutions which serve to maintain it. The image which she frequently adopts to represent woman's role in society (man's too, on occasion) is the puppet. As well as carrying Hoffmannesque associations of the fantastic,[8] the image has connotations of the 'coded mannequin',[9] the metaphor employed by Hélène Cixous to represent the robotic state to which human beings are reduced by a process of psychic repression. The focus on the celebratory and utopian is something of a new departure in Carter's fiction. It does not fully emerge until the texts published in the late 1970s and 1980s, *The Bloody Chamber* (1979) and *Nights at the Circus* (1984). Here she treats themes relating to liberation and change, in the organisation of personal life and the social formation. Acts of resistance against patriarchy are represented. The deconstruction of femininity and masculinity is explored and, in keeping with the shifts in contemporary feminist thought,[10] the perspective becomes increasingly woman-centred. A reevaluation of female experience takes place and the emergence of a female counter-culture is celebrated. The image of the puppet is no longer central to the text. It is replaced by the images of Fevvers' miraculous wings which, she observes, make her body 'the abode of limitless freedom' (p.41),[11] and the egg from which she claims to have been hatched. These images represent ideas of liberation and rebirth; they evoke, in Cixous' words, 'the possibility of radical transformations of behaviour, mentalities, roles, and political economy'.[12, 13] □

Palmer's subsequent discussion of *Nights at the Circus* proceeds to examine this 'woman-centred' text in more detail, arguing that, although it is as intertextually sophisticated as any of Carter's previous works, its spirit is essentially different. In expressing the nature of this alteration in tone, she employs the adjective which has now become almost mandatory in any critical reference to this novel: 'carnivalesque'. Although the common meaning of the word 'carnival' – a street festival or travelling fair – is certainly applicable to a text which centres around the motif of the circus ring, it is also used by Carter's critics in a more specialised sense, where it refers to the work of the Russian theorist Mikhail Bakhtin. In *Rabelais and His World* (1965) Bakhtin examined carnival as an emancipatory event which liberated participants from social restraints, and which stressed the materiality of the body by rendering it grotesque through the excesses of celebration. In Palmer's analysis, the carnivalesque mood of *Nights at the Circus* leads Carter towards the adoption of a feminist utopian spirit, embodied in the image of the winged Fevvers.

■ *Nights at the Circus* has been rightly acclaimed by critics as 'a glorious enchantment', 'a spell-binding achievement'.[14] Like several other of Carter's fictions, it represents a skilfully contrived exercise in inter-textuality. Shakespeare, Milton, Poe, Ibsen and Joyce are some of the writers to whom she alludes, with the effect of creating a polyphonic interplay of European cultural attitudes and moments.[15] The voices of these writers interact in, to cite the Russian critic Mikhail Bakhtin, a medley of 'paradoxically reconstructed quotations'.[16] This medley unites the serious and the comic, the high and low. It subverts any single, unified utterance, in typical carnivalesque manner. The 'carnivalistic', as Bakhtin points out in his discussion, is not a particular kind of genre but a 'flexible form of artistic vision'.[17] Reference to his analysis of this vision is instrumental in illuminating certain significant facets of Carter's novel. It also indicates the way carnivalistic perspectives may be adapted as a vehicle for the treatment of important feminist themes, including an analysis of patriarchal culture and the represen-tation of female community. The imagery and terminology which Carter employs in the novel accord with the spirit of carnival. Ma Nelson, the Madame of the brothel where Fevvers spends her child-hood, is described as 'The Mistress of the Revels' (p.49); Buffo, the chief clown, is 'the Lord of Misrule' (p.117); and God is represented as 'the great ringmaster in the sky' (p.120). Other features of the novel which are in consonance with Bakhtin's analysis include: the mingling of sacred and profane materials; the introduction of utopian elements, such as the reference to taming tigers with music; and the emphasis Carter places on the relativity of experience. The latter is apparent in the variety of different versions of reality which the protagonists accept. A juxtaposition is achieved between the attitudes and ideo-logies of figures as disparate as Colonel Kearney (a capitalistic entre-preneur), the escaped convict (a believer in the innate goodness of humanity) and the Shaman (who is ignorant of history and geography). In Bakhtin's words, the carnival spirit 'proclaims the jolly relativity of everything';[18] it 'offers the chance to have a new outlook on the world, to realize the relative nature of all that exists, and to enter a completely new order of things'.[19]

Carter's interest in exploring 'a completely new order of things', psychic and social, is apparent from the motifs on which the novel is structured. She exploits the image which Bakhtin terms 'the grotesque body, the body in the act of becoming'.[20] Her description of Buffo the clown deconstructing himself in the circus ring, wearing 'his insides on his outside' (p.116), agrees with Bakhtin's account of the way 'carnival objects are turned inside out', in a manner symbolic of 'the destruction of the old and the birth of the new world' which carnival celebrates.[21] However, unlike Bakhtin, Carter takes the unusual step of giving a feminist critique of certain carnivalistic images and values. Instead of regarding the beatings and thrashings associated with carnivalistic mirth[22] as manifestations of playful exuberance, she uses them to represent the violence which is rife in a male-dominated culture. The brutal slapstick in which the clowns engage verges on the murderous. Their dances take the form of 'cheerless arabesques as of the damned' (p.243). There is nothing playful about the behaviour of the ape-man who is represented as 'beating his woman as though she were a carpet' (p.115). In fact, in the course of the narrative, the circus ring, with its hierarchy of male performers and 'carnival-like proceedings' (p.146), becomes an effective symbol of the patriarchal social order. It is associated with a spirit of competition, a preoccupation with financial profit and an oppressive treatment of subordinates, including women and animals.

Characteristic of carnivalistic perspectives is the focus placed on abnormal states of mind, including mental breakdown, split personality and dreams. These phenomena, as Bakhtin comments, may give the individual an insight into 'the dialogical attitude of man to himself'; they 'contribute to the destruction of his integrity and finalizedness', by revealing the possibility of him becoming 'a different person'.[23] These phrases are relevant to Carter's novel, since they give a strikingly accurate description of the process of mental breakdown and subsequent reconstruction of masculinity experienced by Walser, the journalist who accompanies the circus troupe to Russia. He joins the troupe with the aim of discovering whether or not Fevvers' wings are fake, and is subsequently chosen by her as her 'New Man, fitting mate for the New Woman' (p.281). Unlike Buffo the clown who deconstructs himself physically, Walser achieves the task mentally. He is not the only member of the troupe to move towards a state of redefined masculinity. The ape-man also renounces his machismo and starts to learn gentleness.

[... T]he most powerful image of liberation and transformation in the novel is Fevvers herself and her magnificent wings. The image of the winged bird-woman which she represents is, however, more complex in significance than it appears. It is 'transparent' in the sense that a number of contradictory meanings are constructed on it. Though it is predominantly an image of liberation, the male protagonists impose on it stereotypical interpretations of femininity, invented by a patriarchal culture. 'Angel of death', 'queen of ambiguities', 'spectacle' and 'freak' are some of the conventional feminine roles which they attribute to Fevvers in the novel. The egg from which she claims to have been hatched is an image which is similarly ambiguous. On the one hand, it represents psychic rebirth. On the other, it provides a vehicle for Lizzie to theorise about the oppressive nature of reproduction and child-care under patriarchy. Suspecting Fevvers of becoming interested in marriage and domesticity, she rebukes her with the words: 'I've raised you to fly up to the heavens, not to brood over a clutch of eggs' (p.282).

The motifs of liberation and change around which Carter structures the novel apply not only to the individual but also to the community and the group. A central theme in the text is the conventional patriarchal representation of woman in terms of polarities, a device which results in her being depicted either by symbols of transcendence (goddess and angel) or by symbols of the sub-human (nature and animals).[24] In order to highlight the latter, Carter constructs a witty parallel between the subordinate position of the troupe of performing apes in the circus and the position of the woman performers. Both are forced to endure frequent indignities and brutalities. Moreover, at a similar stage of the narrative, both rebel against their captors and succeed in liberating themselves from the tyranny of the circus.

In achieving freedom from male-dominated institutions, the female protagonists are represented as challenging, to a degree, patriarchal divisions and roles. In keeping with the feminist slogan 'the personal is political', Fevvers and her foster-mother Lizzie are revealed, in the course of the narrative, to be political comrades, as well as friends. The brothel where Fevvers spends her adolescence becomes, during the day in the absence of male clients, a miniature women's centre, humming with feminist activity. And the female inmates and warders of Countess P's horrific asylum join together to form 'an army of lovers' (p.217). Having successfully vanquished their oppressor, they escape, committing themselves to the project of creating a female Utopia in the taiga. On walking out into the Siberian wilderness, they discover that 'the white world around them looked newly made, a blank sheet of fresh paper on which they could inscribe any future they wished' (p.218). The image evokes connotations of prelapsarian [the period before Adam and Eve were expelled from the Garden of Eden] (and pre-patriarchal) existence. It also relates to Carter's description of Walser's mind becoming 'a perfect blank' (p.222), in preparation for the subsequent reconstruction of his masculinity. Carter's treatment of the women's journey is celebratory, emphasising the theme of female community. She describes how they 'set off hand in hand, and soon started to sing, for joy' (p.218).

The novel contains a number of episodes focusing on woman-identification and female collectivity, themes which, in her earlier texts, Carter either marginalised or ignored. The most notable is the representation of the lesbian relationship between Mignon, the wife of the ape-man, and the princess of Abyssinia. The relationship between the two women is presented in utopian terms. It is associated with the Orpheus-like capacity to tame wild beasts (in this case, tigers) with music, which the women possess. Carter describes music as 'their language, in which they'd found their way to one another' (p. 168). Commenting on the emotional unity which they have achieved, she portrays them as 'beings who seemed, as a pair, to transcend their individualities' (pp. 202–3).[25] □

Perhaps it is not surprising that, in a study devoted to aligning Carter as a writer of 'rationalist' rather than 'fantastic' fictions, Aidan Day takes issue with such readings of *Nights at the Circus*. Although he does not reject the notion of carnival out of hand, he expresses a suspicion that too much stress on the carnivalesque elements of the text would compromise what he believes is the novel's ultimate adherence to a materialistic examination of the position of women at a precisely pinpointed moment in history.

■ The idea that Carter's writing in *Nights at the Circus* is carnivalesque captures something of the slipperiness and subversiveness of the novel. But the danger with seeing the novel as formally entirely carnivalesque would, by definition, be that the novel then became thematically entirely carnivalesque and that it could be seen as endorsing an *unregulated* subversion of established codes and conventions, as legitimating a chaos of relative perspectives. In my reading, the fantastic in *Nights at the Circus* is, in principle, like the fantastic in Carter's other fictions. Obviously not realist in mode it is, however, deployed and regulated from a rational, materialist, feminist base. And this base is not only an explicit part of the content or theme of *Nights at the Circus*, it also helps direct the novel at a formal level. For all the superficially 'carnivalesque' features of the work it has also to be said that *Nights at the Circus* is, at a deeper level, formally or generically quite traditional. Or, perhaps it would be better to say that it invokes and depends upon – even as it re-imagines – highly traditional narrative forms. Carter commented to John Haffenden that 'the idea behind *Nights at the Circus* was very much to entertain and instruct, and I purposely used a certain eighteenth century fictional device – the picaresque, where people have adventures in order to find themselves in places where they can discuss philosophical concepts without distractions'.[26] This eighteenth-century fictional device is invoked, it seems to me, in something other than a postmodern spirit. It is not invoked to be parodied or to be relativised as a narrative device. It is invoked straight, as it were, because Carter is using the device to explore issues and to say something about those issues in a way that she herself believes in. The issues raised and the responses to those issues explored through the fiction are neither ironised nor relativised. In the second – and in some respects more important – place, there is a sense in which *Nights at the Circus* falls simultaneously within the tradition of the historical novel. Except that it might be more appropriate to call *Nights at the Circus* an 'her-storical' novel. Carter may have said herself that it is rarely possible for new ideas to find adequate expression in old forms. Yet a part of the ambition and achievement of *Nights at the Circus* is that it does not settle just for hybridity and fragmentariness but successfully appropriates and reinvents entire traditional forms in its expression of new ideas. [... ...]

With a fable like this – comic, absurdly comic, in its mad extravagance as well as in its resolution – it is not unreasonable to ask what on earth historicism has to do with it. Well, there is the fundamental period setting: the very end of the nineteenth century. This is not a gratuitous or romantic choice of period. Carter herself observed that *Nights at the Circus*

> is set at exactly the moment in European history when things began to change. It's set at that time quite deliberately, and [Fevvers] is the new woman. All the women who have been in the first brothel with her end up doing these 'new women' jobs, like becoming hotel managers and running typing agencies, and so on, very much like characters in [George Bernard] Shaw.[27]

When Fevvers first spreads her wings she is described by Ma Nelson, the mistress of the brothel Fevvers was brought up in, as 'the pure child of the century that just now is waiting in the wings, the New Age in which no women will be bound down to the ground' (p. 25) [...] Fevvers is associated with the issue of emergent women's rights, and the period of the late nineteenth century, as Carter remarks, was a critical phase in the dawning of consciousness about and agitation for women's rights. The late nineteenth century laid the ground for what would be, in part at least, consolidated and crystallised and turned into British parliamentary legislation in the twentieth century. The issue then at centre-stage was, of course, women's suffrage. In 1865 John Stuart Mill was elected Member of Parliament for Westminster, having put the matter of women's suffrage in his election address. Mill's campaigning for women's rights was profoundly influenced by the woman he had married in 1851, Harriet Taylor. From the point of Mill's election as MP the issue of women's suffrage came to occupy an important place in parliamentary business in each successive parliament. Numerous bills or amendments to bills were proposed with the intention of conferring the franchise upon women; all were defeated by one parliamentary ruse or another. Perhaps most disappointing to radicals was the Liberal W. E. Gladstone's refusal to accept an amendment to the Reform Bill of 1884 which would have granted women's suffrage. It was not, of course, until 1918 that women of a certain age (thirty and over) finally gained the vote.

Nights at the Circus carefully, not obtrusively, sketches in this historical context for its fantasy. There are, in the first place, several general allusions to actual historical personages from the period. When Fevvers, recently returned to London from a triumphant tour on the Continent, is first talking to Walser about her life and career she mentions the late Victorian music hall comedian Dan Leno [...]. In the account of her Continental tour several French names associated with experimental work in the 1890s are dropped, such as the painter Henri Toulouse-Lautrec, the dramatist Alfred Jarry, and the novelist Colette, before reference is indirectly made to the work of Sigmund Freud:

> On that European tour of hers, Parisians shot themselves in droves for her sake; not just Lautrec but all the post-impressionists vie to paint her; Willy gave her supper and she gave Colette some good advice. Alfred Jarry proposed marriage ... In Vienna, she deformed the dreams of that entire generation who would immediately commit themselves wholeheartedly to psychoanalysis. (p. 11)

Back in London, Fevvers gains the attention – though no more – of the infamously lecherous Prince of Wales [...].

More important, however, are the specifically political references sprinkled throughout the text. Such as when Fevvers remarks to Walser that the prostitutes of her childhood home were all sympathetic to the women's movement:

> 'We were all suffragists in that house; oh, Nelson was a one for "Votes for Women", I can tell you!'
>
> 'Does that seem strange to you? That the caged bird should want to see the end of cages, sir?' queried Lizzie, with an edge of steel in her voice. (p. 38)

Or there is Rosencreutz, whose real name Fevvers secretly reveals to Walser before citing 'Rosencreutz' as the type of those parliamentary men who consistently succeeded in the later years of the nineteenth century in opposing the extension of the franchise to women:

> 'You must know this gentleman's name!' insisted Fevvers and, seizing his notebook, wrote it down ... On reading it:

'Good God,' said Walser.

'I saw in the paper only yesterday how he gives the most impressive speech in the House on the subject of Votes for Women. Which he is against. On account of how women are of a different soul-substance from men, cut from a different bolt of spirit cloth, and altogether too pure and rarefied to be bothering their pretty little heads with things of *this* world, such as the Irish question and the Boer War.' (pp. 78–9)

Then there is Lizzie. Lizzie is fondly drawn in a serio-comic spirit as the epitome of the English radical tradition. At the end of the novel Fevvers explains that she had never made a good prostitute in Ma Nelson's house because of

her habit of lecturing the clients on the white slave trade, the rights and wrongs of women, universal suffrage, as well as the Irish question, the Indian question, republicanism, anti-clericalism, syndicalism, and the abolition of the House of Lords. With all of which Nelson was in full sympathy but, as she said, the world won't change overnight and we must eat. (p. 292)

Whilst in Russia Lizzie had persuaded Walser to include some of her own letters in the journalistic packets he was sending back to Britain. It turns out that these were not just personal communications but news of Russian internal politics to Russian dissidents in exile; dissidents who would eventually produce the Revolution of 1917 [...]. The historical roots of Lizzie's radicalism are with the English radical movement of the 1790s, a movement associated with the names, among others, of William Godwin and Mary Wollstonecraft. This historical background to Lizzie's thought is briefly alluded to after Lizzie has been hearing how the women planning to set up a lesbian community had intended to procreate:

These women planned to found a female Utopia in the taiga and asked a favour of the Escapee; that he should deliver 'em up a pint or two of sperm ... With this request, he had complied. I could see he was a perfect gentleman.

'What'll they do with the boy babies? Feed 'em to the polar bears? To the *female* polar bears?' demanded Liz, who was in a truculent mood and clearly thought herself back in Whitechapel at a meeting of the Godwin and Wollstonecraft Debating Society. (pp. 240–1)

The most important thing about the fantasy dimension of *Nights at the*

Circus is that, for all its flamboyant craziness, it makes sense specifically in relation to the historical context that is sketched in by Carter. It is not gratuitous or surrealist fantasy, but fantasy whose symbolic meaning can be recovered in rational historical terms.[28] □

At an earlier point in his argument, Day cites Palmer as an example of a critic who reads *Nights at the Circus* as a carnivalesque text, and, as the above extract demonstrates, positions himself as resistant to such interpretations. However, a comparison of Day's and Palmer's discussions demonstrates that Day's position is not as sharply differentiated from Palmer's as he seems to imply. The crux of Palmer's argument is that, while *Nights at the Circus* shows 'the way the carnivalistic perspectives may be adapted as a vehicle for the treatment of important feminist themes', it also offers 'a feminist *critique* of certain carnivalistic images and values'. This opinion is distinctly reminiscent of Day's final statement that the novel 'hints at some kind of connection between masculinist values and the carnivalesque'.[29] As he argues: 'The herstoricism of *Nights at the Circus* never loses sight of the material realities of women's lives at the end of the nineteenth century. It never carnivalises its preoccupation with women's suffering and disempowerment. The novel offers, in fact, within its narrative, a critique and mockery of the principle of carnival'.[30]

Indeed, both Palmer and Day arrive at similar conclusions: that the novel ends by envisaging a utopian order within which women are no longer confined to male-defined stereotypes. Palmer cites the lesbian relationship between the two circus performers Mignon and the Princess of Abyssinia as 'prefigur[ing] a new feminist era'. It is for this reason, says Palmer, that:

■ The novel concludes aptly on a note of carnivalistic mirth. In the penultimate paragraph, Fevvers' peal of loud laughter is described as uniting her in spirit with the whole cosmos, giving rise to a gust of universal merriment. [...] However, the function of Fevvers' laughter is more than merely festive. As well as irreverently mocking the existing political order, it is socially and psychically liberating. Bakhtin's discussion of the subversive potential of laughter helps to explicate its various levels of meaning. He points out that laughter signifies 'the defeat of power, of earthly kings and of all that oppresses and restricts ... It liberates not only from external censorship but, first of all, from the great interior censor'.[31,32] □

Although Day steers clear of any mention of Bakhtin in his analysis, he nevertheless makes much the same point. He examines Carter's portrayal of Fevvers in order to argue that, while she is an undeniably fantastic – even carnivalesque – creation, the continual stress the text places on Fevvers' earthiness accentuates the fact that she is also a real flesh-and-blood woman, thus enabling Carter to critique the way in which conventional historical narratives (which are authored by men) omit the material realities of women's lives. For Day, therefore, the end of the novel represents a radical redefinition of history itself:

■ The anvil of traditional history must itself be changed if new possibilities for human lives are to be released. There must be an alternative or a reconceived history or herstory within which people may grow. In such a new his/herstory Fevvers and New Woman may be able to realise herself and Jack – Jack-the-Lad – Walser can do what, we are told at the very end of the novel, he has done: 'Walser took himself apart and put himself together again' (p. 294). At the end of their story, Walser and Fevvers, in love, make love with Fevvers on top because her wings make it impossible for her to adopt another position. The scene alludes to an old favourite of Carter's: the story of the rape of Leda by Zeus in the guise of a swan, a story already alluded to at the opening of *Nights at the Circus* [...]. The difference at the end of *Nights at the Circus* is that this scene inverts the classical stereotype of a male figure with wings overwhelming a woman. But it is not just an inversion, as if the feminism of this novel were inscribed within what Carter termed a 'female supremacist' mode.[33] The relationship between Walser and Fevvers is based not on the principle of dominator and dominated but on the idea of love between equals. The cancelling of the traditional patriarchal icon of male dominance is necessary to emblematise this new relationship. Carter is indicating that a new his/herstory is possible because of this new kind of relationship between a woman and a man.

And while it is primarily, it is not *only* a heterosexual model that Carter uses to imagine the possibilities of a new his/herstory. There is in *Nights at the Circus* the further story of two of the female circus artistes, Mignon and the Princess of Abyssinia. Mignon is the partner of the 'Ape-Man' and she is not treated well [...]. Mignon escapes the Ape-Man and she and the Princess of Abyssinia start a loving relationship in which they 'seemed, as a pair, to transcend their individualities' (pp. 202–3). The new his/herstory will be large enough to accommodate sexual orientations not articulated in patriarchal history. [...]

In the closing paragraphs of *Nights at the Circus*, Fevvers starts laughing [...]. How are we to read this laughter? At one level, it is simply personal. Fevvers is ecstatically happy to have found someone to love who loves her in return. But we must also remember that *Nights at the Circus* is a his/herstorical novel. The twentieth century that it looks forward to had, by the time Carter wrote the novel, already substantially happened. I read Fevvers' laughter as, in part, the delight of the victor,

the delight that Carter herself has retrospectively and that her character has prophetically, in knowing that the war for women's rights,
even if not ultimately won, would score up notable victories in the
twentieth century.[34] □

Not all critics share the optimism voiced by Palmer and Day. One of the
most perceptive pieces written on this novel does not appear in the context of a specific study of Carter's work, but in Mary Russo's book, *The
Female Grotesque* (1995), where the final chapter is devoted to a detailed
analysis of *Nights at the Circus*. Russo maintains that a straightforward
interpretation of the novel as utopian is untenable, since female-centred
associations and groupings are not permitted to separate from social
structures and disappear into a utopian 'elsewhere', but are placed in a
position of continual negotiation with dominant ideologies. The compromise struck by the text between utopian aspirations and hard-nosed
realism is represented by Fevvers herself, described by Russo as 'an exhilarating example of the ambivalent, awkward and sometimes painfully
conflictual configuration of the female grotesque'.[35] A woman who both
transcends and is defined by patriarchal structures, Fevvers combines the
contradictory impulses of celebration and critique, and, in the novel's
dominant metaphor of flight, holds them, quite literally, in suspension.

■ *Nights at the Circus* is unique in its depiction of relationships between
women *as* spectacle, *and* women as producers *of* spectacle. To the
extent that female countercultures are depicted in the novel, they are
placed within larger social and economic histories and fictions. The
point I want to make here is simply that to the extent that value is contested in the production of images of women in this novel, it is contested socially. One body as production or performance leads to
another, draws upon another, establishes hierarchies, complicities,
and dependencies between representations and between women.
Conflict is everywhere. Female figures such as Madame Schreck, 'the
scarecrow of desire', organize and distribute images of other women
for the visual market. Her disembodied presence suggests the extreme
of immateriality and genderless politics; she may, as the narrator suggests, be only a hollow puppet, the body as performance *in extremis*.[36]
   It is with great irony that Carter reproduces aspects of Juliette and
the libertarian tradition in *Nights at the Circus*. In a series of critical
counterproductions of the affirmative women 'who will have wings
and who will renew the world', Fevvers is born and born again, as an
act (in the theatrical sense) of serial transgression. [...] Fevvers [... is a]
figure of ultimate spectacularity, a compendium of accumulated cultural clichés, worn and soiled from circulation. Yet, poised as she is on
the threshold of a new century, her marvellous anatomy seems to offer

endless possibility for change. Seeing her wings for the first time, Ma Nelson, whose whorehouse gives Fevvers a comfortable girlhood, identifies in 'the pure child of the century that just now is waiting in the wings, the New Age in which no woman will be bound down to the ground' (p.25).[37]

Ironically, in the context of the whorehouse, this means only that Fevvers will no longer pose as Cupid with a bow and arrow, but will now act as the Winged Victory, a static performance of her femininity 'on the grand scale', but hardly a pure or transformative vision. The magnificent Nike of Samothrace from the second century B.C., long thought to be the greatest example of Hellenistic sculpture, is deservedly famous for its activation of the space around it. Standing eight feet tall, the figure of the victorious goddess leans out into the spatial illusion of onrushing air, still in motion, barely touching the ground. This icon of classical culture was much reproduced as a collectible souvenir and model of classicism. Through the techniques of miniaturization and reproduction [...], Nike reemerged in the late nineteenth century as Victorian bric-a-brac. It is in this guise that she is reproduced and reenlarged by the young Fevvers, whose domestic portrayal (on the whorehouse mantel) of this art object-souvenir in the *tableau vivant* for male visitors would seem merely to set the terms for their accession to, and repeatable acquisition of, the other women who service them. Like Trilby, Fevvers poses as the advertisement and model for similar commodities; not exactly a prostitute herself, she nonetheless installs the myth of femininity as virgin space in the displaced aura of the art work, while suggesting the comfort of the already-used, the 'sloppy seconds' of womanhood waiting, for a price, in the upper chambers.[38] □

As the mention of Juliette in the above extract suggests, Russo regards *The Sadeian Woman* as a crucial intertext as far as *Nights at the Circus* is concerned. The cruel excesses of de Sade's dominatrix bring her freedom, but at the price of her identification with other women, whereas her antithesis, Justine, is representative of *all* women who suffer at the hands of men. Although Juliette's role may superficially appear the preferable one, it is actually as circumscribed as Justine's, for both remain subject to the ultimate law of the male libertine. Fevvers represents a new stage in Carter's examination of this conundrum, for while her profession as *aerialiste* places her physically above the male spectator, it also renders her a fetishistic object. The dualism of this dominant/submissive role is highlighted in the part of the novel narrated by Walser, who, while occupying the voyeuristic position of male spectator, also finds his misogynistic assumptions perpetually confounded by the essential ambiguity of Fevvers' act. Russo argues that, although Fevvers plays up to male fantasies in her performance, she ultimately also subverts them by foregrounding the labour involved in flight.

■ To recapitulate briefly the relationship between the aerial sublime and the female grotesque, I want to return to Fevvers in the midst of her circus act. By way of reference, I turn to the paradigm of the trapeze act as analyzed by Paul Bouissac in his work on the semiotics of the circus. Once in the air, the act is a negotiation, with interruptions, between two stations, with a certain expenditure of energy by the velocity of flight (up to 60 mph), permitting the human body to offer a certain illusion of suspension. Bouissac fails to note that in the case of the female performer, her negotiation of space is often interrupted by a male performer who catches her. Fevvers in the air, however, travels alone.

An additional model of normativity for the flying act is provided by Thomas Aquinas who notes, writing of 'real' angels, 'their motion can be as continuous or as discontinuous as it wishes. And thus an angel can be in one instant in one place and at another instant in another place, not existing at any intermediate time'. I am assuming that in relation to identity, Fevvers has equal claim to either of these models yet no full claim at all to either, since her act seems to dissimulate failure to occupy either time or space in these modes. Quoting the novel, from the point of view of the informed male spectator:

> When the hack *aerialiste*, the everyday wingless variety, performs the triple somersault, he or she travels through the air at a cool sixty miles an hour; Fevvers, however, contrived a contemplative and leisurely twenty-five, so that the packed theater could enjoy the spectacle, as in slow motion, of every tense muscle straining in her Rubenesque form. The music went much faster than she did; she dawdled. Indeed, she did defy the laws of projectiles, because a projectile cannot *mooch* along its trajectory; if it slackens its speed in mid-air, down it falls. But Fevvers, apparently, pottered along the invisible gangway between her trapezes with the portly dignity of a Trafalgar Square pigeon flapping from one proffered handful of corn to another, and then she turned head over heels three times, lazily enough to show off the crack in her bum. (p. 17)

For Walser, semiotician and connoisseur of the hoax, it is precisely the limitations of her act which allow him momentarily to suspend disbelief and grant her a supernatural identity, for no mere mortal could effect such incompetence in the air without dire consequences. Walser observes:

> For, in order to earn a living, might not a genuine bird-woman – in the implausible event that such a thing existed – have to pretend she was an artificial one? (p. 17)

What is more interesting to me than this sophisticated insight which, after all, only goes so far as to permit him the pleasure of a naïve spectator's night at the circus, is that Fevvers reveals what angels and circus stars normally conceal: *labor* and its bodily effects in the midst of simulated play and the creation of illusion. Her body dawdles lazily (the hardest work of all in the air) and yet, unlike her angelic sisters, she never seems to occupy discrete spots on her trajectory; she does not rest. She vamps in the musical sense, filling in the intervals with somersaults. The one time she is static in the air, perched on the swing, the rope breaks and she is stranded. What is revealed in her routine is at one level economic: the Victorian working girl is not the angel (in the house), and the novel is in many ways about working girls.[39] This is not to say that here finally a materiality has emerged from underneath an illusion, that with the appearance of work, we have a ground, that we are no longer, so to speak, in the air. Rather, I would read Fevvers' act as a reminder that the spectacle which conceals work is itself produced, and revamping spectacle shows up and diverts this cultural production.[40] □

Russo does not refer to many of Carter's critics in the course of her argument. However, she concludes it by singling out Palmer's analysis for specific comment, juxtaposing her materialist reading of the novel with Palmer's utopian one:

■ It is tempting to read this novel and even Carter's entire *oeuvre* as a progression, as one critic sees it, from the alienation of the femininity of the 'coded mannequin' to the liberatory prospects of the woman with wings.[41] Indeed, towards the end of the novel, Fevvers looks forward to the day when 'all the women will have wings, the same as I':

> The dolls' house doors will open, the brothels will spill forth their prisoners, the cages, gilded or otherwise, all over the world, in every land, will let forth their inmates singing together the dawn chorus of the new, the transformed (p. 285).

But Carter never lets this optimistic progressivism stand unchallenged:

> 'It's going to be more complicated than that,' interpolated Lizzie. 'This old witch sees storms ahead, my girl. When I look to the future, I see through a glass, darkly. You improve your analysis, girl, and *then* we'll discuss it.' (pp. 285–6)

Lizzie's view of the future is not forward-looking but rather – like the angel of history in a powerful and much-quoted passage from Walter Benjamin – a look backwards to see the future in the past, not as 'sequence of events' but as 'a catastrophe which keeps piling wreckage upon wreckage'.[42] To Lizzie and to the angel of history, 'a storm is blowing from paradise' (p.257). And there is no going back. In Benjamin's image, borrowed from [Paul] Klee's painting *Angelus Novus* [1920], the angel is caught by the storm with his wings blown open; the storm 'propels him into the future to which his back is turned, while the pile of debris before him grows skyward. *This storm is what we call progress*' (emphasis mine).[43]

Only if Lizzie's story comments are read as merely cynical or extraneous can the exchange be made to stand for a developmental antithesis in Carter's writing rather than an apocalyptic intersection of incommensurate discourses, resulting in a 'blow-up' of the narrative and a breakup of two women's narrative partnership. To side provisionally with Lizzie, who represents an ever-present but minority voice in the novel, it is more complicated than that.

I would prefer to read their differences as part of an ongoing dialogue, filled with conflict and repetition – a difficult friendship and an improbable but necessary political alliance.[44] At this point in the novel, the conversation is about losses and making do. Fevvers has 'mislaid her magnificence on the road from London; one wing is bandaged and the other has faded to drab. She is no longer commercially viable. God knows if she will ever fly again'. Lizzie's anarchic power, 'her knack for wreaking domestic havoc', is lost. As the designated heroine of the novel, Fevvers is trading in her wings for marriage with what she hopes will be a transformed Jack Walser ('I'll sit on him, I'll hatch him out. I'll make him into the New Man, in fact, a fitting mate for the New Woman'). And Lizzie, of course is skeptical: '"Perhaps so, perhaps not", she said, putting a damper on things'.[45] For Lizzie, it is necessary to think twice 'about turning from a freak into a woman' (p.283).[46]

This exchange between Lizzie and Fevvers is, like everything in the novel, inconclusive. As Susan Suleiman has written, Carter's strategy '*multiplies* the possibilities of linear narrative and of "story", producing a dizzying accumulation that undermines the narrative logic by its very excessiveness'.[47] There is always something left over, something as untimely as subjectivity itself, that forms the basis of a new plan, perhaps another flight.

Like Fevvers' excessive body itself, the meaning of any possible flight lies in part in the very interstices of the narrative, as the many-vectored space of the here and now, rather than a utopian hereafter.[48] □

Carter followed *Nights at the Circus* with another collection of short stories, *Black Venus*. It has attracted some critical attention, although, as in the case of *Fireworks*, what criticism exists tends to trace connections between specific stories and the novels: thus, the majority of it appears in the book-length surveys of Carter's work, such as my own *Angela Carter: Writing From the Front Line*, Linden Peach's *Angela Carter*, and Aidan Day's *Angela Carter: The Rational Glass*. As the rest of this chapter will demonstrate, however, the associations that are developed by these various critics very much depend on which story one looks at – a point underscored by the fact that all the narratives in the collection had already appeared separately in a variety of publications between 1977 and 1982, and thus can't be viewed as representative of a particular 'moment' in Carter's career.

Aidan Day's analysis of the title story, 'Black Venus', appears in the middle of his chapter on *Nights at the Circus*, where he uses it as another illustration of Carter's desire 'to rehumanise and rehistoricise figures of the female'. 'Black Venus' is an imaginative reconstruction of the life of Charles Baudelaire's mistress Jeanne Duval, and Day finds many parallels between Jeanne and Fevvers.

■ In 'Black Venus' Carter takes the woman Jeanne Duval who was turned into a metaphor by Baudelaire and restores her to life. In his poetry Baudelaire transformed Jeanne Duval into the figure of his own satanically inspirational muse. [...] Carter quotes from Baudelaire's *Fleurs du mal* (1857) as she first describes Baudelaire's poetic colonisation of Jeanne Duval before going on to point out how this colonisation deprived Duval of any real presence and how Duval herself did not wish any of the things ascribed to her in Baudelaire's construction of her as a muse [...].

Not only imaginatively colonised as a woman by Baudelaire, Duval is at once the product of that literal, masculine European colonisation of other peoples and other parts of the world. [...] Compounded with Baudelaire's imaginative imperialism, this shattered history of Duval's amounted to an obliteration of her autonomy, an obliteration of her identity itself – an identity which Carter reinscribes by stressing, as she did with Fevvers in *Nights at the Circus*, Duval's sheer humanity. In 'Black Venus', Baudelaire's poetic idealisation and misrepresentation of Duval extend into his daily treatment of her. The beginning of the story pictures the two of them living out depressing autumn days in Paris. Baudelaire's will to dream survives even these. His romanticising impulse involves a patronisation of Duval:

On these sad days, at those melancholy times, as the room sinks into dusk, he ... will ramble on: 'Baby, baby, let me take you back where you belong, back to your lovely, lazy island where the jewelled parrot rocks on the enamelled tree ... My monkey, my pussy-cat, my pet ... think how lovely it would be to live there.' (pp.231–2)[49]

This kind of nonsense is immediately debunked: 'But, on these days, nipped by frost and sulking, no pet nor pussy she; she looked more like an old crow with rusty feathers in a miserable huddle by the smoky fire which she pokes with spiteful sticks' (p.232). Again, Carter stresses the necessary materialism of a woman for whom the practical exigencies of life contradict romantic fantasy [...].

Carter thus rehumanises Duval but she cannot give her back an uncompromised African history. What she does do is picture Duval's survival and the money she made out of Baudelaire after his death. Just as Fevvers plainly understands that autonomy is not some transcendent condition but something which has to be purchased, so Duval purchases an autonomy that mocks its financial origin in the person who wilfully cooperated in her dispossession. Duval takes ship for the Caribbean with a man 'who called himself her brother' (p.243):

They'd salted away what the poet managed to smuggle to her, all the time he was dying ...

She was surprised to find out how much she was worth.

Add to this the sale of a manuscript or two, the ones she hadn't used to light her cheroots with ... Later, any memorabilia of the poet, even his clumsy drawings, would fetch a surprising sum ...

Her voyage was interrupted by no albatrosses. She never thought of the slaver's route, unless it was to compare her grandmother's crossing with her own, comfortable one. You could say that Jeanne had found herself ... She decided to give up rum, except for a single tot last thing at night, after the accounts were completed. (p.243)

Carter's disdain for masculine constructions of the female, whether as Winged Victory, as muse or whatever, surfaces in her interview with Kerryn Goldsworthy in 1985, where she refers specifically to the 'Black Venus' story:

Jeanne Duval didn't want to be a muse as far as one can tell, she had a perfectly horrid time being a muse. She felt that she should take Baudelaire for as much as she could get. He treated her, as they say, Quite Well, except that he appears not to have taken her in any degree seriously as a human being. I mean you can't take a muse seriously as a human being, or else they stop being a muse; they start being something that hasn't come to inspire you, but a being with all these problems ...

I think the muse is a pretty fatuous person. The concept of the muse is – it's another magic Other, isn't it, another way of keeping women out of the arena. There's a whole book by Robert Graves dedicated to the notion that poetic inspiration is female, which is why women don't have it. It's like haemophilia; they're the transmitters, you understand. But they don't suffer from it themselves.[50, 51] □

For Aidan Day, therefore, 'Black Venus' is another illustration of Carter's concern with replacing women within the historical context denied to them in their traditionally static role of men's ahistorical, never-changing Other. In a rare essay that takes this story as its sole focus, 'Blonde, Black and Hottentot Venus: Context and Critique in Angela Carter's "Black Venus"', Jill Matus makes the same general point, although her analysis adopts a rather more interrogative stance in its examination of Carter's intentions:

■ Does Carter's story claim to be a substituting or superseding version, presenting a new and improved Jeanne Duval? The concerns raised in this question are perhaps allayed by the narrator's awareness of the problem, for the narrative voice continually dissolves the illusions it creates and disputes its own authority (along with that of Baudelaire, Nadar [the main source of information concerning Jeanne's fate after Baudelaire's death] or anyone else) to tell the real story about this woman.[52]

Yet even as it disclaims the truth of its own representations, and teases out the racist and colonialist assumptions that inform traditional versions of Jeanne Duval, Carter's fiction appropriates and reconstructs Jeanne in its own politically-interested image.[53] □

Whereas Day interprets the story's primary interest as being the recovery of the historical Jeanne Duval from the myth created around her by Baudelaire, Matus regards Carter's text as rather more ambitious than that. In her essay, she argues that the object of Carter's interrogation is not only Jeanne Duval herself, but also the entire iconography surrounding the mythological figure of Venus within which Duval's misrepresentation is anchored. Matus proceeds to investigate the cultural meanings traditionally attached to this figure, and the historical association between 'Venus' and the adjective 'black':

■ Venus, goddess of love, has a long history as the signifier of feminine beauty and purity. Mythology, visual representation and literature show, however, that the figure of Venus has also been used to suggest whorish seductiveness and voluptuousness, narcissistic female self-absorption, and a variety of other denigrating versions of woman. The context of the label 'Black Venus' is frequently colonial, where it reveals much about colonial perceptions of race and gender. Its range of associations is wide, from the virulence of Jef Geeraert's *Gangrene* [1975], subtitled 'Black Venus', to the benign paternalism of Stephen Gray's poem 'Black Venus' [1976], in which the speaker implores an island beauty not to yearn for the white man's world, sure to spoil her charms.[54] Both idealization and denigration may be suggested by the term 'Black Venus' – Baudelaire's friend [Théodore de] Banville captures its quality when he describes Jeanne as both bestial and divine.[55] But like 'Hottentot Venus', the term is often employed in a bitterly ironic or oxymoronic [the yoking together of two oppositional terms] way – as if to say, 'How can what is black also be Venus-like?'.[56] □

The term 'Hottentot Venus' refers to a historical figure, of whom Matus believes Carter to have been aware: 'In the second decade of the nineteenth century a young African woman called Saartjie Baartman was exhibited in London and then Paris to show the peculiar and "typical" physiognomy of the African woman. [...] About five years later she died in Paris and the renowned Georges Cuvier wrote up his observations on her cadaver [...]'.[57] Baudelaire knew of Cuvier's work, referring to it in an anti-Belgian poem entitled 'Cuvier's Verdict'. Matus says: 'Although Baudelaire did not write a poem about Cuvier's verdict on the Hottentot Venus, Carter's implication is that he nevertheless inscribed that verdict in the "Black Venus" poems'.[58] Carter's mockery of this association between female sexuality and blackness – a designation which, as Matus points out in her discussion of Emile Zola's character Nana, can function in the metaphorical as well as the actual sense – is also what links 'Black Venus' to novels such as *Nights at the Circus*.

■ Carter's 'Black Venus' situates itself squarely within the contexts of Venus mythology that I have been discussing, and confronts stereotypes with iconoclastic wit. The story displays qualities of much of Carter's work, which has been described by various critics as shocking, intoxicating, revisionist, abrasive. A characteristic procedure of Carter's is to seize upon some image, icon or bit of mythology and draw out its implications, making gorgeous what is denigrated or scorned, blaspheming against what is held sacred, and exposing what is usually kept covert. Carter's fiction relishes the so-called freaks excluded from the Western pantheon of Venuses and relegated to circuses and sideshows. Carter is interested in women larger than life, the giantesses of myth and history and fiction – Helen, Venus, Josephine Baker, Jeanne Duval and Sophia Fevvers, the birdwoman in *Nights at the Circus*, in whom the associations of gross size, deformity and sexual licentiousness, for example, are brought gloriously together.[59] □

The rest of Matus's discussion looks at the various ways in which Carter undermines Baudelaire's representation of Jeanne Duval. A particularly interesting aspect of her analysis is her examination of Carter's involvement in the perpetuation of yet another misrepresentation of this figure. Matus argues that Carter registers her awareness of this in occupying a narrative position which is located outside the text itself, and is thus capable of ironic reflection on Jeanne's construction through language.

■ In 'Black Venus' one of the problems confronting Carter is how to represent Jeanne without presuming to speak for her or know her mind. Bakhtin's notion of dialogic interchange may help to explain Carter's sense of Jeanne, since Bakhtin emphasizes how the word in language is always half someone else's, 'exists in other people's mouths'. It becomes one's own only when the speaker populates it with intention and 'expropriates' the word, adapting it to his or her own semantic and expressive needs.[60] Jeanne's words, Carter suggests, have been more than half someone else's. A Francophone whose Creole patois made her feel in France as if 'her tongue had been cut out and another one sewn in that did not fit well', Carter's Jeanne is without words, without country, without history (p. 18).[61] Noting that Baudelaire's eloquence has denied Jeanne her language, the narrator is concerned to make the silences of Jeanne's own narrative speak. Since her sugar daddy does not hear her, we should. [...]

   Though Jeanne has been, in effect, silenced by Baudelaire's words and eclipsed by his shadow, Carter does not presume to appropriate Jeanne's story by knowing her mind; rather, she draws attention to other possible representations of her than those we already have by persistently imagining her as an ordinary down-to-earth woman concerned with her own immediate material conditions. Her language cannot speak for Jeanne, but it can compete with and challenge the languages that have sought to possess and exploit her. She attempts to formulate an alternative vocabulary to Baudelaire's and to expose the contingencies of his vocabulary. Carter's habit of unsettling ascriptions and projections manifests itself in making the reader scrutinize language closely and attend to the nuances of apparent tautology and the connotations that make a crucial difference. A good example hinges on how we understand 'promiscuous': 'Her lover assumed she was promiscuous because she was promiscuous' (p. 13). But Jeanne has her own code of honor. To her prostitution was a question of number; of being paid by more than one person at a time. That was bad. She was not a bad girl. When she slept with anyone else but Daddy, she never let them pay. It was a matter of honour. It was a question of fidelity (p. 12).

The passage draws attention to the misconstruction of Jeanne's actions from the point of view of the onlooker. Because she was promiscuous – took many sexual partners – does not mean in her terms that she was promiscuous (unable to discriminate among them).[62] ☐

Day and Matus, therefore, both align 'Black Venus' with *Nights at the Circus* by pointing to the similarities between Jeanne Duval and Fevvers, and in *Angela Carter: Writing From the Front Line*, I too cite 'Black Venus' as exemplifying the demythologising impulse which is characteristic of Carter's work, 'breaking apart received histories specifically in order to find the female experience which has been exiled to the subtext or the margins of the accepted narrative'.[63] However, the story I examine in most detail is 'The Fall River Axe Murders', which is a recovery of another mythologised historical figure – Lizzie Borden, whose murder of her parents is commemorated in a traditional rhyme.

■ Borden was to become a figure which fascinated Carter, for not only did she write a second short story about her, published in 1991,[64] but was also planning a full-length novel on the Borden murders before she died. 'The Fall River Axe Murders' is a subtle, skilfully-constructed narrative, which focuses on the morning before Lizzie murders her parents. The actual murder is not described, for that is the bit of the story everybody knows – instead, Carter is again concerned with revealing what the commonly accepted version of history keeps hidden.

Carter prefaces the narrative with the familiar nursery rhyme in which Lizzie gives her father 'forty whacks', thus drawing attention to Borden's quasi-folkloric status. What she proceeds to construct, however, is not a nursery story, but rather a study in repression related under the shadow of the inevitable foreknowledge both reader and author share which attempts to restore historical specificity to the familiar narrative. In this way, she removes Lizzie's act from the realm of the salaciously horrific and recasts it, more sympathetically, as the release of a repression too great to be contained. The dominant trope within the narrative is that of enclosure; a preoccupation which extends to the text's own formation, for it is generated from within the very narrow space which divides the drawing back of the hammer on top of a clock from its striking the alarm which will set the tragedy in motion. 'Bridget's clock leaps and shudders on its chair, about to sound its own alarm. Their day, the Bordens' fateful day, trembles on the brink of beginning' (p. 121).[65]

The narrative voice itself, however, remains resolutely modern and detached, its awareness of the events to come placing it beyond the narrow temporal space within which the action of the text is itself confined. Instead, it wanders freely between past, present and future in order to build up a picture, almost unbearable in its nightmarish intensity, of confinement and repression. Under its knowing eye, the Borden house itself takes on the surreal quality and distorted perspective of an Escher engraving, 'full of locked doors that open only into other rooms with other locked doors, for upstairs and downstairs, all the rooms lead in and out of one another like a maze in a bad dream' (p. 107). The sleepers enmeshed in this humid, fetid domestic space offer an appearance of peacefulness which is patently no more than an illusion; but the signs of impending catastrophe can be read most clearly in the body of the woman who is to be its perpetrator:

> The hem of the nightdress is rucked up above her knees because she is a restless sleeper. Her light, dry, reddish hair, crackling with static, slipping loose from the night-time plait, crisps and stutters over the square pillow which she clutches as she sprawls on her stomach (p. 113).

Glimpsed in the abandonment of sleep, Lizzie is temporarily released from the constraints of middle-class spinsterhood which constrict her waking hours, but as the static which 'crackles', 'crisps' and 'stutters' her hair indicates, she is dry tinder on the verge of becoming a conflagration born of anger and frustration.

Carter traces the origins of this frustration back to both its local and general sources. The Borden household itself is presented as a peculiar one. It is dominated by the figure of Lizzie's father – a diluted embodiment of the joylessly self-sufficient Sadeian spirit – whose iron-willed repression extends to himself as well as to others, and to every area of his domestic and professional life: 'At night, to save the kerosene, he sits in lampless dark. He waters the pear trees with his urine; waste not, want not … . He mourns the loss of the good organic waste that flushes down the WC' (p. 111).

But Old Borden himself is not the whole story, for behind him lies a whole culture which condemns Lizzie, as a middle-class New England spinster at the end of the nineteenth century, to a pitifully circumscribed form of existence. Her never-varying day begins with the donning of her viciously tight 'whalebone corset that took her viscera in a stern hand and squeezed them very tightly' (p. 103), and proceeds to a tedious round of genteel domestic tasks and charity work undertaken with the sole intention of filling in time ('What would the daughters of the rich do with themselves if the poor ceased to exist?' (p. 117)). In this context, her murder of her father and stepmother is no act of meaningless insanity, but a striking out at a system which cancels out her own will and desires and forces them to conform to the pattern of another's.[66] □

As far as I am concerned, therefore, 'The Fall River Axe Murders', rather than representing a progression in Carter's representation of her female characters, is – in a sense – retrogressive, since Lizzie Borden cannot be compared to Fevvers or any other of the female figures in Carter's later fiction. Instead, I argue that this story looks back to Carter's portrayals of female victimisation which predate the publication of *The Bloody Chamber* in 1979: 'Denied the risky opportunity of progression represented in these tales by the figure of the wolf, the female subject can herself become a monster; a glassy-eyed automaton with an axe'.[67]

In contrast, Linden Peach, by focusing on yet another story from *Black Venus*, looks even beyond *Nights at the Circus* in order to establish a connection with Carter's next novel, *Wise Children* (1991). Although he regards *Black Venus* as a whole as occupying an intermediate position between *Nights at the Circus* and *Wise Children*, particularly in its role of perpetuating 'Carter's interest in the illegitimate and its relationship to the carnivalesque',[68] the only story he examines in any detail is 'Overture and Incidental Music for *A Midsummer Night's Dream*', a story which anticipates Carter's use of Shakespearean references in *Wise Children*.

■ Carter suggests that the Court of Oberon and Titania has been ideal-ised over the centuries and that the original Court was a much less sedate place. Like the wind which Dora observes whips around back-stage, Carter exposes what is hidden behind the scenes: the Golden Herm is an hermaphrodite – lusted after by Oberon who sees him/her as a boy – through which Carter pursues her interest in the blurring of sexual boundaries. In a carnivalesque spirit, Carter gives us the 'reality' – the fairies all have head colds – behind the English mid-summer fantasy:

> Puck is no more polymorphously perverse than all the rest of these sub-microscopic particles, his peers, yet there is something particu-larly rancid and offensive about his buggery and his undinism and frotteurism and his scopophilia and his – indeed, my very paper would blush, go pink as an invoice, should I write down upon it some of the things Puck gets up to down in the reeds by the river, as he is distantly related to the great bad god Pan and, when in the

wood, behaves in a manner uncommon in an English wood, although familiar in the English public school. (p. 70)[69]

It is important to appreciate the full implications of the relationship between the two texts which Carter encourages us to question by calling her story an 'overture and incidental music'. An 'overture' is normally an introduction, which reverses the chronological relationship between the two texts, and does not have to have a close relationship in style to the main piece of music. Carter is really saying that *Midsummer Night's Dream* is predicated on an absence. If Shakespeare's play is situated in a dream-world, the ever present absence is what the Grimm brothers realised in their 'dark necromantic forest'.[70] □

Fairy tale and Shakespeare, therefore, combine in Carter's final novel, *Wise Children*, a riotous and typically irreverent celebration of life, death, family and theatricality.

CHAPTER EIGHT

Wise Children (1991) and American Ghosts and Old World Wonders (1993)

A NGELA CARTER'S last novel, *Wise Children*, appeared six years after *Nights at the Circus*. It was received with general enthusiasm – Lynne Truss, reviewing it for *The Literary Review*, described *Wise Children* as 'a magnificently vivid and funny first-person narrative [...], an exuberant book [...] about theatre, about family and about the manifold interesting places where acting and kinship intersect. In particular it is about the role of the father'. Truss presents *Wise Children* as a riotous text which ends on a suitably resounding note:

■ Carter builds up to a fifth act (well, Chapter Five) of Shakespearean proportions, with the great birthday party turning into a place of reve-lation, reconciliation and rebirth, all of it immensely satisfying. And then, remembering to stand up for bastards, she contrives to exit on a song, a dance, a smile, and a very acceptable curtain line. What a shame you can't give a standing ovation to a novel.[1] □

A review in the *New York Times* written by the American novelist Joyce Carol Oates maintained that although '*Wise Children* may not be Angela Carter's most provocative and arresting work of fiction', it was great fun nonetheless: 'a giddy soufflé of a novel, mock memoir, mock confession, mock romance, a post-modernist parody of a familiar genre'.[2] For Salman Rushdie, on the other hand, *Wise Children* is Carter's 'finest' novel, for:

■ In it, we hear the full range of her off-the-page, real-life voice. The novel is written with her unique brand of deadly cheeriness. It cackles gaily as it impales the century upon its jokes. Like all her works, it is a celebration of sensuality, of life. More particularly, it celebrates wrong-side-of-the-trackness, and wrong-side-of-the-blanketness too.

It is a raspberry blown by South London across the Thames, a paean to bastardy.[3] □

The publication of *Wise Children* was also marked by a number of interviews with its author, several of which were published, not in academic journals or literary magazines, but in the mainstream Sunday broadsheets. Like the reviews, these interviews laid stress on the novel's irreverent theatricality, and also explored Carter's sources. Interviewed by Peter Kemp for the *Sunday Times*, Carter talked of the use she had made of her own family history in the plotting of the novel, in terms which recall one of the major motivating forces behind both *Nights at the Circus* and *Black Venus* – the desire to fight against the obscurity allocated to women in a male-dominated culture:

■ At the centre of *Wise Children*, another rumbustious rummage into the property-basket of yesteryear, are prodigies of another kind; identical twins in the form of septuagenarian ex-song-and-dance-girls, Dora and Nora Chance. The inspiration for these veteran hoofers, now living in Bard Road, Brixton, was, it turns out, close to home: 'I had an aunt, my mother's sister, who probably should have gone on the halls. She didn't have a very good life at all. She was a clerk in a rather Dickensian office, and she had a most miserable fading away. I suppose I wanted to give her a happier life.'[4] □

Yet Carter also differentiates *Wise Children* from her earlier work, sending herself up as a mellowing writer who, all desire to shock now firmly behind her, is settling into an avuncular middle age:

■ As [Dora] (and the novel) go out in high-kicking gusto, the sadistic voluptuaries and impaled brides of Carter's earlier fiction seem to have been left jubilantly behind. Asked about this blooming into geniality, Carter tells you it's because 'I'm nicer as a middle-aged person than I was as a girl. When I was 18 or 19, I became self-inducedly very thin and morbid. But after I had my little boy,' (he's now seven) 'I was just fatter in the way one often is, and I felt so much better for it.' A warm advocate of avoirdupois [weight] ('If only Kafka had eaten more, he could have turned into Frankie Howerd'), she mockingly sighs. 'All these years, I've been fighting the Falstaff in my soul. All these years, I've had this deep conviction that I was the Prince of Denmark when, really and truly, I was Juliet's Nurse.'[5] □

Carter's interview with Susannah Clapp, published in the *Independent on Sunday* on the same day as Kemp's article, covers some of the same ground. Here, too, she spoke of the novel as, in part at least, an imaginative

revision of family history, granting her aunt the opportunities that she
was tragically denied in reality:

■ In re-creating past lives of the city [London], the novel also invents a
happier life for the author's Aunt Kit, who, having failed her exams,
was expected by her parents to 'go on the Halls', but was instead
pushed by a prim headmistress into a life as clerkess. Kit was dippy –
in the war she took to roaming the streets during the blackout, 'she
adored seeing those flying bombs' – and was 'rabidly frigid'. She had a
miserable life and a bleak death. The narrator of *Wise Children*, who goes
from the Halls to Hollywood and back, has a more eventful time.[6] □

Where Clapp's interview differs from Kemp's, however, is that it discusses the influence of Shakespeare upon the text in more depth:

■ One of the things [Carter] likes about Shakespeare is that he's
'vulgar ... he functions perfectly well without the language. People
weep and gnash their teeth over Ophelia in Peru. They're just terrific
plays, very good pieces of drama'.
  Her original plan had been to write a novel in which all the
Shakespeare plots were to be replayed by her Cockney song-and-
dance heroines and their family. In the end she couldn't get them all
in: there's no *Two Noble Kinsmen*, and, unless a fierce cook counts as
standing for a reference to pie, no *Titus Andronicus*: 'Shakespeare's a bit
of a vegetarian, good on fruit and veg, but rotten on meals'. But there
are, for example, two Falstaffs, one male and one female, and two
Lears. And there are twins everywhere, the result of an interview Iris
Murdoch gave years ago in which she said she liked Shakespeare and
her interviewer, A. S. Byatt, remarked that that must be the reason for
the number of twins in her books: 'That stuck in my mind, and I
thought I'd write a novel composed entirely of twins'.[7] □

However, the most detailed interview arising from the publication of
Wise Children is one given by Carter to her old friend Lorna Sage.
Published in Malcolm Bradbury and Judith Cooke's *New Writing*, this
article is less introductory and more concerned with addressing an
informed, and probably academic, audience. Therefore, although it lays
as much stress on the novel's carnivalesque elements as the reviews and
the popular interviews, it is also more analytically involved, allowing
Carter to get really expansive on the subject of Shakespeare:

■ Angela Carter's new novel *Wise Children* is a Shakespearean soap
opera about a British stage dynasty in which the men belong to the
legitimate theatre and the women to vaudeville. It's an acrobatic romp

through the branches of the family tree, posing questions about gender and generation and about the genres of the novel – the latest instalment in an oeuvre that unravels the romance of exclusion.

'I've always covered a lot of ground', she says. This time, she wanted lightness: '*Nights at the Circus* hasn't got enough air in it, it's a big thick heavy nineteenth-century novel. There should be more holes in the text, it should be airy, with spaces on the page. One of the most difficult things about writing this book was that I wanted to have a transparent prose that just ran, and I wanted it to be very funny, and at the same time I wanted the complex of ideas about paternity, and the idea of Shakespeare as a cultural ideology.'

[...] The new novel's Shakespearean rag coincides with a renewed public debate about the national bard's centrality or otherwise, sparked off by Prince Charles – 'his roots are ours, his language is ours, his culture is ours' – an assertion that immediately raises awkward questions about who 'we' are. For Carter, the short answer is that Shakespeare is anybody's and everybody's:

When I was writer in residence in Sheffield [in the mid 1970s] there were some Chilean refugee kids staying in the same house, finishing off school. One of them, Cecilia, was shown the Olivier *Hamlet*, and when she came home we said – because we very much wanted her to enjoy her first Shakespeare – 'Well, did you enjoy it?' and she said, 'What do you mean enjoy it, I *hated* it, I hated every minute of it!' and we were crestfallen. She said, 'That Ophelia, he shouldn't have done it to her, that Hamlet, I cried my eyes out, and now you ask me did I *enjoy* it!' I'm sure that Shakespeare would have been very pleased after four hundred years. She was having exactly the same reaction to it that Dr Johnson had to the end of *Lear*. What was really interesting was that Cecilia homed in immediately on the bit that was made for her, for teenage girls. I do think there's something about Shakespeare that converts the most sophisticated person into the naïve observer: *this time*, you know, Othello will see sense about the handkerchief. They played *Lear* with a happy ending for two hundred years, and it's perfectly possible that *Lear* with a happy ending would have sent you from the theatre with a great surge of joy, it would turn into a late comedy, a successful *Cymbeline* ...

Criticism – or praise – of Shakespeare as the homogenising factor in the national heritage doesn't, consequently, move her. She says, with some irony,

It's a real shame that we've got Shakespeare as opposed to, say,

Goethe, who was a great poet and a great dramatist and a great intellectual, and a rather good diplomat besides being a snappy little natural philosopher. Shakespeare just isn't an intellectual, and I think this is one of the reasons why intellectuals get so pissed-off with him. They are still reluctant to treat him as popular culture. It's altogether too carnivalesque, there's still the shadow of Leavis, we still feel we have to take it seriously. The extraordinary thing about English literature is that actually our greatest writer is the intellectual equivalent of bubble-gum, but can make twelve-year-old girls cry, can foment revolutions in Africa, can be translated into Japanese and leave not a dry eye in the house. You mention folk culture and people immediately assume you're going to talk about porridge and clog-dancing, there's this William Morris and Arnold Wesker prospect – truly the bourne from which no traveller returns. Shakespeare, like Picasso, is one of the great hinge-figures that sum up the past – one of the great Janus-figures that sum up the past as well as opening all the doors towards the future. I tend to agree that his politics were diabolical. I think I know the sort of person he was, the sort of wet war-hating liberal who was all gung-ho for the Falklands, who in taking sides would have said, you know, it's a sorry business, but once we have embarked on it … signed William Shakespeare, Highgate Village. That sort of intellectual dishonesty seems to me to *reek* from all the political aspects of the plays, but the plays themselves add up to something else. You can play them any way you want. It must be obvious that I *really like* Shakespeare.

It's equally obvious that popular culture is for her neither innocent nor crudely representational. Her Shakespeare is in the tradition of Chaucer and Boccaccio, ribald, magical and a bricoleur.[8] The play that's at the centre of the new novel is *A Midsummer Night's Dream*, restaged with loving irreverence as a 1930s Hollywood spectacular.

I like *A Midsummer Night's Dream* almost beyond reason, because it's beautiful and funny and camp – and glamorous, and cynical. It's not sophisticated like *Love's Labours Lost*, which I think is Shakespeare's only attempt at a sort of campus novel. English popular culture is very odd, it's got some very odd and unreconstructed elements in it. There's no other country in the world where you have pantomime with men dressed as women and women dressed as men, and everybody thinks this is perfectly suitable entertainment for children. It's part of the great tradition of British art, is all that 'smut' and transvestism and so on.[9] □

Critics of this novel have followed Carter's lead in examining the use she makes of Shakespeare – in particular, her critiquing of the way in which his work has been instrumental in the formation of an imperialist ideology, and employed as the determinator of 'high' culture. In a particularly readable and detailed essay, Kate Webb offers a comprehensive analysis of *Wise Children* which concentrates especially on Carter's humorous undermining of Shakespeare's cultural respectability. Webb argues that Carter's playful appropriation of his plot-lines has the effect of reworking him as a two-faced symbol. On the one hand, Shakespeare functions as the iconographic symbol of British imperialism, legitimising hierarchical divisions in class and culture; on the other hand, the carnivalesque elements in this novel allow him to be seen in a quite different light – as a writer of earthy comedy which challenges all notions of respectability and propriety.

■ If it is relatively easy (and Carter has a lot of fun doing this) to show how we foster and exploit binary oppositions in culture in order to justify the domination and exclusion of others, and to sustain elite privilege in society, it is a much more complicated thing to respond to the fictions, the romances – family and otherwise – which we have built upon the idea of legitimacy and illegitimacy. Master of this dialectic is William Shakespeare, whose 'huge overarching intellectual glory'[10] dominates the English literary canon and whose work, like Carter's own, is brimful with ideas of doubleness, artificiality and parody. In *Wise Children*, Carter not only weaves Shakespeare's stories in and out of her own, she also reminds us of the extent to which his words and ideas impregnate English culture and life: his face is on the £20 note that Dora doles out to the fallen comic, Gorgeous George; and contemporary television programmes that poach their names from him, like *The Darling Buds of May*, *May to September* and *To the Manor Born*, all make pointed, if somewhat disguised, appearances in the novel.

Part of what attracts Carter to Shakespeare is his playing out of the magnetic relationship of attraction and repulsion that exists between the legitimate and the illegitimate, between energy and order. This occurs most famously, perhaps, in the sliding friendship of Prince Hal and Falstaff. Near the close of her story, Dora tries to reimagine one of Shakespeare's cruellest moments: what if Hal, on becoming king, had not rejected Falstaff, but dug him in the ribs and offered him a job instead? What if order was permanently rejected, and we lived life as a perpetual carnival? These questions are not answered directly [...] but this challenge to order, to the legitimate world, is made throughout the novel. [... ...]

Throughout *Wise Children* Carter celebrates the vital and carnivalesque in life. 'What a joy it is to dance and sing!' is Dora's refrain, but she is aware of the effect that the enthusiasm and self-absorption of carnival can have upon others: aware, too, of the ways in which this power can be harnessed by a dominant group and brought to bear upon a weaker one. So she celebrates craziness, 'a kind of madness', that drives old Ranulph to travel the world taking Englishness to foreigners, yet deftly shows how intimately connected are Shakespeare's cultural domination and British imperialism.

Carter's connecting of art and religion reinforces this idea: Ranulph sees it as his 'mission' in life to perform Shakespeare throughout the world in order to persuade other people of the greatness of the Bard's words, just as missionaries took the Bible and tried to persuade 'natives' of the truth of God's Word. Ranulph Hazard's theatre troupe literally follow in the steps of religious evangelicalism – his 'patched and ragged tent went up in the spaces vacated by the travelling evangelicals'. They perform in 'wild, strange and various places', and their costumes are 'begged or improvised or patched and darned'. Cultural hegemony may have been an important part of the imperial vision, but acting, Carter reminds us, has always been an illegitimate profession: peripatetic, thrown-together, made-up and sexually ambivalent (in Central Park, Estella plays Hamlet in drag). Theatre, and particularly the theatre of Shakespeare, has played its role in colonising the minds of other countries, but it is also a potentially destabilising and subversive force.[11] □

However, Webb identifies other literary voices at work in the text apart from Shakespeare's. As she says,

■ a huge part of the fun of reading *Wise Children* lies in seeing how far you can unpack the layers of meaning. How far, too, you can unpick the words of others that have been woven into Carter's/Dora's own. There is Shakespeare everywhere, but other writers also: Milton, Sterne, Wordsworth ('If the child is father of the man ... then who is the mother of the woman?'), Dickens, Lewis Carroll making an appearance as a purveyor of 'kiddiporn', Samuel Butler, Shaw, Dostoevsky ('My crime is my punishment'), Henry James and Tennessee Williams ('They lived on room service and the kindness of strangers') are just a random selection.[12] □

Webb singles Milton out for particular mention, arguing that the preoccupation with dualism of Carter's novel – the dualism that the allusions to Shakespeare simultaneously shore up and undermine – can be traced back to *Paradise Lost* (1667). In its retelling of the Biblical story of the fall of Lucifer from heaven and the expulsion of humanity from Eden, it represents a simple schema, in which one is either for the patriarch or against him.

■ If Shakespeare provides English literary culture with a model for plurality, it is in Milton, particularly in *Paradise Lost*, that we find a model for dualism in the world, a dualism resulting from the patriarchal and monistic vision of Christianity. One of Dora's refrains (she has a few up her sleeve) is the Miltonic phrase 'Lo, how the mighty are fallen', which is both a silly semantic joke and a serious intimation of the world she inhabits. Many of the descriptions of fallenness in *Wise Children* are specifically Miltonic or Christian: for instance, both Melchior and Peregrine are figured as Godlike *and* Satanic. Peregrine lands into the lives of the naked, innocent, unselfconscious and therefore Eve-like Nora and Dora as Adam arrived on earth: out of nowhere. And it is of Adam that Dora thinks when she sees him, because this is to be her First Man, the man who, like the fallen angel Lucifer, will first seduce her. In the same way, Melchior, 'our father' who 'did not live in heaven' but who, God-like, is worshipped by the girls from afar, is also given a Satanic side: he appears 'tall, dark and handsome' with 'knicker shifting' eyes, dressed in 'a black evening cape with a scarlet lining'. Later he is Count Dracula (a late-nineteenth-century Satanic pretender), ordering Dora and Nora to carry dirt over from Stratford – as Dracula had carried it from Transylvania – to scatter on the Hollywood set of his film of *A Midsummer Night's Dream*.[13] □

This patriarchal order, however, is systematically and thoroughly deconstructed in *Wise Children* – for how can the authority of the father be sustained in a world in which he cannot even be identified? Webb argues for a link between this absence of the figure of the father and the text's carnivalesque elements:

■ [I]t is the errant behaviour of fathers that creates, among the Hazards and the Chances, so much opportunity for the breakdown of order, for transgression. It seems that in some way fatherly absence is what creates the carnival. That men are such recalcitrant parents stems from their carnival instincts, a sense of narcissism (Peregrine is far too self-involved to be able to give himself permanently as a parent); selfishness (Melchior is more interested in his work than in his children); and a desire not to be controlled or determined within a family order which limits the patriarch just as it confines women. [... ...]

Such fatherly ambivalence, Carter suggests in *Wise Children*, might be rooted not only in carnival selfishness but in the anxiety of paternity: the eternal 'gigantic question mark over the question of their paternity'. It is this forever unresolved uncertainty about their role in biological creativity that has led men to create a mystique around artistic, and especially literary, creativity: as critics like Gilbert and Gubar have shown, the anxiety of paternity is translated into the anxiety of authorship. Here, however, Carter seems to be arguing that women, whose role in biological creativity is not in doubt ('"Father" is a hypothesis but "mother" is a fact') should now begin to shrug off the male anxiety that they, as writers, have been made to assume, and stop asking questions such as 'Is the pen a phallus?'[14] Dora does not romanticise or transform sex into something other than it is (which is what men do in their mystifying of the creative process, to cover their feelings of inadequacy); she enjoys it for what it is. A straight-thinking woman, Dora would never mistake a pen for a penis.[15] □

In the last chapter we looked at the debates surrounding *Nights at the Circus* as to whether Carter's utilisation of the carnivalesque mode supports the ideal of a feminist utopia. Likewise, Webb argues that *Wise Children* exposes the limits of the carnivalesque even while it appropriates it. She argues that female experience is elided in Bakhtin's theories, which allocate no specific role to women in the overturning of established order. Examining the role of each of the main female characters in turn, she argues that *Wise Children*, rather than ending on an uncomplicated note of carnivalesque mirth and breakdown, actually demonstrates that such anarchism may not always work to women's advantage.

■ As I suggested above, the Bakhtinian idea of carnival is central to *Wise Children*. In particular, Carter plays out ideas about sexuality's relationship to the carnivalesque transgression of order – a transgression that is, according to Bakhtin, at once both sanctioned and illegitimate. Jane Miller has argued in a collection of essays[16] that because of the breakdown of all barriers, particularly linguistic and bodily ones, that carnival entails, women do not appear in Bakhtin's work as distinct from men: carnival's amassing experience, which collapses laughter with fear, pleasure with nausea, where the world becomes 'infinitely reversible and remakeable',[17] ends up denying female difference. The reason Miller tenders for 'the inability of even those writers [Bakhtin, Volosinov and other Formalists who are interested in power] to make gender difference and sexual relations central to their work' is that they are limited by their 'particular history and their own place in it'. What Carter seems to suggest in *Wise Children*, however, is a prior problem. It is not just a question of Bakhtin denying difference, denying 'those pains and leakages that are not common to both sexes',[18] but that women and carnival might, ultimately, be inimical because female biology and the fact of motherhood make women an essentially connecting force, while carnival is essentially the celebration of transgression and breakdown.

Without entering into the debate about whether transgression can be revolutionary if it is sanctioned by authority,[19] perhaps it is in this seeming paradox in Bakhtin's argument – that carnival's transgressions are both allowed and disallowed – that we can see how well suited a model carnival is to masculinity, and how ill suited it is to femininity.

Although some women in *Wise Children* possess characteristics that might be thought of as carnivalesque, it is a man, Peregrine, who embodies it: he is 'not so much a man, more of a travelling carnival'. Peregrine is red and rude, a big man and, in the classic Rabelaisian manner, a boundary-buster, growing bigger all the time. To Dora and Nora he is the proverbial rich American uncle, a sugar daddy whose fortunes dramatically rise and fall but who, when he is in the money, spreads his bounty around with extravagance and enjoyment. He is a big bad wolf of an uncle, too, a randy old devil who seduces the pubescent Dora when she is just thirteen. He is a multiple man, and his multiplicity makes him as elusive as the butterflies he ends up pursuing as a lepidopterist in the Brazilian jungle: to Dora and Nora 'He gave ... all his histories, we could choose which ones we wanted – but they kept on changing, so. That was the trouble'. He is a contradictory presence, a very 'material ghost', in whom Dora sees all her lovers pass by as she and he make love at Melchior's tumultuous birthday party.

If Peregrine's history is unknowable because it is so multiple, Grandma's origins are unknown because she refuses to reveal them: 'our maternal side founders in a wilderness of unknowability'. Grandma arrived in Bard Road at the beginning of the century with no past but enough money to set her going for a year. She is a mystery woman, dateless, nameless, 'She'd invented herself, she was a one-off', just as later she invents her family. And like Perry, she is a woman of contradictions, a naturist who happily reveals her naked body to the world, yet speaks with an elocuted voice, a disguise that sometimes slips as she forgets herself and 'talks up a blue streak'. She and Perry get along famously – they are kindred spirits who joke about the idea of their being married.

Estella, Dora and Nora's 'real' grandmother, also comes close to one of the few descriptions of womanhood in Bakhtin's work ('she represents ... the undoing of pretentiousness, of all that is finished, completed, exhausted'): Estella's 'hair was always coming undone ... tumbling down her back, spraying out hairpins in all directions, her stockings at half-mast, her petticoat would come adrift in the middle of the street, her drawers start drooping. She was a marvel, and she was a mess'. And through her affair with a younger man, Estella is the undoing of Ranulph's old order. But unlike Perry, who is able to skip away from all his sexual transgressions, Estella is destroyed in the *Othello*esque orgy of jealousy and retribution that ensues from her affair.

In the same way, Saskia is a force who wreaks havoc, but like Estella she, too, pays a price. If Saskia's disruptiveness is carnivalesque, there is little of the carnival's laughter in her. Saskia's anger, as it commonly is in women, is directed to the domestic sphere of food and cooking. As a child she'd played a witch in her father's *Macbeth*, 'but she'd shown more interest in the contents of her cauldron than her name in lights'. In later life she continues to be an 'unnatural' witchy woman who, rather than nurturing, seems intent upon poisoning people. From the age of five, when she's seen under a bush devouring the bloody carcass of a swan, to her twenty-first birthday party, when she serves up a duck 'swimming in blood', her conspicuous consumption of meat is perhaps some sort of profane attempt to make herself feel legitimate, to be flesh of her father's flesh. But finally, Melchior's marriage to her best friend forces Saskia to recognise herself as a terminal outsider and, unable to gain the love she needs from her father, she sets about poisoning him instead. [...]

The Lady Atlante Lynde, Melchior's first wife, after falling downstairs (or was she pushed by Saskia and Imogen?), comes to life in Dora and Nora's basement, and is rechristened Wheelchair in honour of her new invalid status. Once at Bard Road she seems to undergo some sort of a transformation: losing her upper-class tightness, she becomes another bawdy, bardy woman [...]. But her transformation isn't only psychological [...] – the woman becomes her wheelchair, or at least, they become part of one another. Welded together they now, like twins, contain something of the other's personality. [...]

All these women, and Dora too, have elements of carnival in them, but none of them personifies it as Peregrine does. Perhaps this has something to do with carnival's relationship to order. Carter has argued that in the 'real' world, 'to be a woman is to be in drag'.[20] If, in the carnival world, by putting on masks and being other than what we are, we transgress the order of the 'real' world, then what does this play-acting mean for women who, in the 'real' world, already exist in a duplicitous state of affectation? The idea of carnival seems to presuppose a monistic world: the experience of femininity contradicts this, implying that the 'real' world is itself a place of diversity, of masks and deception.

We can understand better the idea of carnival being both licensed and illicit if we see how masculinity operates within it. In *Wise Children* the anarchic solipsism of carnival allows a forty-year-old man (Peregrine) to seduce/rape a thirteen-year-old girl (Dora). It could be argued that patriarchy relies upon such masculine transgression of order as a reminder and a symbol of the very force which shores it up. This is what Carter seems to be saying in *Wise Children* about the function of war in society: that patriarchy legitimates the violent disorders of war in order to sustain itself. Attractive as carnival's disorder can be to women who have been trapped by patriarchy, when women become the object of this disorder – as they are in war, or in rape, or in 'kiddiporn' – then the idea of carnival becomes much more problematic for them, and their relation to it becomes an inevitably ambivalent one: as with Estella and Saskia, carnival is as likely to defeat women as it is to bring down order.[21] □

Because of this association with patriarchy, argues Webb, the ending of *Wise Children* pulls away from an unequivocal endorsement of the carnival spirit, signifying the text's regretful conclusion that there are certain things in life that carnival is powerless to change.

■ There are 'limits to the power of laughter' – the carnival can't rewrite history, undo the effects of war or alter what is happening on the 'news'. And there is no transcendence possible in life, Carter tells us, from the materiality of the moment, from the facts of oppression and war. But carnival does offer us the tantalising promise of how things might be in a future moment, if we altered the conditions which tie us down. It is only the carnival which can give us such imagined possibilities, which is why the creative things that make it up in life are so precious: laughter, sex and art.[22] □

Gerardine Meaney's discussion of *Wise Children*, which appeared a year before the publication of Webb's essay in her book (*Un*)*Like Subjects: Women, Theory, Fiction* (already quoted in Chapter Three of this Guide), raises very much the same issues. For Meaney, as for Webb, the novel 'focuses on the fictionality of paternity', although Meaney lays greater stress on its scepticism concerning maternity, arguing that the fact that the Chance sisters are unable to establish the identity of either their mother or their father means that 'Maternity too moves out of the realm of biological certainty'. For both critics, too, the question of origins is inseparable from the question of authorship. Just as Webb, as we have seen, argues that the greater surety surrounding the matriarchal principle in the text, even while it does not apply to the Chance sisters in the literal sense, nevertheless frees them from the male anxiety of authorship, so Meaney asserts that such a 'concern with biological origin and the questions of identity it raises is [...] inextricable from the problem of literary authority for the woman writer'.[23] She goes on to argue that the literary allusions within the book constitute a dualistic exchange between realism and modernism: 'In *Wise Children*, Carter plays legitimate and traditional authority, in the form of Shakespeare, off against illegitimate and modernist literary authority, in the form of Joyce.'[24]

■ In the Hazard family's attachments to Shakespeare and the public's attachment to the Hazards, Carter satirizes 'British patriotic and national identities, as they appear mediated through the cultural reproduction of Shakespearean drama'.[25] The phenomenon partakes fully of that 'nostalgia, a craving, unappeasable hunger for what is irretrievably lost', that Graham Holderness has identified as the source of a peculiarly British form of postmodern and post-colonial 'patriotism' centred on key cultural icons, most notably Shakespeare. It is not surprising then that Carter seeks to demystify traditional and patriarchal authority through the Shakespearean figure of Melchior.[26] □

Ultimately, Melchior is revealed as an ineffectual figure, whose 'kingdom is already lost' – a loss represented in *Wise Children* in the appropriation of Shakespeare for the American dream machine:

■ It is in Hollywood, during the exhausting filming of *A Midsummer Night's Dream*,[27] that Dora, wiser than her father, realizes that the cultural icons he venerates are commodities, as indeed Melchior, Nora and Dora herself are commodities in the cultural market-place [...]. When she finds Shakespeare on a bank-note Dora recognizes that the culture on which the earlier generation of Hazards had sought to capitalize has 'turned into actual currency' (p. 191).[28] It is not only the daughters, but also the fathers who are units of exchange.[29] □

If Melchior is the representative of an already exhausted imperialist impulse that draws on Shakespeare as a legitimating force, then it is Peregrine who embodies its opposite mode, modernism. Although in her essay Webb cites a number of literary sources upon which *Wise Children* draws, she does not mention the author who, for Meaney, provides the principal modernist subtext of the novel. The extract cited below argues that the work of James Joyce is central to *Wise Children*, surfacing particularly in the web of allusions surrounding Melchior's brother Peregrine. In addition, Dora's narrative constitutes an ironic play on Joycean concepts of the female and of 'feminine' discourse.

■ Melchior is a Shakespearean hero: Peregrine's name identifies him with a minor character in Jonson and an outsider at that. He is a teller of tales, as well as a conjuror: 'He gave us all histories, we could choose which ones we wanted – but they kept on changing, so' (p. 31). His Joycean connections surface gradually. He addresses Nora and Dora as 'floradora', linking the singing and dancing sisters with Joyce's 'Sirens' [an episode in *Ulysses*].[30] His name, which has such an excess of connections and meanings, is also that of two of the compilers of the Annals of the Four Masters, 'the Gaelic book which is most frequently mentioned in *Finnegans Wake*.[31] Peregrine's most striking Joycean feature, however, is his resurrection on the occasion of his brother's (and his own) hundredth birthday: '"Thunder and lightning!", sang our Peregrine. "Did yez think I was dead?"' (p.206). [...]

Wise Children does more than displace traditional by modernist literary authority, though such a displacement occurs. Melchior, who cannot compete with his brother's Lazarus act, is finally 'upstaged' (p.207) and 'with his crown still on, though much askew' (p.228), he presides over the closing carnival less as the ghost of imperial majesty than as lord of misrule. Both Melchior and Peregrine are characters in Dora's fiction, their stories told 'inadvertently' (p.11) in 'the course of assembling notes towards my own autobiography'. Peregrine supplies the pulp romance and Melchior is no more substantial. [...]

Peregrine is not the only fabulist in this tale. It is not coincidental that Dora has an identical twin called Nora, but Dora distances herself from the Joycean female. 'She [Nora] said, "Yes!" to life and I said, "Maybe ..."' (p.5). Dora is no Molly Bloom then, but a variety of Joycean female roles are suggested. Her description of Peregrine in terms of 'pulp romance' can be read as a kind of retort by Gerty McDowell. The 'Nausicaa' episode in *Ulysses* parodies certain elements in the 'demon lover' motif: 'She could see at once by his dark eyes that he was a foreigner'.[32] This episode is on one level the epitome of the feminization of popular culture and the appropriation of the aesthetic to the masculine 'author'. It is the implication of such an authorial presence that ironically frames Gerty's fantasy and makes her story and particularly her way of telling it the debased opposite of that authority. There is a double irony, however, for the distance from which the avant-garde artist views Gerty's 'marmalady drawsery'[33] prose is also the distance from which Bloom views Gerty. In effect, Joyce's parody of 'women's fiction' is identified as a male masturbatory fantasy, an identification which not only undermines the hierarchy of prose style and gender initially proposed, but also opens up the possibility of reciprocity. 'Still it was a kind of language between us', thinks Bloom. Karen Lawrence has recently claimed that 'in "Nausicaa", Joyce opened up the possibility of female desire', though she must admit that 'the fantasy was rooted in the patriarchal view'.[34]

Wise Children inverts the terms of the parody. Peregrine plays 'demon lover' to Dora's demystified version of both the heroine and narrator of women's fiction. There are strong parallels with *Heroes and Villains*. Ironic distance is a property of literary authority, but in both these novels it is improperly centred on feminine protagonists, Marianne and Dora. In the wedding scene in *Heroes and Villains*, this prevented the frank exchange of women and signifiers, [and] was linked with incest [...]. In *Wise Children*, the consequence of transgression is suspended, the threat of madness or death replaced by a 'laughing apocalypse'[35] that never quite happens.[36] □

Through reference to the theories of the French feminist Julia Kristeva, who 'posit[s] a special relationship between the maternal, the subversive and the poetic',[37] Meaney argues that the female writing subject – in this case, Dora, whose 'autobiography' *Wise Children* purports to be – ironically appropriates the work of Joyce in order to instate the figure of the mother, rather than the father, as the figure which legitimates the act of authorship and functions as the source of meaning. Of particular importance in Meaney's discussion is her use of the term 'thetic', which in Kristevan theory refers to a break in the boundary which divides the symbolic order (the realm of language, law and the authority of the father) from the semiotic order (the pre-Oedipal experience of union with the mother's body). Meaney argues that Carter's use of Joycean texts such as *Finnegans Wake* 'facilitates the comic approach to the thetic boundary [...] (re)turn[ing] to a text which is a highly significant site of the modernist confrontation with meaning and a site of infinite transpositions between sign systems in order to produce a new articulation of the thetic'.[38] However, Meaney points to the abrupt halt Dora places on the carnivalesque conclusion of *Wise Children* in order to indicate the novel's resistance to the complete overthrow of the symbolic.

■ The collapse of this project into chaos seems ecstatically and dangerously close when Dora briefly contemplates the possibility that her carnivalesque coupling with Peregrine might have brought her father's house down, 'sent it all sky high, destroyed all the terms of every contract, set all the old books on fire, wiped the slate clean' (p. 222). This is the tragic conclusion of *Heroes and Villains* replayed as comedy. But at this point, when all boundaries appear to have been transgressed, Dora acknowledges she can go no further: 'There are limits to the power of laughter and though I may hint at them from time to time, I do not propose to step over them' (p. 220).

Wise Children draws back from the limit where carnival ends (p. 222). For inextricable from the novel's celebration of the irrelevance of biological origins is the denial of death implicit in all resurrection stories. In answer to her 'Wither goest we?', Dora initially answers 'Oblivion' (p. 11), but by novel's end she and Nora have realized that 'if we've got those twins to look out for, we can't afford to die for at least another twenty years' (p. 230). Carter draws attention to these limitations in her attempt to exceed the law of the father and the rebellion of the son. 'The carnival's got to stop, some time', Dora admonishes Peregrine (p. 222). Claiming affinity with yet another literary predecessor, a female one this time, Dora passes over the war in her memoir: 'Let other pens dwell on guilt and misery. A., for Austen, Jane. *Mansfield Park*. I do not wish to talk about the war. Suffice [it] to say it was no carnival, not the hostilities. No carnival' (p. 163). In her use of Bakhtin, as well as Joyce, Carter has found a mode of celebrating difference, releasing its subversive potential. In one sense she has gone further than Kristeva, who associates carnival with a subversive under-current within the patriarchal tradition. [...] But there is still a limit. Dora leaves her father's house standing, her story pauses before the possibility of a transgression from which there could be no recovery:

> But truthfully, these glorious pauses do, sometimes, occur in the discordant but complementary narratives of our lives and if you choose to stop the story there, at such a pause, and refuse to take it any further, then you can call it a happy ending. (p. 227)[39] □

Meaney's conclusion has, however, been criticised by Clare Hanson in her essay '"The Red Dawn Breaking Over Clapham": Carter and the Limits of Artifice', in which Hanson argues that 'a tension [...] runs throughout Carter's work [...] between a radical will and sceptical pessimism' which is often ignored by 'the celebratory tendency in Carter criticism, a tendency that tends to obscure the depth and complexity of her later work'.[40] The quotation in Hanson's title is taken from a letter Carter wrote to Lorna Sage in 1977, in which she said that 'the notion that one day the red dawn will indeed break over Clapham, is the one thing that keeps me going'.[41] Hanson takes this as

■ an extremely revealing remark [...]. On the one hand is a socialist commitment to and belief in the possibility of a revolution which will overturn restrictive and repressive social practices; on the other is an underling sense of pessimism, even despair ('the *one* thing that *keeps me going*') which puts pressure on any firm faith in the possibility of social change.[42] □

Hanson goes on to cite Elaine Jordan's and Merja Makinen's analyses of *Nights at the Circus* as examples of the way in which the later novels are characteristically read as signifying a new and refreshing note of optimism on Carter's part. According to Hanson, such interpretations draw on

■ the strand in contemporary feminist thought that sees poststructuralism, and deconstruction in particular, as helpful and liberating for feminism. [...] Deconstruction is linked with that questioning of the 'grand narratives' of Western thought that Jean-François Lyotard identifies as *the* characteristic of the postmodern condition; it thus shades into the unmasking or 'delegitimation' of the dominant narratives of patriarchy and imperialism.[43] To deconstruct is to oppose or contest these narratives, and Carter's later work is often thought of as 'deconstructive' in this sense.[44] ☐

As far as Hanson is concerned, however, Carter's later work is more nihilistic than most critics have realised, and she discerns limits to the kind of celebratory readings which regard Carter as breaking down the structures of power and patriarchy in order to establish a new liberatory order. *Nights at the Circus*, she concludes, 'is ambivalent about the possibility of social change [and] *Wise Children* shares this ambivalence' through its focus 'on an indictment of (or melancholy acceptance of?) the binary oppositions that structure social existence'.[45] This is a very different view to that voiced by Kate Webb, who regards the dualism that pervades the text as posing an implicit challenge to order and legitimacy. For Hanson, the primary dualism in the text is the opposition of comedy and tragedy; a distinction which she links to gender difference. 'In *Wise Children* comedy, the improper and the feminine are [...] linked to resistance, to the spirit of "making do" and "making the best of it". Tragedy, on the other hand, is linked with automatic (unthinking) authority, with legitimacy and, of course, with masculinity.'[46] This point of view differs very little from the arguments presented by critics such as Webb and Meaney – however, it is at this point that Hanson singles out Gerardine Meaney as an example of a critic who, in her desire to pursue a celebratory reading of the novel, has taken the association a little too far:

■ Following up these overlapping associations, it is possible to read *Wise Children* as interweaving two opposing strands: on the one hand, comedy, illegitimacy, the feminine and the carnivalesque; on the other, tragedy, legitimacy, the masculine and a history punctuated by war. Given the existence of these oppositions, it would obviously be possible to argue that the novel accomplishes a feminist, carnivalesque subversion of the symbolic order of patriarchy. This is to some extent the reading Gerardine Meaney offers in her interesting discussion of the novel. She reads *Wise Children* through the theory of Julia Kristeva, arguing that the novel represents a 'comic approach to the thetic boundary' – in other words, that it moves towards the boundary or threshold between semiotic and symbolic modes. She also argues that the novel draws on and deploys Bakhtinian notions of the carnival in which conventional rules of behaviour are suspended, hierarchies are overturned and opposites mingle. Through her use of Bakhtin, she suggests, Carter has found 'a mode of celebrating difference, releasing its subversive potential'.[47] I would argue, however, that Meaney's own desire to celebrate subversive potential leads her to misunderstand Carter's view of the ultimate purpose and efficacy of carnival, and to misread what is ultimately an elegiac text. Although *Wise Children* offers moods of celebration and reconciliation which are not only stated, as it were, but enacted through the generous rhythms of the prose, the novel is also marked by constant reminders of war and death – the facts we cannot laugh away. Any mood of celebration is further undercut by Dora's sharp reminder that tragedy always upstages comedy:

> Of course, we didn't know, then, how the Hazards would always upstage us. Tragedy, eternally more class than comedy. How could mere song-and-dance girls aspire so high? We were destined, from birth, to be the lovely ephemera of the theatre, we'd rise and shine like birthday candles, then blow out. (p. 58)[48]

Dora also points out that 'there are limits to the power of laughter', thus offering an implicit critique of the optimistic ending of *Nights at the Circus*. *Wise Children* emphasizes instead the implacability and inescapability of the operation of power. This is most vividly illustrated in this novel by the difference in the ultimate fates of Melchior Hazard and Grandma Chance. Grandma Chance, point of origin for an 'alternative' female genealogy in the text, the one who attempts to 'write' a different history, is presented in the end as attaining the status only of a *comic* version of Lear. A naturist, she continues in later life to do the housework naked, and is laughed at by her daughters. After she dies, Dora makes the connection with Lear, telling us that 'when we remembered how we'd mocked her nakedness in her old age we were ashamed' (p. 164). Grandma Chance has not a chance of making the real narrative, the 'tragic' narrative, and is accordingly and appropriately taken out by a flying bomb in the Second World War. Melchior, on the other hand, representative of patriarchal genealogy and the law, is connected with the sublime Lear, a role he plays to acclaim both in 'real' life and on the stage. Knighted and honoured, he never loses either status or patriarchal power, but survives to his 100th birthday, on which occasion he looks 'regal, but festive', with rings on his fingers 'like a king, or pope' (p. 198). To associate femininity with comedy is thus, ultimately, to stress its powerlessness. In a sense, the true tragedy in *Wise Children* is that of Grandma Chance, and perhaps that of Carter, too – what could be called the radical tragedy of a disappointed will-to-change. Official 'tragedy' in this novel simply represents the dominant cultural (patriarchal) narrative.

Through the figures of Melchior and Grandma Chance, Carter stresses, retrospectively, the power of power and the vulnerability of those who attempt to subvert or circumvent it. In this respect, *Wise Children* continues and intensifies the Foucauldian strain which, I would argue, runs right through Carter's work. For if *Nights at the Circus* is concerned with ways of contesting the symbolic order, then *Wise Children* emphasizes much more strongly the persistence and pervasiveness of power itself. It is a novel in which the principles of legitimacy and legitimation may be questioned, but in which the structures of both remain intact. It is also a novel in which the power of art itself is called into question. In 'Notes from the Front Line', Carter writes that language is 'power, life and the instrument of culture, the instrument of domination and liberation'.[49] The implication is that, by intervening in the symbolic order, art can help to redefine that order. In *Wise Children*, published eight years later, there is a more pessimistic view of the role and utility of art. In this novel, we see Shakespeare being used as a commodity to shore up an economy and culture that are in decline. The implication is surely not that this is a misuse of Shakespeare, but that there was always, as Carter might have put it, something pretty dodgy about Shakespeare, hence his enduring popularity.[50] The artists from 'the other side of the tracks' in this novel are doomed to be no more than 'lovely ephemera' who will leave no enduring mark on culture: even Dora Chance is characterized at the end of the novel as little more than a pub bore.

In this novel, Carter thus comes rudely up against the limits of artifice, specifically *her* artifice. The melancholy subtext of the novel is that it will take more than artifice, and art, to bring the red dawn to Clapham. In making this point, I'm not in any way questioning Carter's committed socialism, but I am suggesting that her radical will was, increasingly, counterbalanced by a rueful scepticism both about the possibility of social change and about the effectiveness of art in bringing about that change. To present Carter's fiction as unproblematically 'deconstructive' is thus, I'd argue, both to underestimate and to underread her. One of the most important things that Carter's speculative fiction does is to document and exemplify the tension between a radical will and a sceptical Nietzchean pessimism that is such a central feature of the postmodern condition.[51] So it is entirely fitting that Carter's last novel, ending with the words 'What a joy it is to dance and sing', should be one in which the limitations of (its own) carnivalesque art have been so thoroughly canvassed.[52] □

Hanson's article is theoretical in focus, drawing on the work of Judith Butler and Michel Foucault in order to make its point that Carter's later fiction is more sceptical and fatalistic than it tends to be given credit for. However, although Hanson lays an unusual amount of stress on Carter's spirit of fatalism, she is not, as the views discussed in this chapter have demonstrated, alone in her belief that the text turns away from an unequivocal endorsement of the spirit of carnival. Some critics, though, have endowed this view with a biographical significance, regarding it as an uncannily apt conclusion to a book written by an author who was to die of cancer only a few months later. It is worth stressing, however, that these are strictly retrospective readings, for according to Lorna Sage, Carter's cancer was not diagnosed until the spring of 1991, too late to have influenced the formation of *Wise Children* in any significant way.[53] In '*Wise Children*: Angela Carter's Swan Song', however, Beth A. Boehm writes of the novel's fatalistic fascination with mortality, and the strategies it adopts to defer the inevitable end for as long as possible, in terms which recast the novel as Carter's own *memento mori*.

According to Boehm, feminist issues which have dominated Carter's previous work, such as the exposure of 'the male bias behind literary and cultural constructs, in particular the construction and representation of "femininity"', are 'clearly and self-consciously relegated to the back burner' in *Wise Children*. Instead, 'Carter turns her attention to such grand Shakespearean themes as the power of love and illusion and the mystery of origins and ends.'[54] As far as Boehm is concerned, it is Shakespeare's comedies which have particular resonance for this text, which for her functions as a more benign form of the Bakhtinian carnival spirit:

■ As Shakespeare illustrated in comedies like *Twelfth Night* and *A Midsummer Night's Dream* (plays richly alluded to and parodied in *Wise Children*), the special dispensation of comedy is that it allows us to escape from time and death by creating a space for the magic of carnival, a magic that protects us from the demons outside the world of comedy. Puck's speech near the end of *A Midsummer Night's Dream* calls forth images of illness and death, only to reassure us that his fairy play (like the play within the play – a tragedy transformed into farce by Bottom and the rude mechanicals) has kept these night fears at bay.

In *Wise Children* Carter self-consciously goes about the business of creating a singularly safe comic space. Quoting another comic genius, Dora writes '"Let other pens dwell on guilt and misery." A., for Austen, Jane. *Mansfield Park*. I do not wish to talk about the war. Suffice it to say it was no carnival, not the hostilities. No carnival' (p.163).[55] Similarly, when Dora very reluctantly agrees to perform the '"substitute bride" bit, as in *Measure for Measure* and *All's Well That Ends Well*', when she agrees, in other words, to act as Nora and marry Ghengis Khan, the sleazy Hollywood producer of the film version of *A Midsummer Night's Dream*, she refuses to act tragically: 'Sad. Nothing more than sad. Let's not call it a tragedy; a broken heart is never a tragedy. Only untimely death is a tragedy. And war, which, before we knew it, would be upon us; replace the comic mask with the one whose mouth turns down and close the theatre, because I refuse point-

blank to play in tragedy' (pp. 153–54). But refusing to play in tragedy
is distinct from refusing to acknowledge the tragic. Dora's uncle
Peregrine, a master illusionist, is all for fun and games; his biography
is 'a Chinese banquet of options' (p. 31), implausible and impossible
to substantiate. Dora, however, knows that demons exist outside the
comic world: '"The carnival's got to stop, some time, Perry", I said.
"You listen to the news, that'll take the smile off your face"' (p. 222).
'"And wars are facts we cannot fuck away, Perry; nor laugh away,
either"' (p. 221). Dora understands what Peregrine does not: comedy,
like the storyteller, gets its authority from death. The comic world is
powerful precisely because it is juxtaposed to the mortal world; the
safe place of comedy is made necessary by the dangers that lurk outside. As Feste, the wise clown in *Twelfth Night*, tells the revellers, the
time of holiday is by its very nature not eternal: 'Present mirth hath
present laughter;/ What's to come is still unsure./ ... Youth's a stuff
will not endure' (2:3.48–9, 52).[56] ☐

Boehm regards the ending of the novel as embracing a comedic world-
view, thus showing that 'Carter has successfully made Shakespearean
comic form her own and has found a way to cheat, for the time being,
the inevitability of the final curtain'.[57] Such a celebration, however, is
not unqualified, since it is predicated on the certainty of death – 'Nora
and Dora, by the special dispensation of comedy, are able to escape from
death and time, but the power of this joyful ending, unfortunately, lies in
part in its recognition that someday the singing will end, in its recognition that death is the end of all stories.'[58]

   In Carter's case, however, death did not quite mark the end of her story-
telling, as another collection of short stories, *American Ghosts and Old World
Wonders*, was published posthumously in 1993. To date, this collection has
received scant critical attention, although, as in the case of *Black Venus*,
the monographs on Carter's work mention individual stories in passing.
Linden Peach aligns her rewriting of a Jacobean tragedy as a screen-play
for a Western, 'John Ford's *'Tis Pity She's a Whore'*, with *The Passion of New
Eve*, in an analysis which reveals many similarities between them:

■ America in 'John Ford's *'Tis Pity She's a Whore'* is riddled, like America
in *The Passion of New Eve*, with confusion, pretence and illusion: in *The
Passion of New Eve*, Tristessa is a woman in a man's body masquerading
as Woman and Evelyn becomes a man in a woman's body: in 'John
Ford's *'Tis Pity She's a Whore'*, Annie-Belle 'cross-dresses' as her brother's
wife, the community believe her to be pregnant by the Minister's son
and Johnny is mistakenly regarded as a shamed member of her family.
At the centre of both texts, there is a void, metaphorically and literally
and a concern with oppression and a claustrophobic masculinity.[59] ☐

Both Aidan Day and myself, however, draw connections between *American Ghosts and Old World Wonders* and *Wise Children*. As discussed in Chapter Seven of this Guide, Day, rather like Clare Hanson, is sceptical of how far the carnivalesque can be employed in readings of Carter's work. Here, he draws on Carter's last interview with Lorna Sage, as well as the story 'In Pantoland', in order to make an important point:

■ [T]he carnivalesque is no solution to anything, as Carter pointed out in discussion with Lorna Sage, when she also observed that Bakhtin on carnival was someone she had read very late and only then because so many readers had declared that her work was carnivalesque in Bakhtin's definition of the term. But while she quite liked Bakhtin, she could not take him as an authority:

> she is characteristically sceptical about the vogue for the carnival-
> esque: 'It's interesting that Bakhtin became very fashionable in the
> 1980s, during the demise of the particular kind of theory that
> would have put all kinds of question marks around the whole idea
> of the carnivalesque. I'm thinking of Marcuse and repressive
> desublimation, which tells you exactly what carnivals are for. The
> carnival has to stop. The whole point about the feast of fools is that
> things went on as they did before, after it stopped.'[60]

Carter makes the same point at the end of a piece, 'In Pantoland', included in her posthumous, 1993 collection of short stories, *American Ghosts and Old World Wonders*:

> As Umberto Eco once said, 'An everlasting carnival does not work.'
> You can't keep it up, you know; nobody ever could. The essence of
> the carnival, the festival, the Feast of Fools, is transience. It is here
> today and gone tomorrow, a release of tension not a reconstitution
> of order, a refreshment ... after which everything can go on again
> exactly as if nothing had happened.
>   Things don't change because a girl puts on trousers or a chap
> slips on a frock, you know. Masters were masters again the day
> after Saturnalia ended; after the holiday from gender, it was back to
> the old grind.[61]

Carnival is no reconstitution of order.[62] □

In *Angela Carter: Writing From the Front Line*, I similarly argue that 'In Pantoland'

■ carries with it distinct echoes of *Wise Children* in its exploration and exposure of theatricality. Carter defines Pantoland as a place of 'illusion and transformation' (p. 99)[63] where 'everything is excessive and gender is variable' (p. 100). If the real does intrude – in the form, say, of real dogs or horses – it is rendered so insignificant by the garish exaggeration of its fictional surroundings, that:

> 'large as life' isn't the right phrase at all, at all. 'Large as life' they might be, in the context of the auditorium, but when the proscenium arch gapes as wide as the mouth of the ogre in *Jack and the Beanstalk*, those forty white horses pulling the glass coach of the princess look as little and inconsequential as white mice. (p. 99)

The scenery may be two-dimensional and distinctly shaky, but this is carnival, which hinges on the reversal and inversion of accepted hierarchies, including that which privileges the authentic over the fake.

However, in spite of the freewheeling anarchy inherent in pantomime, the piece nevertheless ends with acquiescence to the real. It may be with a certain reluctance, but it has to be done, no question, for

> As Umberto Eco once said, 'An everlasting carnival does not work.' You can't keep it up, you know; nobody ever could. The essence of the carnival, the festival, the Feast of Fools, is transience. It is here today and gone tomorrow, a release of tension not a reconstitution of order, a refreshment ... after which everything can go on again exactly as if nothing had happened. (p. 109)

There are, in other words, no new stories and no fresh starts to be had – we're stuck with what we've got.[64] ☐

Sadly, as far as Carter's critics and readers are concerned, there are indeed no new stories now to be had. However, Carter always argued that narrative was an inescapable element of human existence; an activity which should be carried on till the very end:

■ A good writer can make you believe time stands still.

Yet the end of all stories, even if the writer forebears to mention it, is death, which is where our time stops short. Sheherezade knew this, which is why she kept on spinning another story out of the bowels of the last one, never coming to a point where she could say: 'This is the end'. Because it would have been. We travel along the thread of narrative like high-wire artistes. That is our life.[65] ☐

NOTES

INTRODUCTION

1 Quoted in Peter Kemp, 'Magical History Tour', *The Sunday Times*, 9 June 1991, pp. 6–7.

2 Paul Barker, 'The Return of the Magic Story-Teller', *The Independent on Sunday*, 8 January 1995, pp. 14, 16 (p. 14).

3 Quoted in John Haffenden, 'Magical Mannerist', *The Literary Review*, November 1984, pp. 34–8 (p. 36).

4 Quoted in Lorna Sage, 'The Savage Sideshow', *New Review*, 4:39/40, July 1977, pp. 51–7 (p. 51).

5 Haffenden (1984), p. 36.

6 Angela Carter, 'Notes from the Front Line' (1983), in Angela Carter, *Shaking a Leg: Collected Journalism and Writings*, London: Chatto & Windus, 1997, p. 37.

7 Ibid., p. 37.

8 Haffenden (1984), p. 38.

9 Nicci Gerrard, 'Angela Carter is Now More Popular than Virginia Woolf', *Observer Life*, 9 July 1995, pp. 20, 22–3 (p. 22).

10 Quoted in Mary Harron, '"I'm a Socialist, Damn It! How Can You Expect Me to be Interested in Fairies?"', *The Guardian*, 25 September 1984, p. 10.

11 Carter (1997), p. 38.

12 Quoted in Harron (1984), p. 10.

13 Carter (1997), p. 38.

14 Quoted in Kemp (1991). Page number unavailable.

15 Sage (1977), p. 55.

16 Elaine Jordan, 'Afterword' to Joseph Bristow and Trev Lynn Broughton, eds, *The Infernal Desires of Angela Carter: Fiction, Femininity, Feminism*, London: Longman, 1997, p. 216.

17 Quoted in Helen Cagney Watts, 'An Interview with Angela Carter', *Bête Noire*, 8, August 1985, pp. 161–76 (p. 163).

CHAPTER ONE

1 [*O'Day's note*] See, for instance, 'Angela Carter', in John Haffenden, *Novelists in Interview*, London: Methuen, 1985, p. 76.

2 [*O'Day's note*] The most notable example is John Bayley, 'Fighting for the Crown', *The New York Review of Books*, 23 April 1992, pp. 9–11.

3 [*O'Day's note*] See Haffenden [1985], p. 80; Helen Cagney Watts, 'An Interview with

Angela Carter', *Bête Noire*, 8, August 1985, p. 165; and Angela Carter, 'Truly, It Felt Like Year One', in Sara Maitland, ed., *Very Heaven: Looking Back at the 1960s*, London: Virago, 1988. What isn't clear from published statements is whether Carter consciously intended to work over the same local territory three times. She once referred to *The Passion of New Eve* as the second in a 'project of three speculative novels', which suggests that she did sometimes conceive of things in threes: see Lorna Sage, 'The Savage Sideshow: A Profile of Angela Carter', *New Review*, 4, 39/40 (1977), p. 56. And it can scarcely be accidental that the Trilogy comprises her first, third and fifth published novels, interspersed with the earliest of the speculative fictions, *The Magic Toyshop* (1967) and *Heroes and Villains* (1969). *Toyshop*, strictly, is the crossover text: its initial 1950s setting allies it with the realism of the Bristol Trilogy, but the period details and the laws of nature obtaining in its fictional world become far less certain once the action moves into the toyshop, marking the advent of the speculative tendency in Carter's fiction. The novel's 'magical realist' potential is fully exploited in the 1986 film version.

4 Roland Barthes, 'The Reality Effect' (1968), repr. in Roland Barthes, *The Rustle of Language*, trans. Richard Howard, Oxford: Blackwell, 1986, p. 141.

5 Margaret McDowell, in James Vinson, ed., *Contemporary Novelists*, London: Macmillan, 1982, p. 129.

6 John Haffenden, *Novelists in Interview*, London: Methuen, 1985, p. 80.

7 Helen Cagney Watts, 'An Interview with Angela Carter', *Bête Noire*, 8, August 1985, p. 165.

8 Lorna Sage, 'The Savage Sideshow: A Profile of Angela Carter', *New Review*, 4:39/40, 1977, pp. 51–7 (p. 55).

9 Angela Carter, *Honeybuzzard*, London: Pan, 1968. All page numbers in O'Day's discussion refer to this edition – he was writing before the re-release of the novel by Virago Press in 1994 under its original title of *Shadow Dance*.

10 [*O'Day's note*] Carter, quoted in Watts [1985], p. 165. She refers to her early sixties self as 'a wide-eyed provincial beatnik' in Sage [1977], p. 54. For slightly contradictory statements on the drafting and typing up of *Shadow Dance*, see Watts [1985], p. 166; and Ian McEwan, 'Sweet Smell of Excess', *The*

Sunday Times Magazine, 9 September 1984, p. 43.

11 Angela Carter, *Nothing Sacred: Selected Writings,* London: Virago Press, 1982, p. 84.

12 [*O'Day's note*] On the revision of *Love,* see Carter, 'Living in London – X', *London Magazine,* 10 (March 1971), p. 55.

13 Sage (1977), p. 54.

14 Marc O'Day, 'Mutability is Having a Field Day: The Sixties Aura of Angela Carter's Bristol Trilogy', in Lorna Sage, ed., *Flesh and the Mirror: Essays on the Art of Angela Carter,* London: Virago Press, 1994, pp. 24–8.

15 Ibid., p. 57.

16 Lorna Sage, *Angela Carter,* Plymouth: Northcote House, 1994, p. 22.

17 Angela Carter, *Honeybuzzard,* London: Pan Books, 1968. All page numbers in Sage's discussion refer to this edition.

18 The Marquis de Sade (1740–1814) spent over 27 years in prison and lunatic asylums because of his sexually perverse lifestyle. He was the author of several pornographic novels which were considered too obscene to be published in his lifetime. His writing greatly influenced Carter, who published a critique of two of his novels, *Justine* (1791) and *Juliette* (1798), in *The Sadeian Woman* (1979). Sage's usage of the term 'radical pornographer' is a reference to this work. For more on Carter's views on de Sade, see Chapter Six of this Guide.

19 Susan Sontag, 'Notes on Camp' (1964), in Susan Sontag, *A Susan Sontag Reader,* New York: Vintage Books, 1983, pp. 105–19 (pp. 116–7).

20 Angela Carter, 'Notes from the Front Line' (1983), in Angela Carter, *Shaking a Leg: Collected Journalism and Writings,* London: Chatto & Windus, 1997, p. 40.

21 Sage (1994), pp. 11–12.

22 Angela Carter, *Love,* London: Rupert Hart-Davis, 1971. Unless otherwise indicated, all page numbers in Sage's discussion refer to this edition, although she also quotes from the revised edition of 1987.

23 Sage (1994), pp. 20–1.

24 Sarah Gamble, *Angela Carter: Writing From the Front Line,* Edinburgh: Edinburgh University Press, 1997, p. 39.

25 Andrew Ross, *No Respect: Intellectuals and Popular Culture,* London: Routledge, 1989, p. 149.

26 Gamble (1997), p. 41.

27 Ibid., p. 51.

28 Ross (1989), p. 151.

29 Angela Carter, *Love,* London: Picador, 1988 (revised edition). All page numbers in Gamble's discussion refer to this edition.

30 Carter (1988), p. 215.

31 Gamble (1997), pp. 52–3.

32 Leslie A. Fiedler, *Love and Death in the American Novel,* London: Granada-Paladin, 1970, p. 126.

33 Marina Warner, 'Angela Carter: Bottle Blonde, Double Drag', in Sage, ed. (1994), pp. 244–5.

34 Elizabeth MacAndrew, *The Gothic Tradition in Fiction,* New York: Columbia University Press, 1979, p. 8.

35 Steven Connor, *The English Novel in History 1950–1995,* London and New York: Routledge, 1996, p. 136.

36 Linden Peach, *Angela Carter,* Basingstoke: Macmillan, 1998, pp. 27–9.

37 Angela Carter, *Love,* London: Picador, 1988. All page numbers in Peach's discussion refer to this edition.

38 Peach (1998), pp. 68–70.

39 James Wood, 'Bewitchment', *London Review of Books,* 16, 8 December 1994, pp. 20–1 (p. 20).

40 Susannah Clapp, 'On Madness, Men and Fairy-Tales', *The Independent on Sunday,* 9 June 1991, pp. 26–7 (p. 26).

41 Sage (1994), p. 12.

42 Olga Kenyon, *The Writer's Imagination,* Bradford: University of Bradford Print Unit, 1992, p. 25.

43 Mary Russo, *The Female Grotesque: Risk, Excess and Modernity,* London: Routledge, 1995, p. 6.

44 Gamble (1997), pp. 54–5.

45 Peach (1998), pp. 49–50.

46 Richard Boston, 'Logic in a Schizophrenic's World', *The New York Times Book Review,* 2 March 1969, p. 42.

47 This reference is to a passage from the work of the eighteenth-century Scottish philosopher David Hume (1711–76), from which Carter drew the title of her novel, and which she includes as its opening epigraph: *'The mind is a kind of theatre, where several perceptions successively make their appearance, pass, re-pass, glide away and mingle in an infinite variety of postures and situations'* (Carter's italics). Hume was a controversial philosopher whose best-known work was the three-volume *A Treatise of Human Nature* (1739–40). A religious sceptic, he argued that human beings were not distinct, autonomous individuals, but collections of shifting 'perceptions'.

48 Peach (1998), pp. 58–9.
49 Angela Carter, *Several Perceptions*, London: Virago Press, 1995. All page numbers in Day's discussion refer to this edition.
50 Aidan Day, *Angela Carter: The Rational Glass*, Manchester: Manchester University Press, 1998, pp. 38–9.
51 Angela Carter, *Love*, London: Chatto & Windus, 1987 (revised edition). Unless otherwise indicated, all page numbers in Sage's discussion refer to this edition.
52 Angela Carter, *Love*, London: Hart-Davis, 1971.
53 Lorna Sage, *Women in the House of Fiction: Post-War Women Novelists*, Basingstoke: Macmillan, 1992, pp. 170, 171, 172–3.
54 Carter (1988), p. 213.
55 Janet Todd, *Sensibility: An Introduction*, London: Methuen, 1986, p. 4.
56 Patricia Juliana Smith, 'All You Need is Love: Angela Carter's Novel of Sixties Sex and Sensibility', *The Review of Contemporary Fiction*, 14:3, Fall 1994, pp. 24–9 (pp. 24–5).
57 Ibid., p. 25.
58 Smith (1994), p 26.
59 Angela Carter, *Love*, New York: Penguin, 1988 (revised edition). All page numbers in Smith's discussion refer to this edition.
60 Smith (1994), p. 28.
61 O'Day, in Sage, ed. (1994), p. 55.
62 Smith (1994), p. 25.
63 O'Day, in Sage, ed. (1994), p. 52.

CHAPTER TWO

1 Catherine Stott, 'Runaway to the Land of Promise', *The Guardian*, 10 August 1972, p. 10.
2 Olga Kenyon, *The Writer's Imagination*, Bradford: University of Bradford Print Unit, 1992.
3 Roland Barthes, *Image, Music, Text*, New York: Hill & Wang, 1977, p. 146.
4 Angela Carter, 'Notes from the Front Line', in Michelene Wandor, ed., *On Gender and Writing*, London: Pandora Press, 1983, p. 71.
5 Angela Carter, *The Magic Toyshop*, London: Virago Press, 1981. All page numbers in Palmer's discussion refer to this edition.
6 E. T. A. Hoffmann, *Tales of Hoffmann*, trans. R. J. Hollingdale, Harmondsworth: Penguin Books, 1982, pp. 85–125.
7 Sigmund Freud, 'The Uncanny', in *The Standard Edition of the Complete Psychological Works of Sigmund Freud*, trans. James Strachey, London: Hogarth, 1953–73, Vol. XVII.

8 See John Haffenden, 'Magical Mannerist', *The Literary Review*, November 1984, pp. 34–8.
9 [*Palmer's note*] See Hélène Cixous, 'The Character of Character', trans. Keith Cohen, *New Literary History* 5, 1974, 383–402. Other relevant discussions include Catherine Belsey, *Critical Practice*, London: Methuen, 1980, pp. 56–85; and Julia Kristeva, *Desire in Language: A Semiotic Approach to Literature and Art*, trans. Thomas Gora et al., Oxford: Blackwell, 1981, pp. 125–209.
10 [*Palmer's note*] See E. Ann Kaplan, 'Is the Gaze Male?', in Ann Snitow et al., eds, *Desire: The Politics of Sexuality*, London: Virago, 1984, pp. 321–38.
11 Paulina Palmer, 'From "Coded Mannequin" to Bird Woman: Angela Carter's Magic Flight', in Sue Roe, ed., *Women Reading Women's Writing*, Brighton: Harvester Press, 1987, pp. 179–205 (pp. 183–6).
12 Angela Carter, *The Magic Toyshop*, London: Virago Press, 1982. All page numbers in Mills et al.'s discussion refer to this edition.
13 Sara Mills, Lynne Pearce, Sue Spaull and Elaine Millard, *Feminist Readings/Feminists Reading*, Hemel Hempstead: Harvester Wheatsheaf, 1989, pp. 135–6.
14 Ibid., p. 136.
15 Ibid., p. 138.
16 Susan Gubar, '"The Blank Page" and the Issues of Female Creativity', *Critical Inquiry*, 8, Winter 1981.
17 Mills et al. (1989), p. 139.
18 Angela Carter, *The Magic Toyshop*, London: Virago Press, 1981. All page numbers in Sage's discussion refer to this edition.
19 Lorna Sage, *Angela Carter*, Plymouth: Northcote House, 1994, pp. 15–16.
20 Helene Deutsch, *Psychology of Women*, Vol. 1, New York: Grune & Stratton, 1944, pp. 251–2; Eleanor Maccoby and Carol Jacklin, *The Psychology of Sex Differences*, Stanford, CA: Stanford University Press, 1974, p. 329; quoted in Nancy Chodorow, *The Reproduction of Mothering: Psychoanalysis and the Sociology of Gender*, Berkeley, CA: University of California Press, 1978, p. 139.
21 Jessica Benjamin, 'Master and Slave: The Fantasy of Erotic Domination', in Ann Snitow, Christine Stansell and Sharon Thompson, eds, *Powers of Desire: The Politics of Sexuality*, New York: Monthly Review Press, 1983, p. 86.
22 Simone de Beauvoir, *The Second Sex*, trans. H. M. Parshley, New York, 1989, p. 287. Name of publisher unavailable.

23 [*Wyatt's note*] As [Luce] Irigaray says, 'In the last analysis, the female Oedipus complex is woman's entry into a system of values that is not hers, and in which she can "appear" and circulate only when enveloped in the needs/desires/fantasies of others, namely men' (*This Sex Which is Not One*, trans. Catherine Porter [Ithaca, NY, 1985], p.134).

24 [*Wyatt's note*] Bram Dijkstra, *Idols of Perversity: Fantasies of Feminine Evil in Fin-de-Siècle Culture* [Oxford, 1986], documents the popularity of the dead beauty in nineteenth-century paintings; the dead woman represents 'the apotheosis of an ideal of feminine passivity and helplessness' (p.36). See also Elizabeth Bronfen, *Over Her Dead Body: Death, Femininity, and the Aesthetic* [New York, 1992], pp.59–64.

25 Amy Richlin, 'Reading Ovid's Rapes', in Amy Richlin, ed., *Pornography and Representation in Greece and Rome*, New York: Oxford University Press, 1992, p.158.

26 Jean Wyatt, 'The Violence of Gendering: Castration Images in Angela Carter's *The Magic Toyshop, The Passion of New Eve*, and "Peter and the Wolf"', in Alison Easton, ed., *Angela Carter*, Basingstoke: Macmillan, 2000, pp.58–83 (pp.67–8).

27 Angela Carter, *The Magic Toyshop*, London: Virago Press, 1981. All page numbers in Wyatt's discussion refer to this edition.

28 Kaja Silverman, *Male Subjectivity at the Margins*, New York: Routledge, 1992, p.135.

29 Lorna Sage, 'The Savage Sideshow', *New Review*, 4:39/40, 1977, pp.51–7 (p.56).

30 Gayle Rubin, 'The Traffic in Women: Notes on the "Political Economy" of Sex', in Rayna Reiter, ed., *Toward an Anthropology of Women*, New York: Monthly Review Press, 1975, pp.79–80.

31 Benjamin, in Snitow et al., eds (1983), p.288.

32 Ibid., p.283.

33 Silverman (1992), p.42.

34 Wyatt, in Easton, ed. (2000), pp.72–5.

35 Aidan Day, *Angela Carter: The Rational Glass*, Manchester: Manchester University Press, 1998, p.23.

36 Ibid., p.23.

37 Lorna Sage, 'Angela Carter', in Malcolm Bradbury and Judith Cooke, eds, *New Writing*, London: Minerva Press, 1992, pp.185–93 (p.190).

38 Angela Carter, *The Magic Toyshop*, London: Virago Press, 1990. All page numbers in Day's discussion refer to this edition.

39 Miriam Allott, ed., *The Poems of John Keats*, London: Longman, 1970, p.62.

40 Day (1998), pp.31–2.

41 Linden Peach, *Angela Carter*, Basingstoke: Macmillan, 1998, pp.73–4, 75.

42 John Haffenden, *Novelists in Interview*, London: Methuen, 1985, p.80.

43 Thomas Crow, *The Rise of the Sixties: American and European Art in the Era of Dissent*, London: George Weidenfield & Nicolson, 1996, p.47.

44 Peach (1998), pp.84–5.

45 Dora, whose real name was Ida Bauer, was sent to Freud by her father for treatment in 1900, suffering from hysterical symptoms. Her father was having an affair with the wife of a friend, Herr K., who had himself attempted to seduce Dora when she was only fourteen. Dora's belief was that her father wanted her treated in order to avoid her betraying his sexual indiscretions. However, Freud regarded her hysteria as arising from repressed sexual fantasies – in particular, an incestuous desire for her father. Dora never accepted Freud's interpretation of her situation, and eventually terminated her analysis. Freud published her case history in 'Fragment of an Analysis of a Case of Hysteria' (1905). Dora has become an iconographic figure in the writing of modern feminists, such as Clare Kahane, Hélène Cixous and Jane Gallop, for her refusal to allow her account of her condition to be revised through the 'authoritative' narrative of the male psychoanalyst.

46 Lucie Armitt, *Contemporary Women's Fiction and the Fantastic*, Basingstoke: Macmillan, 2000, p.200.

47 Angela Carter, *The Magic Toyshop*, London: Virago Press, 1981. All page numbers in Armitt's discussion refer to this edition.

48 Armitt (2000), pp.202–3.

49 Ibid., p.205.

50 Ibid., p.206.

51 Ibid., pp.210–11.

CHAPTER THREE

1 Lorna Sage, 'The Savage Sideshow', *New Review*, 4:39/40, 1977, pp.51–7 (p.52).

2 Les Bedford, 'Angela Carter: An Interview', Sheffield University Television, February 1977.

3 Ibid.

4 Roz Kaveney, 'New New World Dreams: Angela Carter and Science Fiction', in Lorna

Sage, ed., *Flesh and the Mirror: Essays on the Art of Angela Carter*, London: Virago Press, 1994, p. 176

5 Ibid., pp. 171–2

6 Ibid., p. 175.

7 Ibid., p. 171

8 David Punter, *The Literature of Terror: A History of Gothic Fictions from 1765 to the Present Day*, London: Longman, 1980, p. 374.

9 Angela Carter, *Heroes and Villains*, London, 1969. Name of publisher unavailable. All page numbers in Punter's discussion refer to this edition of the text.

10 [*Punter's note*] It is, in particular, one of the clichés which lie behind the 'sword-and-sorcery' fiction of Michael Moorcock and others. There is unfortunately no room here for discussion of this school of writing, but it is worth noting as another fruitful offshoot from the central stem of Gothic: Moorcock especially demonstrates a considerable power in the manipulation of mythic and quasi-mythic materials, which is in no way harmed by the simple nature of his dualistic universe.

11 Punter (1980), pp. 396–8.

12 Robert Clark, 'Angela Carter's Desire Machines', *Women's Studies*, 14, 1987, pp. 147–61 (pp. 153–4).

13 Ibid., p. 152.

14 [*Clark's note*] The novel begins with a brilliant exemplification of Freud's family romance. Melanie dresses up in the roles of famous women, then one night puts on her mother's wedding dress, accidentally locks herself out of the house, tears the dress to shreds and re-enters the house by climbing a tree naked. The next morning she wakes to hear that her parents have died and considers herself the symbolic cause, rightly so in that she has usurped her mother's past, torn her hymeneal garb and climbed the phallic tree of knowledge to enter her father's house.

15 Angela Carter, *Heroes and Villains*, Harmondsworth: Penguin, 1981. All page numbers in Clark's discussion refer to this edition.

16 Sage (1977), p. 56.

17 Clark (1987), pp. 150–2.

18 Angela Carter, *Heroes and Villains*, Harmondsworth: Penguin, 1981. All page numbers in Palmer's discussion refer to this edition of the text.

19 [*Palmer's note*] Beatrice Faust discusses the genre 'Sweet Savagery' in *Woman, Sex and Pornography*, Harmondsworth: Penguin, 1981, pp. 137–46.

20 Frankie Rickford, 'No More Sleeping Beauties and Frozen Boys', in Eileen Phillips, ed., *The Left and the Erotic*, London: Lawrence & Wishart, 1983, p. 142

21 [*Palmer's note*] Annette Kuhn, *Women's Pictures: Feminism and Cinema*, London: Routledge & Kegan Paul, 1982, p. 15. See also Michèle Barrett, 'Feminism and the Definition of Cultural Politics', in Rosalind Brunt and Caroline Rowan, eds, *Feminism, Culture and Politics*, London: Lawrence & Wishart, 1982, pp 37–58.

22 Palmer, in Roe, ed. (1987), pp. 187–9.

23 Elizabeth Mahoney, 'But Elsewhere?: The Future of Fantasy in *Heroes and Villains*', in Bristow and Broughton, eds (1997), p. 73.

24 Ibid., p. 3.

25 Ibid., pp. 84–5.

26 Palmer, in Roe, ed. (1987), p. 181.

27 Mahoney, in Bristow and Broughton, eds (1997), p. 76.

28 Ibid., p. 77.

29 [*Mahoney's note*] State decriminalisation of sexual violence against women is part of the bad place in much dystopian writing by women. See, for example, Katharine Burdekin, *Swastika Night* (1937); Suzy McKee Charnas, *Walk to the End of the World* (1974); Zoe Fairbairns, *Benefits* (1979); and Rebecca Brown, *The Terrible Girls* (1990).

30 Angela Carter, *Heroes and Villains*, Harmondsworth: Penguin, 1986. All page numbers in Mahoney's discussion refer to this edition of the text.

31 Mahoney, in Bristow and Broughton, eds (1997), pp. 81–3.

32 [*Mahoney's note*] Gerardine Meaney focuses upon the relations between gender, time, space and history in her reading of *Heroes and Villains*. Through a discussion of Kristeva's categories of time ('cyclical' and 'monumental'), she argues that in *Heroes and Villains* Carter 'attempted to "wind back" the clock of history, perhaps to uncover something undetermined'. In other words, if history is interrogated from a gender perspective (wound back on itself), oppressive myths of origin – here, psychoanalytic 'myths' of feminine sexuality – can be uncovered and subverted. Meaney, *(Un)Like Subjects* [London: Routledge, 1993], p. 217.

33 [*Mahoney's note*] 'Monstrous' is used here to signal an unruly, powerful and threatening presence contained in the representation of the feminine body. Mary Russo's article 'Female Grotesques: Carnival and Theory' re-reads Bakhtin's theory of the carnival to

argue that the woman's body which is coded as 'monstrous' has the potential power to disrupt not only limits of representation, but wider social formations. See Teresa de Lauretis, ed., *Feminist Studies/Critical Studies*, Basingstoke: Macmillan, 1986, pp. 213–29.

34 Mahoney, in Bristow and Broughton, eds (1997), pp. 83–4.

35 Julia Kristeva, 'Women's Time', in Toril Moi, ed., *The Kristeva Reader*, Oxford: Blackwell, 1986, p. 191.

36 Angela Carter, *Heroes and Villains*, Harmondsworth: Penguin, 1981. All page numbers in Meaney's discussion refer to this edition.

37 Simone de Beauvoir, *The Second Sex*, trans. H.M. Parshley, Harmondsworth: Penguin, 1972, p. 94.

38 Ibid., p. 63.

39 Kristeva, in Moi, ed. (1986), p. 191. *Jouissance* is a term used extensively by Kristeva, although its exact meaning is difficult to define. Roughly speaking, it indicates the existence of a female energy centred in the pleasure provided by the maternal body, which cannot be fully incorporated into the male-dominated symbolic order of language, law and sequential time.

40 Gerardine Meaney, *(Un)Like Subjects: Women, Theory, Fiction*, London: Routledge, 1993, pp. 89–91. This part of Meaney's argument has been reprinted under the title 'History and Women's Time: *Heroes and Villains*' in Alison Easton, ed., *Angela Carter*, Basingstoke: Macmillan, 2000.

41 Ibid., p. 95.

42 Ibid., p. 98.

43 Meaney's allusion here is to the French theorist Roland Barthes: in particular, his work *Mythologies* (1957), in which he argued that myth, in its evocation of eternal 'truths', works to eliminate historical particularities. Bourgeois culture thus depends on myth in order to make its world-view appear 'natural' and eternal, rather than contingent and, hence, subject to change.

44 Angela Carter, *The Sadeian Woman: An Exercise in Cultural History*, London: Virago Press, 1979, p. 148.

45 Ibid., p. 111.

46 Meaney (1993), pp. 99–100.

47 Kristeva (1986), p. 192.

48 Meaney (1993), p. 109.

49 Anna Katsavos, 'An Interview with Angela Carter', *The Review of Contemporary Fiction*, 14:3, Fall 1994, pp. 11–17 (pp. 12–13).

CHAPTER FOUR

1 Linden Peach, *Angela Carter*, Basingstoke: Macmillan, 1998, p. 20.

2 Ibid., p. 19.

3 Ibid., pp. 21–2.

4 Angela Carter, *Fireworks*, London: Virago Press, 1987 (revised edition).

5 Sarah Gamble, *Angela Carter: Writing From the Front Line*, Edinburgh: Edinburgh University Press, 1997, p. 104.

6 Roland Barthes, *Empire of Signs*, trans. Richard Howard, London: Jonathan Cape, 1983, p. 62.

7 Ibid., p. 9.

8 Ibid., p. 10.

9 Angela Carter, *Fireworks*, London: Virago Press, 1988. All page numbers in Sage's discussion refer to this edition.

10 Lorna Sage, *Angela Carter*, Plymouth: Northcote House, 1994, pp. 26–7.

11 Angela Carter 'Afterword to *Fireworks*', in Angela Carter, *Burning Your Boats: Collected Short Stories*, ed. Salman Rushdie, London: Chatto & Windus, 1995, p. 459. The 'Afterword' appeared only in the first edition of *Fireworks*.

12 Susan Rubin Suleiman, 'The Fate of the Surrealist Imagination in the Society of the Spectacle', in Sage, ed. (1994), p. 100.

13 Catherine Stott, 'Runaway to the Land of Promise', *The Guardian*, 10 August 1972, p. 10.

14 Alex Hamilton, 'Sade and Prejudice', *The Guardian*, 30 March 1979, p. 15.

15 Susannah Clapp, 'On Madness, Men and Fairy-Tales', *The Independent on Sunday*, 9 June 1991, pp. 26–7 (p. 26).

16 Lorna Sage, 'The Savage Sideshow', *New Review*, 4:39/40, 1977, pp. 51–7 (p. 53).

17 Elaine Jordan, 'Enthralment: Angela Carter's Speculative Fictions', in Linda Anderson, ed., *Plotting Change: Contemporary Women's Fiction*, London: Edward Arnold, 1990, p. 31.

18 Sage (1977), p. 52.

19 Sage (1994), p. 35.

20 Jordan, in Anderson, ed. (1990), p. 31.

21 Angela Carter, *The Infernal Desire Machines of Doctor Hoffman*, Harmondsworth: Penguin, 1982. All page numbers in Jordan's discussion refer to this edition.

22 Jordan, in Anderson, ed. (1990), p. 34.

23 Angela Carter, *Nothing Sacred: Selected Writings*, London: Virago Press, 1982, p. 84.

24 Patricia Waugh, *Metafiction: The Theory and*

Practice of Self-Conscious Fiction, London: Methuen, 1984, p.6.

25 Linda Hutcheon, *A Poetics of Postmodernism: History, Theory, Fiction*, London: Routledge, 1988, p.93.

26 The concept of the *flâneur* was developed by the cultural theorist Walter Benjamin in his book *Charles Baudelaire: A Lyric Poet in the Era of High Capitalism* (1973). The *flâneur* (a word taken from the French *flâner* – to saunter) is an urban figure, who, in order to preserve his individuality, withdraws from the crowd to assume the position of detached observer.

27 Walter Benjamin, *Charles Baudelaire: A Lyric Poet in the Era of High Capitalism*, trans. Harry Zohn, London: Verso, 1983, p.69.

28 Sage (1994), p.33.

29 Mario Vargas Llosa, 'Social Commitment and the Latin American Writer', in Doris Meyer, ed., *Lives on the Line: The Testimony of Contemporary Latin American Authors*, Berkeley: University of California Press, 1988, pp.128–38 (p.133).

30 Gamble (1997), p.109, pp.110–12.

31 Angela Carter, *The Infernal Desire Machines of Doctor Hoffman*, Harmondsworth: Penguin, 1982. All page numbers in Day's discussion refer to this edition.

32 Hans Bertens, *The Idea of the Postmodern: A History*, London: Routledge, 1995, p.11.

33 Aidan Day, *Angela Carter: The Rational Glass*, Manchester: Manchester University Press, 1998, pp.76–8.

34 Angela Carter, *The Infernal Desire Machines of Doctor Hoffman*, London, 1972. Name of publisher unavailable. All page numbers in Punter's discussion refer to this edition.

35 [*Punter's note*] See, e.g., Flann O'Brien, *The Third Policeman* (London, 1967).

36 [*Punter's note*] See Gilles Deleuze and Félix Guattari, *Anti-Oedipus: Capitalism and Schizophrenia*, trans. R. Hurley et al. (New York, 1977).

37 [*Punter's note*] I shall be returning at several points to this subtext: that there is a clear relation between the anxieties of the 1970s and the ambivalent heritage of the 1960s. See also my 'The Moral Majority', in *For Life on Earth: Writings against War*, ed., Maggie Gee (Norwich, 1982), pp.55–6.

38 [*Punter's note*] I am assuming that Desiderio's foreign name and location are displacements of a type familiar in Gothic and neo-Gothic fiction.

39 David Punter, *The Hidden Script: Writing and the Unconscious*, London: Routledge, 1985, pp.29–32.

40 Suleiman, in Sage, ed. (1994), p.107.

41 Ibid., p.108.

42 Ricarda Smith, 'The Journey of the Subject in Angela Carter's Fiction', *Textual Practice*, 3:1, 1990, note 5.

43 Herbert Marcuse, *Eros and Civilization*, with a new Preface by the Author, New York: Vintage, 1962, p.135.

44 Suleiman, in Sage, ed. (1994), pp.108–9.

45 Guy Debord, *La Société du spectacle*, Paris: Champ Libre, 1971, p.9. Quoted in Suleiman, in Sage, ed. (1994), p.110.

46 Suleiman, in Sage, ed. (1994), p.111.

47 Ibid., p.112.

48 Angela Carter, *The Infernal Desire Machines of Doctor Hoffman*, Harmondsworth: Penguin, 1982. All page numbers in Suleiman's discussion refer to this edition.

49 Suleiman, in Sage, ed. (1994), pp.113–6.

50 Angela Carter, 'Once More into the Mangle', in Angela Carter, *Shaking a Leg: Collected Journalism and Writings*, London: Chatto & Windus, 1997, p.247.

51 Ibid.

52 Angela Carter, *The Sadeian Woman: An Exercise in Cultural History*, London: Virago Press, 1979, p.15.

53 Sally Robinson, *Engendering the Subject: Gender and Self-Representation in Contemporary Women's Fiction*, Albany, NY: State University of New York Press, 1991, p.102.

54 Peach (1998), p.111.

55 [*Bonca's note*] George Bataille, *Eroticism*, trans. Mary Dalwood (San Francisco: City Lights, 1986), p.16; Camille Paglia, *Sexual Personae: Art and Decadence from Nefertiti to Emily Dickinson* (New York: Vintage, 1990), p.3.

56 Angela Carter, *The Infernal Desire Machines of Doctor Hoffman*, London: Rupert Hart-Davis, 1972. All page numbers in Bonca's discussion refer to this edition.

57 Carter (1979), p.19.

58 Cornel Bonca, 'In Despair of the Old Adams: Angela Carter's *The Infernal Desire Machines of Dr. [sic] Hoffman*', *The Review of Contemporary Fiction*, 14:3, Fall 1994, pp.56–62 (pp.59–61).

CHAPTER FIVE

1 Peter Ackroyd, 'Passion Fruit', *Spectator*, 26 March 1977, pp.23–4 (p.23).

2 Quoted in Olga Kenyon, *The Writer's*

Imagination, Bradford: University of Bradford Print Unit, 1992, p. 31.

3 Lorna Sage, *Angela Carter*, Plymouth: Northcote House, 1994, p. 36.

4 Quoted in Kenyon (1992), p. 31.

5 Ibid.

6 John Haffenden, 'Magical Mannerist', *The Literary Review*, November 1984, pp. 34–8 (p. 36).

7 Angela Carter, 'Notes from the Front Line', in Michelene Wandor, ed., *On Gender and Writing*, London: Pandora Press, 1983, p. 71.

8 Carter, in Wandor, ed. (1983), p. 70.

9 [*Jordan's note*] I'm indebted to conversation with Richard Crane about his play on Eisenstein, *Red Magic*, for this analogue (the play was presented at the Edinburgh Festival Fringe and at the South Bank Museum of the Moving Image in the Summer of 1988).

10 Elaine Jordan, 'The Dangers of Angela Carter', in Isobel Armstrong, ed., *New Feminist Discourses: Critical Essays on Theories and Texts*, London: Routledge, 1992, pp. 122–3.

11 David Punter, *The Hidden Script: Writing and the Unconscious*, London: Routledge, 1985, p. 36.

12 Ibid., p. 37.

13 Angela Carter, *The Passion of New Eve*, London: Virago Press, 1977. All page numbers in Punter's discussion refer to this edition.

14 Punter (1985), pp. 38–9.

15 Alison Lee, 'Angela Carter's New Eve(lyn): De/Engendering Narrative', in Kathy Mezei, ed., *Ambiguous Discourse: Feminist Narratology and British Women Writers*, Chapel Hill: University of North Carolina Press, 1996, pp. 238–49 (p. 238).

16 Shlomith Rimmon-Kenan, *Narrative Fiction: Contemporary Poetics*, London: Routledge, 1983, p. 95.

17 Angela Carter, *The Passion of New Eve*, London: Virago Press, 1982. All page numbers in Lee's discussion refer to this edition.

18 Lee, in Mezei, ed. (1996), pp. 244–5, 246.

19 Rachael Blau DuPlessis, *Writing Beyond the Ending: Narrative Strategies of Twentieth-Century Women Writers*, Bloomington: Indiana University Press, 1985, p. 34. Quoted in Lee, in Mezei, ed. (1996), p. 239.

20 Lee, in Mezei, ed. (1996), p. 239.

21 Judith Butler, *Gender Trouble: Feminism and the Subversion of Identity*, New York: Routledge, 1990, p. 33.

22 Ibid.

23 Ibid., p. 138.

24 Lee is referring here to Mieke Bal, *On Story-Telling: Essays in Narratology*, ed. David Jobling, Sonoma, CA: Polebridge, 1991.

25 Susan S. Lanser, 'Towards a Feminist Narratology', *Style*, 20:3, 1986, pp. 341–63 (p. 346).

26 Lee, in Mezei, ed. (1996), pp. 246–7, 248.

27 Sandy Stone, 'The Empire Strikes Back: A Posttransexual Manifesto', in Julia Epstein and Kristina Straub, eds, *Body Guards: The Cultural Politics of Gender Ambiguity*, London and NY: Routledge, 1991, p. 291.

28 [*Johnson's note*] See Kate Bornstein, *Gender Outlaw: On Men, Women, and the Rest of Us* (London: Routledge, 1994), and also Bernice L. Hausman, *Changing Sex: Transsexualism, Technology and the Idea of Gender* (Durham, NC: Duke University Press, 1995).

29 Heather L. Johnson, 'Unexpected Geometries: Transgressive Symbolism and the Transsexual Subject in Angela Carter's *The Passion of New Eve*', in Bristow and Broughton, eds (1997), pp. 166–83 (p. 167).

30 Angela Carter, *The Passion of New Eve*, London: Virago Press, 1982. All page numbers in Johnson's text refer to this edition.

31 [*Johnson's note*] Jane Gallop, *Thinking Through the Body* (NY: Columbia University Press, 1988), p. 20.

32 [*Johnson's note*] Renée Richards, *Second Serve*, quoted in Marjorie Garber, *Vested Interests: Cross-dressing and Cultural Anxiety* (London: Penguin, 1993), p. 105. Garber includes this as an example of the elusiveness of the subject position.

33 Robert J. Stoller, *Presentations of Gender*, London and New Haven, CT: Yale University Press, 1985, p. 149.

34 Johnson, in Bristow and Broughton, eds (1997), pp. 170–2, 173–4.

35 [*Armitt's note*] As argued by Jean Baudrillard, *America* (London: Verso, 1988), p. 125.

36 Angela Carter, *The Magic Toyshop* (1981), p. 1.

37 Iain Chambers, *Border Dialogues: Journeys into Postmodernism*, London: Routledge, 1990, p. 88.

38 Angela Carter, *The Passion of New Eve*, London: Virago Press, 1982 All page numbers in Armitt's discussion refer to this edition.

39 Lucie Armitt, *Theorising the Fantastic*, London: Edward Arnold, 1996, p. 164.

40 Jean Baudrillard, *America*, London: Verso, 1988, pp. 28–9, 96.

41 [*Armitt's note*] Carter's definition of surrealism is taken from John Haffenden, ed., *Novelists in Interview* (London: Methuen, 1985), p. 92. The definition of the hyperreal is Raman Selden and Peter Widdowson's. See *A Reader's Guide to Contemporary Literary Theory* (Hemel Hempstead: Harvester Wheatsheaf, 1993), p. 180.

42 Baudrillard (1998), pp. 9, 28, 32.

43 Armitt (1996), pp. 172–4.

44 Ibid., p. 174.

45 Ibid., p. 176.

46 Ibid.

47 Donna J. Haraway, 'The Promises of Monsters: A Regenerative Politics for Inappropriate/d Others', in Grossberg et al., eds, *Cultural Studies*, New York: Routledge, 1992, pp. 295–337 (p. 297).

48 Donna J. Haraway, 'A Cyborg Manifesto: Science, Technology, and Socialist-Feminism in the Late Twentieth Century', in *Simians, Cyborgs and Women: The Reinvention of Nature*, London: Free Association Books, 1991, pp. 149–81 (pp. 149–54 *passim*).

49 Hélène Cixous and Catherine Clément, *The Newly Born Woman*, trans. Betsy Wing, Manchester: Manchester University Press, 1987, pp. 63–4.

50 William Blake, 'Milton', in P. H. Butter, ed., *William Blake: Selected Poems*, London: J. M. Dent, 1982, pp. 143–63.

51 Butter, ed. (1982), p. 244n.

52 [*Armitt's note*] As stated in the Book of Genesis 2:24.

53 David Howarth, 'Reflections on the Politics of Space and Time', *Angelaki*, Vol. 1, 1993, pp. 43–56 (p. 47).

54 Jean Baudrillard, 'The Automation of the Robot', in Larry McCaffery, ed., *Storming the Reality Studio: A Casebook of Cyberpunk and Postmodern Science Fiction*, Durham: Duke University Press, 1991, pp. 178–81 (p. 180).

55 Carter (1979), p. 5.

56 Armitt (1996), pp. 176–9.

57 Angela Carter, *The Passion of New Eve*, London: Virago Press, 1982. All page numbers in Gamble's discussion refer to this edition.

58 Jean Baudrillard, *Simulations*, trans. Paul Foss, Paul Patton and Philip Beitchman, New York: Semiotext(e), 1983, p. 23.

59 Sarah Gamble, *Angela Carter: Writing From the Front Line*, Edinburgh: Edinburgh University Press, 1997, p. 129.

60 Jordan (1990), pp. 19–40 (p. 37).

61 Aidan Day, *Angela Carter: The Rational Glass*, Manchester: Manchester University Press, 1998, p. 128.

62 Angela Carter, *The Passion of New Eve*, London: Virago Press, 1992. All page numbers in Day's discussion refer to this edition.

63 Day (1998), pp. 129, 130–1.

64 Lorna Sage, 'Angela Carter: The Fairy Tale', in Danielle M. Roemer and Cristina Bacchilega, eds, *Angela Carter and the Fairy Tale*, Detroit, MI: Wayne State University Press, 2001, pp. 65–81 (p. 65).

CHAPTER SIX

1 Lorna Sage, *Angela Carter*, Plymouth: Northcote House, 1994, p. 40.

2 Margaret Atwood, 'Magic Token through the Dark Forest', *Observer*, 23 February 1992, p. 61; Lorna Sage, 'The Soaring Imagination', *The Guardian*, 17 February 1992, p. 37; *The Late Show*, presented by Tracy McLeod, BBC2, 18 February 1992.

3 Angela Carter, *The Sadeian Woman: An Exercise in Cultural History*, London: Virago Press, 1979, p. 5.

4 Merja Makinen, 'Angela Carter's *The Bloody Chamber* and the Decolonization of Feminine Sexuality', *Feminist Review*, 42, Autumn 1992, pp. 2–15 (pp. 2–3). This essay has also been reprinted in Alison Easton, ed., *Angela Carter*, Basingstoke: Macmillan, 2000.

5 Ibid., p. 3.

6 Helen Cagney Watts, 'An Interview with Angela Carter', *Bête Noire*, 8, August 1985, pp. 161–76 (p. 170).

7 Ibid., p. 162.

8 Sage (1994), p. 38.

9 Margaret Atwood, 'Running with the Tigers', in Lorna Sage, ed., *Flesh and the Mirror: Essays on the Art of Angela Carter*, London: Virago Press, 1994, pp. 117–35 (p. 120).

10 Les Bedford, 'Angela Carter: An Interview', Sheffield University Television, February 1977.

11 [*Keenan's note*] See Hélène Cixous's use of maternal metaphors to represent *écriture feminine* (the practice of a specifically feminine writing) in 'The Laugh of the Medusa' (1975), and Julia Kristeva's conception of maternity as a potential challenge to phallogocentricism in 'Héréthique de l'amour' (1977). I believe that Carter makes explicit reference to the maternal theories of Cixous

and Kristeva in *The Passion of New Eve*, and an implicit criticism of them underpins her attack on the mythicization of motherhood in *The Sadeian Woman*. 'The Laugh of the Medusa' appears in Elaine Marks and Isabelle de Courtivron, eds, *New French Feminisms: An Anthology* (Amherst: University of Massachusetts Press, 1980), trans. Keith Cohen and Paula Cohen, pp. 245–64. 'Héréthique de l'amour' appears as 'Stabat Mater' in Toril Moi, ed., *The Kristeva Reader*, trans. Léon S. Roudiez (Oxford: Basil Blackwell, 1986), pp. 161–86.

12 [*Keenan's note*] I would like to thank Lisa Day of Virago Press for access to the following cuttings from the Virago library: Jan Tomczyk, review of *The Sadeian Woman* in *The Birmingham Sun*, 29 May 1979; Rachel Billington, 'Beware women', in the *Financial Times*, 31 March 1979; Marsaili Cameron, 'Whip Hand', in *Gay News*, March 1979; Ann Oakley, review in *British Book News*, August 1979; Julia O'Faolain, 'Chamber music', in *London Magazine*, August/September 1979; Sara Maitland, review in *Time Out*, 4 May 1979; anonymous review in *Women's Report*, June 1979. Page numbers are not available.

13 Sally Keenan, 'The Sadeian Woman: Feminism as Treason', in Joseph Bristow and Trev Lynn Broughton, eds, *The Infernal Desires of Angela Carter: Fiction, Femininity, Feminism*, London: Longman, 1997, pp. 132–48 (pp. 134–5). This essay has also been reprinted in Easton, ed. (2000), pp. 37–57.

14 Carter (1979), p. 19.

15 Anna Katsavos, 'An Interview with Angela Carter', *The Review of Contemporary Fiction*, 14:3, Fall 1994, pp. 11–17 (p. 16).

16 Nanette Altevers, 'Gender Matters in The Sadeian Woman', *The Review of Contemporary Fiction*, 14:3, Fall 1994, pp. 18–23 (p. 20).

17 Robert Clark, quoted in Altevers (1994), pp. 18–19.

18 Angela Carter, *The Sadeian Woman: An Exercise in Cultural History*, London: Virago Press, 1979. All page numbers in Altevers' discussion refer to this edition.

19 Katsavos (1994), pp. 16, 13–14.

20 Altevers (1994), p. 20.

21 Keenan, in Bristow and Broughton, eds (1997), p. 138.

22 Andrea Dworkin, *Pornography: Men Possessing Women*, London: The Women's Press, 1981, p. 84.

23 Roland Barthes, *Image, Music, Text*, trans. Stephen Heath, London: Fontana, 1977, p. 42.

24 Angela Carter, *The Sadeian Woman: An Exercise in Cultural History*, London: Virago Press, 1979. All page numbers in Kappeler's discussion refer to this edition.

25 Susanne Kappeler, *The Pornography of Representation*, Cambridge: Polity Press, 1986, pp. 133–5.

26 Angela Carter, 'Afterword' to *Fireworks*, London: Quartet Books, 1974, p. 122.

27 Angela Carter, *The Sadeian Woman: An Exercise in Cultural History*, London: Virago Press, 1979. All page numbers in Duncker's discussion refer to this edition.

28 Andrea Dworkin, 'The Politics of Fear and Courage', in *Our Blood: Prophecies and Discourses on Sexual Politics*, London: The Women's Press, 1982, p. 62.

29 Patricia Duncker, 'Re-Imagining the Fairy Tales: Angela Carter's Bloody Chambers', *Literature and History*, 10:1, 1984, pp. 3–14 (p. 8).

30 Ibid., pp. 6–7.

31 Atwood, in Sage, ed. (1994), pp. 117–35 (p. 118).

32 Ibid.

33 Angela Carter, *The Sadeian Woman: An Exercise in Cultural History*, London: Virago Press, 1979. All page numbers in Atwood's discussion refer to this edition.

34 Atwood, in Sage, ed. (1994), pp. 120–2.

35 Ibid., p. 122.

36 Ibid., p. 132.

37 Ibid., p. 135.

38 Duncker (1984), p. 12.

39 References are to Robert Clark, 'Angela Carter's Desire Machine', *Women's Studies*, 14, 1987, pp. 147–61, and Avis Lewallen, 'Wayward Girls but Wicked Women?: Female Sexuality in Angela Carter's *The Bloody Chamber*', in Gary Day and Clive Bloom, ed., *Perspectives on Pornography: Sexuality in Film and Literature*, Basingstoke: Macmillan, 1988, pp. 144–58.

40 Clark (1987), pp. 149, 150.

41 Ellen Cronan Rose, 'Through the Looking Glass: When Women Tell Fairy Tales', in Elizabeth Abel, Marianne Hirsch and Elizabeth Langland, eds, *The Voyage In: Fictions of Female Development*, Hanover, NH: University Press of New England, 1983, pp. 209–27 (p. 211).

42 Bruno Bettelheim, *The Uses of Enchantment*, New York: Alfred A. Knopf, 1976, p. 308.

43 Ibid., p. 279.

44 Cronan Rose (1983), pp. 222–5.

45 Angela Carter, *The Bloody Chamber*, Harmondsworth: Penguin, 1981. All page

numbers in Armitt's discussion refer to this edition.

46 Lucie Armitt, 'The Fragile Frames of *The Bloody Chamber*', in Joseph Bristow and Trev Lynn Broughton, eds, *The Infernal Desires of Angela Carter: Fiction, Femininity, Feminism*, Harlow: Addison Wesley Longman, 1997, pp. 88–99 (p. 98).

47 Armitt is referring here to Elaine Jordan, 'The Dangers of Angela Carter', in Isobel Armstrong, ed., *New Feminist Discourses: Critical Essays on Theories and Texts*, London: Routledge, 1992, and Merja Makinen, 'Angela Carter's *The Bloody Chamber* and the Decolonization of Feminine Sexuality', in *Feminist Review*, 42, 1992, pp. 2–15. Makinen's essay has also been reprinted in Easton, ed. (2000), pp. 20–36.

48 Makinen (1992), p. 5.

49 [*Armitt's note*] This point is argued in Bruno Bettelheim, *The Uses of Enchantment: The Meaning and Importance of Fairy Tales* (Harmondsworth: Penguin, 1991), p. 44.

50 [*Armitt's note*] In other words, genre fiction is perceived to inhabit a safe site of play of its own, shored up by internal rulings and protected at all costs from the far less clear-cut demands of non-formulaic fictional writing. This is often considered to be a desirable state of affairs by critics of fantasy, who place great stress on the importance of distinguishing between folk and fairy/faerie, or the fabulous and the marvellous, losing sight, in the process, of the (perhaps dangerous) pleasures of reading beyond such constraints.

51 Armitt (1997), pp. 88–90.

52 Ibid., p. 92.

53 Ibid., pp. 95–7.

54 Cristina Bacchilega, *Postmodern Fairy Tales: Gender and Narrative Strategies*, Philadelphia: University of Pennsylvania Press, 1997, pp. 140–2.

55 Marina Warner, *From the Beast to the Blonde: On Fairy Tales and Their Tellers*, London: Chatto & Windus, 1994, p. 197. For a more extended version of this argument, see Warner's essay 'Angela Carter: Bottle Blonde, Double Drag', in Sage, ed. (1994), pp. 243–56.

56 Angela Carter, ed., *The Virago Book of Fairy Tales*, London: Virago Press, 1990, p. ix.

57 Warner (1994), p. 195.

CHAPTER SEVEN

1 Robert Nye, 'Daring Young Woman', *The Guardian*, 27 September 1984. Page numbers unavailable.

2 Carolyn See, 'Come On and See the Winged Lady', *The New York Times*, 24 February 1985. Page numbers unavailable.

3 Helen Carr, *From My Guy to Sci-Fi*, London: Pandora Press, 1989.

4 Nicci Gerrard, *Into the Mainstream*, London: Pandora Press, 1989.

5 Merja Makinen, 'Angela Carter's *The Bloody Chamber* and the Decolonization of Feminine Sexuality', *Feminist Review*, 42, Autumn 1992, pp. 2–15 (p. 7).

6 Ian McEwan, 'Sweet Smell of Excess', *The Sunday Times Magazine*, 9 September 1984, pp. 42–4 (p. 44).

7 John Haffenden, 'Magical Mannerist', *The Literary Review*, November 1984, pp. 34–8 (pp. 36–7).

8 [*Palmer's note*] On the relation between E. T. A. Hoffmann and fantasy, see Rosemary Jackson, *Fantasy: The Literature of Subversion* (London: Methuen, 1981), pp. 43–4, 66–7.

9 Hélène Cixous, *Sorties*, trans. in Elaine Marks and Isabelle de Courtivron, eds, *New French Feminisms*, Brighton: Harvester Press, 1981, p. 97.

10 [*Palmer's note*] A survey of these developments is given by Hester Eisenstein, *Contemporary Feminist Thought* (Allen & Unwin, London, 1984), pp. 45–96.

11 Angela Carter, *Nights at the Circus*, London: Chatto & Windus, Hogarth, 1984. All page numbers in Palmer's discussion refer to this edition.

12 Cixous, in Marks and de Courtivron (1981), p. 96.

13 Paulina Palmer, 'From "Coded Mannequin" to Bird Woman: Angela Carter's Magic Flight', in Sue Roe, ed., *Women Reading Women's Writing*, Brighton: Harvester Press, 1987, pp. 179–205 (pp. 179–80).

14 Gillian Greenwood, 'Flying Circus', *The Literary Review*, October 1984, p. 43.

15 [*Palmer's note*] Carter also alludes to art conventions, especially surrealistic ones. Her description of Fevvers' feathered headdress and robe (p. 41) recalls Max Ernst's *The Robing of the Bride*, and her representation of the way the tigers 'scattered their appearance upon the glass' of the mirrors in the train crash (p. 206) may be related to René Magritte's *Découverte* and *Le Faux Miroir*.

16 Mikhail Bakhtin, *Problems of Dostoevsky's Poetics*, trans. R. W. Rotsel, USA: Ardis, 1973, p. 89.

17 Ibid., p. 139.

18 Ibid., p. 103.

19 Mikhail Bakhtin, *Rabelais and his World*, trans. Helene Iswolsky, Massachusetts: MIT Press, 1968, p. 34.

20 Ibid., p. 317.

21 Ibid., pp. 410–11.

22 Ibid., pp. 200–7.

23 Bakhtin (1973), pp. 96, 122.

24 [*Palmer's note*] For a detailed discussion of these symbols and their significance, see Sandra M. Gilbert and Susan Gubar, *The Madwoman in the Attic: The Woman Writer and the Nineteenth-century Literary Imagination* (New Haven: Yale University Press, 1979), pp. 18–20.

25 Palmer, in Roe, ed. (1987), pp. 197–200.

26 Haffenden (1985), p. 87.

27 Anna Katsavos, 'An Interview with Angela Carter', *The Review of Contemporary Fiction*, 14:3, Fall 1994, pp. 11–17 (p. 13).

28 Aidan Day, *Angela Carter: The Rational Glass*, Manchester: Manchester University Press, 1998, pp. 168–9, 172–5.

29 Ibid., p. 194.

30 Ibid., p. 185.

31 Bakhtin (1968), pp. 92, 94.

32 Palmer, in Roe, ed. (1987), p. 201.

33 Angela Carter, 'The Language of Sisterhood', in Leonard Michaels and Christopher Ricks, eds, *The State of the Language*, Berkeley, Los Angeles and London: University of California Press, pp. 226–34 (p. 226).

34 Day (1998), pp. 192–3, 194.

35 Mary Russo, *The Female Grotesque: Risk, Excess and Modernity*, London: Routledge, 1995, p. 159. An edited version of Russo's chapter on this text, 'Revamping Spectacle: Angela Carter's *Nights at the Circus*' is published in Easton, ed. (2000), pp. 136–60.

36 [*Russo's note*] For a very different use of the iconography of the emaciated female body, see for instance the puppetry of Lotte Prinzel, or in the context of feminist art, see Valie Export's performance work described in 'Persona, Proto-Performance, Politics', *Discourse* 14/2 (Spring 1992), pp. 26–35.

37 Angela Carter, *Nights at the Circus*, London: Chatto & Windus, Hogarth, 1994. All page numbers in Russo's discussion refer to this edition.

38 Russo (1995), pp. 105–7.

39 [*Russo's note*] For an account of the female circus performer as Victorian working girl, see Michael Hiley, *Victorian Working Women: Portraits From Life* (Boston: David Godine, 1980). The figure of the female acrobat raises the predictable questions of gender and propriety: 'Ought we forbid her to do these things? … And, though it is not well to see a nude man fling a nude girl about as she is flung, or to see her grip his body in midair between her seemingly bare thighs, I think that an unreflecting audience takes no note … and looks upon these things and looks at him and her only as two performers. Still, the familiar interlacing of male and female bodies in sight of the public, is gross and corrupting, though its purpose be mere athletics' (p. 119).

40 Russo (1995), pp. 176–7.

41 [*Russo's note*] Paulina Palmer's 'From "Coded Mannequin" to Bird Woman: Angela Carter's Magic Flight', in *Women Reading Women's Writing* (New York: St. Martin's Press, 1987), argues that the tension which exists between an impulse to analyze and demythologise gender and the impulse towards utopian celebrations of woman-centered culture is reflected in two 'stages' of Carter's work. From Palmer's perspective, the image of the puppet or 'coded Mannequin' is 'replaced by the image of Fevver's [*sic*] miraculous wings which she observes make her body "the abode of limitless freedom" and the egg from which she claims to have been hatched'. Hoffmann, Freud, and the uncanny are associated with texts published prior to 1978, those 'marred by an element of distortion', and those later texts, including *The Bloody Chamber* and *Nights at the Circus*, are associated with 'the expression of emotions which have a liberating effect'. As an opening illustration of this dichotomy, she cites a passage (which I would agree is crucial) from the conclusion of the novel, in which Fevvers, for the last time, gives an 'enthusiastic if cliché-ridden speech heralding the new age of women's liberation' (Palmer, 179).

42 Walter Benjamin, 'Theses on the Philosophy of History', in *Illuminations*, trans. Harry Zohn, New York: Schocken Books, 1969, p. 257.

43 Ibid., p. 258.

44 [*Russo's note*] The claim that 'an emergence of a female counter-culture is celebrated' in the novel (Palmer, 180) is, in my view, true only as a prefigurative *possibility*. And many female types and institutional contexts are represented in the novel, implicating any definition of female counterculture in the histories and metahistories of violence and oppression by and of women.

Fevvers herself eats caviar in a grand hotel, at the expense of the peasant woman, Baboushka. Countess P., Olga Alexandrovna, and Madame Schreck all partake in criminality and destruction.

45 [*Russo's note*] The prospects for life with Walser, the New Man, have seemed dim for most of my students. Although I have suggested alternative readings, on the numerous occasions when we have discussed his transformations as successively a brash American journalist, a fellow traveller with the clowns, a surrealistic anthropologist who 'goes native', and a new age man, students tend to see him in all these roles as a 'jerk' – something closer to the bad alternatives in Tania Modleski's *Feminism Without Women* than to the nondominant types in Kaja Silverman's *Male Subjectivity at the Margins*.

46 [*Russo's note*] Lizzie's greatest fear is that Fevvers will become the 'tableau' of 'a woman in bondage to her reproductive system, a woman tied hand and foot to that Nature which your physiology denies' (p. 283). Carter never accedes to a definition of even motherhood as the 'natural'; throughout the novel mothers are second-hand representations within fictions, images, and tableaux.

47 Susan Rubin Suleiman, *Subversive Intent: Gender, Politics, and the Avant-Garde*, Cambridge: Harvard University Press, 1990, p. 137.

48 Russo (1995), pp. 179–81.

49 Angela Carter, *Burning Your Boats: Collected Short Stories*, ed. Salman Rushdie, London: Vintage, 1996. All page numbers in Day's discussion refer to this edition.

50 Kerryn Goldsworthy, 'Angela Carter', *Meanjin*, 44:1, Adelaide: March 1985, pp. 4–13 (pp. 11–12).

51 Day (1998), pp. 178–81.

52 [*Matus's note*] *Charles Baudelaire, Oeuvres Complètes*, 2 vols., ed. Claude Pichois (Paris, 1975–76); Baudelaire, *Correspondance*, ed. Claude Pichois and Jean Ziegler (Paris, 1973); Baudelaire, *Flowers of Evil*, trans. George Dillon and Edna St. Vincent Millias (New York, 1936); Felix Nadar, *Charles Baudelaire Intime: Le Poète Vierge* (Paris, 1911).

53 Jill Matus, 'Blonde, Black and Hottentot Venus: Context and Critique in Angela Carter's "Black Venus"', *Studies in Short Fiction*, 28:4, 1991, pp. 467–76 (p. 467). This essay has been reprinted in Easton, ed. (2000), pp. 161–72.

54 [*Matus's note*] Stephen Gray's poem 'Hottentot Venus' begins:
My name is Saartjie Baartman and I come from Kat Rivier
they call me the Hottentot Venus
they rang up the curtains on a classy peepshow two pennies
two pennies in the slot and I'd wind up
shift a fan and roll my rolypoly bum
and rock the capitals of Europe into mirth.
[Stephen Gray, ed., *A World of Their Own: Southern African Poets of the Seventies*, Johannesburg: Donker, 1976, p. 56.]

55 Quoted in Enid Starkie, *Baudelaire*, London: Faber, 1957, p. 87.

56 Matus (1991), p. 468.

57 Ibid., p. 469.

58 Ibid., p. 470.

59 Ibid., pp. 470–1.

60 Mikhail Bakhtin, *The Dialogic Imagination: Four Essays*, trans. Caryl Emerson and Michael Holquist, ed. Michael Holquist, Austin: University of Texas Press, 1981, p. 294.

61 Angela Carter, *Black Venus*, London: Chatto & Windus, 1985. All page numbers in Matus's discussion refer to this edition.

62 Matus (1991), pp. 472–3.

63 Sarah Gamble, *Angela Carter: Writing From the Front Line*, Edinburgh: Edinburgh University Press, 1997, p. 150.

64 [*Gamble's note*] It is included in Carter's final collection of short stories, *American Ghosts and Old World Wonders*.

65 Angela Carter, *Black Venus*, London: Chatto & Windus, 1985. All page numbers in Gamble's discussion refer to this edition.

66 Gamble (1997), pp. 151–3.

67 Ibid., p. 153.

68 Linden Peach, *Angela Carter*, Basingstoke: Macmillan, 1998, pp. 145–6.

69 Angela Carter, *Burning Your Boats: Collected Short Stories*, ed. Salman Rushdie, London: Chatto & Windus, 1995. All page numbers in Peach's text refer to this edition.

70 Peach (1998), p. 146.

CHAPTER EIGHT

1 Lynne Truss, 'Dora and Nora, Two Batty Old Bags', *The Literary Review*, June 1991, pp. 33–4.

2 Joyce Carol Oates, 'Comedy is Tragedy That Happens to Other People', *The New York Times*, 19 January 1992. Page numbers unavailable.

3 Salman Rushdie, 'Angela Carter, 1940–92: A Very Good Wizard, a Very Dear Friend', *The New York Times Book Review*, 8 March 1992, p. 5.

4 Peter Kemp, 'Magical History Tour', *The Sunday Times*, 9 June 1991. Page numbers unavailable.

5 Ibid.

6 Susannah Clapp, 'On Madness, Men and Fairy-Tales', *The Independent on Sunday*, 9 June 1991, pp. 26–7 (p. 26).

7 Ibid., p. 27.

8 The term 'bricoleur' is taken from the work of the anthropologist Claude Lévi-Strauss. In *The Savage Mind* (1962), he describes the 'bricoleur' as a recycler; someone who uses whatever tools and materials are to hand. Sage's reference here, therefore, is to Carter as a recycler of existing texts.

9 Lorna Sage, *Women in the House of Fiction: Post-War Women Novelists*, Basingstoke: Macmillan, 1992, pp. 185–7.

10 'Angela Carter's Curious Room', prod. Kim Evans, London: BBC1 Omnibus Video, 15 September 1992.

11 Kate Webb, 'Seriously Funny: *Wise Children*', in Lorna Sage, ed., *Flesh and the Mirror: Essays on the Art of Angela Carter*, London: Virago Press, 1994, pp. 279–307 (pp. 280–1, 284). This essay has also been reprinted in Alison Easton, ed., *Angela Carter*, Basingstoke: Macmillan, 2000, pp. 192–215.

12 Ibid., p. 295.

13 Ibid., pp. 286–7.

14 See Sandra M. Gilbert and Susan Gubar, *The Madwoman in the Attic*, Yale University Press, 1979.

15 Webb, in Sage, ed. (1994), pp. 299–300.

16 Jane Miller, *Seductions: Studies in Reading and Culture*, Virago Press, 1990. Name of publisher and page numbers are not given by Webb.

17 Ibid.

18 Ibid.

19 [*Webb's note*] I'm thinking here in particular of the New Historicist writing on Shakespeare, and of Linda Hutcheon's *A Theory of Parody*, Methuen, 1985.

20 Omnibus (1992).

21 Webb, in Sage, ed. (1994), pp. 301–5.

22 Ibid., pp. 306–7.

23 Gerardine Meaney, *(Un)Like Subjects: Women, Theory, Fiction*, London: Routledge, 1993, p. 127.

24 Ibid.

25 Graham Holderness, '"What ish [*sic*] my nation?"': Shakespeare and National Identities', *Textual Practices*, 5:1, 1991, 74–93 (p. 75).

26 Meaney (1993), p. 128.

27 [*Meaney's note*] Carter is obviously making reference to the 1935 version directed by Max Reinhardt and William Dieterle.

28 Angela Carter, *Wise Children*, London: Chatto & Windus, 1991. All page numbers in Meaney's text refer to this edition.

29 Meaney (1993), p. 129.

30 James Joyce, *Ulysses* (1922), ed. Declan Kiberd, Harmondsworth: Penguin, 1992, pp. 210–39.

31 J. Atherton, *The Books at the Wake: A Study of Literary Allusions in James Joyce's Finnegans Wake*, New York: Paul P. Appel, 1974, p. 89.

32 *Ulysses* (1992), p. 293.

33 James Joyce, *Letters* (1957), ed. Stuart Gilbert, Vol. 1, London: Faber, 1966, p. 135.

34 Karen Lawrence, 'Joyce and Feminism', in Derek Attridge, ed., *The Cambridge Companion to James Joyce*, Cambridge: Cambridge University Press, 1990, p. 252.

35 Julia Kristeva, *Powers of Horror: An Essay on Abjection*, trans. L. S. Roudiez, New York: Columbia University Press, 1982, p. 206.

36 Meaney (1993), pp. 130–2.

37 Ibid., p. 134.

38 Ibid., p. 139.

39 Ibid., pp. 139–40.

40 Clare Hanson, '"The Red Dawn Breaking Over Clapham": Carter and the Limits of Artifice', in Joseph Bristow and Trev Lynn Broughton, eds, *The Infernal Desires of Angela Carter: Fiction, Femininity, Feminism*, London: Longman, 1997, p. 59.

41 Hanson's citation for this reference is Lorna Sage, 'Death of the Author', in *Granta*, 41, Autumn 1992, p. 241. However, it can also be found in *Angela Carter*, Plymouth: Northcote House, 1994 – Sage's rewriting of that article for the Northcote House 'Writers and their Work' series, p. 22.

42 Hanson, in Bristow and Broughton, eds (1997), p. 22.

43 [*Hanson's note*] See Jean-François Lyotard, *The Postmodern Condition: A Report on Knowledge* (1979), trans. Geoff Bennington and Brian Massumi (Manchester: Manchester University Press, 1984). For Lyotard, 'grand narratives' are those such as Christianity or Marxism, which attempt to find a framework for everything. He argues that the postmodern world-view is characterized by 'little narratives', which present local

explanations but do not claim to explain everything.

44 Hanson, in Bristow and Broughton, eds (1997), p.60.

45 Ibid., p.67.

46 Ibid., p.68.

47 Meaney (1993), pp.139–40.

48 Angela Carter, *Wise Children*, London: Chatto & Windus, 1991. All page numbers in Meaney's text refer to this edition.

49 Angela Carter, 'Notes from the Front Line', in Wandor, ed. (1983), p.77.

50 [*Hanson's note*] Compare Carter's deft debunking of the Shakespeare myth in the Omnibus interview recorded in 1991.

51 [*Hanson's note*] See Elaine Jordan, 'Enthralment: Angela Carter's Speculative Fictions', in Linda Anderson, ed., *Plotting Change* (London: Edward Arnold, 1990), for a discussion of the speculative qualities of Carter's fiction.

52 Hanson, in Bristow and Broughton, eds (1997), pp.69–71.

53 See Lorna Sage, *Angela Carter*, Plymouth: Northcote House, 1994, p.58.

54 Beth A. Boehm, '*Wise Children*: Angela Carter's Swan Song', *The Review of Contemporary Fiction*, 14:3, Fall 1994, pp.84–9 (p.85).

55 Angela Carter, *Wise Children*, New York: Penguin, 1993. All page numbers in Boehm's text refer to this edition.

56 Boehm (1994), pp.86–7.

57 Ibid., p.88.

58 Ibid., pp.88–9.

59 Linden Peach, *Angela Carter*, Basingstoke: Macmillan, 1998, pp.122–3.

60 Sage (1992), p.188.

61 Angela Carter, *Burning Your Boats: Collected Short Stories*, ed. Salman Rushdie, London: Vintage, 1996, p.389.

62 Aidan Day, *Angela Carter: The Rational Glass*, Manchester: Manchester University Press, 1998, pp.202–3.

63 Angela Carter, *American Ghosts and Old World Wonders*, London: Chatto & Windus, 1993.

64 Gamble (1997), pp.187–8.

65 Angela Carter, 'Introduction', *Expletives Deleted: Selected Writings*, London: Chatto & Windus, 1992, p.2.

SELECT BIBLIOGRAPHY

Novels

Shadow Dance (London: Heinemann, 1966; reprinted as *Honeybuzzard*, New York: Simon & Schuster, 1966; London: Pan, 1968; London: Virago Press, 1994).

The Magic Toyshop (London: Heinemann, 1967; New York: Simon & Schuster, 1968; London: Virago Press, 1981).

Several Perceptions (London: Heinemann, 1969; New York: Simon & Schuster, 1968; London: Pan, 1970; London: Virago Press, 1995).

Heroes and Villains (London: Heinemann, 1969; New York: Simon & Schuster, 1969; Harmondsworth: Penguin, 1981).

Love (London: Rupert Hart-Davis, 1971; revised edition, London: Chatto & Windus, 1987; New York: Viking Penguin, 1988; London: Picador, 1988).

The Infernal Desire Machines of Doctor Hoffman (London: Rupert Hart-Davis, 1972; reprinted as *The War of Dreams*, New York: Bard/Avon Books, 1977; Harmondsworth: Penguin, 1982).

The Passion of New Eve (London: Gollancz, 1977; New York: Harcourt Brace Javanovich, 1977; London: Virago Press, 1982).

Nights at the Circus (London: Chatto & Windus, 1984; New York: Viking, 1985; London: Pan, 1985).

Wise Children (London: Chatto & Windus, 1991; New York: Farrar, Straus and Giroux, 1992; London: Vintage, 1992).

Short Stories

Fireworks: Nine Profane Pieces (London: Quartet Books, 1974; New York: Harper & Row, 1981; revised edition, London: Chatto & Windus, 1987; London: Virago Press, 1988).

The Bloody Chamber and Other Stories (London: Gollancz, 1979; New York: Harper & Row, 1980; Harmondsworth: Penguin, 1981).

Black Venus (London: Chatto & Windus, 1985; reprinted as *Saints and Strangers*, New York: Viking Penguin, 1987; London: Pan, 1986).

American Ghosts and Old World Wonders (London: Chatto & Windus, 1993; London: Vintage, 1994).

Children's Stories

Miss Z, the Dark Young Lady, illustrated by Keith Eros (London: Heinemann, 1970; New York: Simon & Schuster, 1970).

The Donkey Prince, illustrated by Keith Eros (New York: Simon and Schuster, 1970).

Martin Leman's Comic and Curious Cats, text by Angela Carter, illustrated by Martin Leman (London: Gollancz, 1979; London: Gollancz Paperback, 1988).

Moonshadow, text by Angela Carter, idea and paintings by Justin Todd (London: Gollancz, 1982).

Verse
Unicorn (Leeds: Location Press, 1966).

Radio Plays
Come Unto These Yellow Sands: Four Radio Plays (Newcastle upon Tyne: Bloodaxe Books, 1985; Newcastle upon Tyne: Bloodaxe Paperback, 1985).

Film and Television
The Company of Wolves, dir. Neil Jordan (ITC Entertainment/Palace Production 1984).
The Magic Toyshop, dir. David Wheatley (Granada TV, 1987).
'The Kitchen Child', *Short and Curlies* (Channel Four, 30 June 1990).
The Holy Family Album (Channel Four, 3 December 1991).

Selected Non-fiction
Foreword to *The Fairy Tales of Charles Perrault*, trans. Angela Carter (London: Gollancz, 1977; New York: Bard Books, 1979).
The Sadeian Woman: An Exercise in Cultural History (London: Virago Press, 1979; reprinted as *The Sadeian Woman and the Ideology of Pornography*, New York: Pantheon, 1979).
'The Language of Sisterhood', in Leonard Michaels and Christopher Ricks, eds, *The State of the Language* (University of California Press, 1980).
Nothing Sacred: Selected Writings (London: Virago Press, 1982; revised edition, London: Virago Press, 1992).
Editor and translator, *Sleeping Beauty and Other Favourite Fairy Tales* (London: Gollancz, 1982; New York: Schocken, 1989; London: Gollancz Paperback, 1991).
'Notes from the Front Line', in Michelene Wandor, ed., *On Gender and Writing* (London: Pandora Press, 1983; reprinted in Angela Carter, *Shaking a Leg: Collected Journalism and Writings*, London: Chatto & Windus, 1997).
Editor, *Wayward Girls and Wicked Women* (London: Virago Press, 1986).
'Truly, It Felt Like Year One', in Sara Maitland, ed., *Very Heaven: Looking Back at the 1960s* (London: Virago Press, 1988).
Editor, *The Virago Book of Fairy Tales* (London: Virago, 1990; reprinted as *Old Wives' Fairy Tale Book*, New York: David McKay, 1987; London: Virago Press, 1991).
Editor, *The Second Virago Book of Fairy Tales* (London: Virago Press, 1992; London: Virago Press, 1993).
Expletives Deleted: Selected Writings (London: Chatto & Windus, 1992; London: Vintage, 1993).

Collected Works
Burning Your Boats: Collected Short Stories, ed. Salman Rushdie (London: Chatto & Windus, 1995). (All the stories from *Fireworks*, *The Bloody Chamber*, *Black Venus* and *American Ghosts and Old World Wonders*, plus some previously uncollected material.)

The Curious Room: Collected Dramatic Works (London: Chatto & Windus, 1996).
(All the radio plays, including those previously published in *Come Unto These Yellow Sands*, screen plays, a libretto and a stage play.)

Shaking a Leg: Collected Journalism and Writings (London: Chatto & Windus, 1997). (Material from *Nothing Sacred* and *Expletives Deleted* as well as a wide range of previously uncollected pieces, including 'Notes from the Front Line'.)

Interviews and Profiles

These are arranged in chronological rather than alphabetical order in order to enable interviews to be linked with specific pieces of work if appropriate. Where interviews with Carter were published posthumously, they are listed under the year in which the interview was given.

1972

Stott, Catherine, 'Runaway to the Land of Promise', *The Guardian* (10 August 1972), p. 10.

1977

Bedford, Les, 'Angela Carter: An Interview' (Sheffield University Television, February 1977).

Sage, Lorna, 'The Savage Sideshow', *New Review*, 4:39/40 (July 1977), pp. 51–7.

1979

Watts, Janet, 'Sade and the Sexual Struggle', *Observer Magazine* (25 March 1979), pp. 54–5.

Hamilton, Alex, 'Sade and Prejudice', *The Guardian* (30 March 1979), p. 15.

1982

Mortimer, John, 'The Stylish Prime of Miss Carter', *The Sunday Times* (24 January 1982), p. 36.

1984

McEwan, Ian, 'Sweet Smell of Excess', *The Sunday Times Magazine* (9 September 1984), pp. 42–4.

Harron, Mary, '"I'm a Socialist, Damn It! How Can You Expect Me to be Interested in Fairies?"', *The Guardian* (25 September 1984), p. 10.

Haffenden, John, 'Magical Mannerist', *The Literary Review* (November 1984), pp. 34–8. (Reprinted in 1985 – see next entry.)

1985

Haffenden, John, ed. *Novelists in Interview* (London: Methuen, 1985), pp. 76–96.

Goldsworthy, Kerryn, 'Angela Carter', *Meanjin*, 44:1 (Adelaide, March 1985), pp. 4–13.

Cagney Watts, Helen, 'An Interview with Angela Carter', *Bête Noire*, 8 (August 1985), p. 161–76.
Smith, Anne, 'Myths and the Erotic', *Women's Review*, 1 (November 1985), pp. 28–9.

1986
Gristwood, Sarah, 'Not a Bad Lot', *The Guardian* (29 October 1986).
Waterson, Moira, 'Flights of Fancy in Balham', *Observer Magazine* (9 November 1986), pp. 42–5.

1987
Appignanesi, Lisa, *Angela Carter in Conversation* (London: ICA Video, 1987).
Women Writers, Channel Four (26 October 1987).

1988
Anna Katsavos, 'An Interview with Angela Carter', *The Review of Contemporary Fiction*, 14:3 (Fall 1994), pp. 11–17.

1989
Snitow, Ann, 'Conversation with a Necromancer', *Village Voice Literary Supplement*, 75 (June 1989), pp. 14–16.

1991
Bradfield, Scott, 'Remembering Angela Carter', *The Review of Contemporary Fiction*, 14:3 (Fall 1994), pp. 90–3.
Clapp, Susannah, 'On Madness, Men and Fairy-Tales', *The Independent on Sunday* (9 June 1991), pp. 26–7.
Kemp, Peter, 'Magical History Tour', *The Sunday Times* (9 June 1991), pp. 6–7.

1992
Sage, Lorna, 'Angela Carter Interviewed by Lorna Sage', in Malcolm Bradbury and Judith Cooke, eds, *New Writing* (London: Minerva Press, 1992), pp. 185–93.
Evans, Kim (producer), 'Angela Carter's Curious Room' (London: BBC1 Omnibus Video, 15 September 1992).

1995
Barker, Paul, 'The Return of the Magic Story-Teller, *The Independent on Sunday* (8 January 1995), pp. 14, 16.
Gerrard, Nicci, 'Angela Carter is Now More Popular than Virginia Woolf', *Observer Life* (9 July 1995), pp. 20, 22–3.

Obituaries
Author unknown, 'Angela Carter', *The Times* (17 February 1992), p. 15.
Sage, Lorna, 'The Soaring Imagination', *The Guardian* (17 February 1992), p. 37.

Coover, Robert, 'A Passionate Remembrance', *The Guardian* (18 February 1992). Reprinted in *The Review of Contemporary Fiction*, 14:3 (Fall 1994), pp. 9–10.

Warner, Marina, 'Obituary: Angela Carter', *The Independent* (18 February 1992).

Webb, W.L., 'Angela Carter, Rich in Rude Grace', *The Guardian* (20 February 1992), p. 25.

Atwood, Margaret, 'Magic Token through the Dark Forest', *Observer* (23 February 1992), p. 61.

Callil, Carmen, 'Flying Jewelry', *The Sunday Times* (23 February 1992), p. 6.

Rushdie, Salman, 'Angela Carter 1940–92: A Very Good Wizard, a Very Dear Friend', *The New York Times Book Review* (8 March 1992), p. 5.

Sage, Lorna, 'Death of the Author', *Granta: Biography*, 41 (Autumn 1992), pp. 233–54. (An expanded version of this article was published as *Angela Carter* by Northcote House in 1993 – see 'Monographs' below.)

Monographs

Day, Aidan, *Angela Carter: The Rational Glass* (Manchester: Manchester University Press, 1998).

Gamble, Sarah, *Angela Carter: Writing From the Front Line* (Edinburgh: Edinburgh University Press, 1997).

Lee, Alison, *Angela Carter* (New York: Twayne Publishers, 1997).

Peach, Linden, *Angela Carter* (Basingstoke: Macmillan, 1998).

Sage, Lorna, *Angela Carter* (Plymouth: Northcote House, 1994).

Collected Criticism

The essays in these collections are cited individually in the 'Essays on Angela Carter' section below.

Sage, Lorna, ed., *Flesh and the Mirror: Essays on the Art of Angela Carter* (London: Virago Press, 1994).

Bristow, Joseph and Broughton, Trev Lynn, eds, *The Infernal Desires of Angela Carter: Fiction, Femininity, Feminism* (Harlow: Addison Wesley Longman, 1997).

Easton, Alison, ed., *Angela Carter: Contemporary Critical Essays* (Basingstoke: Macmillan, 2000).

Roemer, Danielle M., and Bacchilega, Cristina, eds, *Angela Carter and the Fairy Tale* (Detroit, MI: Wayne State University Press, 2001).

Special Issues Devoted to Angela Carter

The Review of Contemporary Fiction, 14:3 (Fall 1994).

Marvels and Tales: Journal of Fairy-Tale Studies, 12:1 (1998). Revised version of this collection published as Danielle M. Roemer and Cristina Bacchilega, eds, *Angela Carter and the Fairy Tale* (Detroit, MI: Wayne State University Press, 2001).

Books with Key Discussions on the Work of Angela Carter

Main novels discussed are in parentheses at the end of each entry.

Armitt, Lucie, *Theorising the Fantastic* (London: Arnold, 1996). (Extensive discussion of *The Passion of New Eve* in relation to modern technotheory.)

Armitt, Lucie, *Contemporary Women's Fiction and the Fantastic* (Basingstoke: Macmillan, 2000). (Carter's work is referenced throughout Armitt's debate, but detailed discussions are on the *Infernal Desire Machines of Doctor Hoffman*, *The Magic Toyshop*, *Nights at the Circus* and *Wise Children*.)

Bacchilega, Cristina, *Postmodern Fairy Tales: Gender and Narrative Strategies* (Philadelphia: University of Pennsylvania Press, 1997). (*The Bloody Chamber* narratives discussed as examples of postmodern feminist fairy tales.)

Cranny-Francis, Anne, *Feminist Fiction: Feminist Uses of Generic Fiction* (Cambridge: Polity Press, 1990). (Discussion of *The Bloody Chamber*.)

Gasiorek, Andrzej, *Post-War British Fiction: Realism and After* (London: Edward Arnold, 1995). (Examines the relationship between fantasy and realism in Carter's fiction.)

Kappeler, Susanne, *The Pornography of Representation* (Cambridge: Polity Press, 1986). (Short but influential attack on Carter's treatment of pornography in *The Sadeian Woman*.)

Kenyon, Olga, *Writing Women* (London: Pluto Press, 1991). (Chapter Two, 'Angela Carter: Fantasist and Feminist', is an accessible introduction to Carter's work.)

Meaney, Gerardine, *(Un)Like Subjects: Women, Theory, Fiction* (London: Routledge, 1993). (Traces connections between Carter's novels and French feminist theory. Texts discussed in detail are *Heroes and Villains*, *The Sadeian Woman* and *Wise Children*.) An edited version of Meaney's discussion of *Heroes and Villains* has been published as 'History and Women's Time: *Heroes and Villains*' in Alison Easton, ed., *Angela Carter* (Basingstoke: Macmillan, 2000), pp. 84–106.

Mills, Sara, Pearce, Lynn, et al., *Feminist Readings/Feminists Reading* (Hemel Hempstead: Harvester Wheatsheaf, 1989). (Readings of *The Magic Toyshop* using Anglo-American and French feminist theory.)

Punter, David, *The Literature of Terror: A History of Gothic Fictions from 1765 to the Present Day* (London: Longman, 1980). (Discusses *Heroes and Villains* and *Love* as examples of contemporary Gothic.)

Punter, David, *The Hidden Script: Writing and the Unconscious* (London: Routledge & Kegan Paul, 1985). (Chapter Two, 'Angela Carter: Supersessions of the Masculine', discusses *The Infernal Desire Machines of Doctor Hoffman*, *The Passion of New Eve* and *The Sadeian Woman*.)

Russo, Mary, *The Female Grotesque: Risk, Excess and Modernity* (London: Routledge, 1995). (Chapter Three, 'Revamping Spectacle: Angela Carter's *Nights at the Circus*'. An edited version of this chapter has been reprinted as 'Revamping Spectacle: Angela Carter's *Nights at the Circus*' in Alison Easton, ed., *Angela Carter* (Basingstoke: Macmillan, 2000), pp. 136–60.)

Sage, Lorna, *Women in the House of Fiction: Post-War Women Novelists*

(Basingstoke: Macmillan, 1992). (Pithy survey of Carter's novels up to *Nights at the Circus*.)

Warner, Marina, *From the Beast to the Blonde: On Fairy Tales and Their Tellers* (London: Chatto & Windus, 1994). (References to various stories from *The Bloody Chamber* throughout.)

Williams, Linda Ruth, *Critical Desire: Psychoanalysis and the Literary Subject* (London: Edward Arnold, 1995). (Chapter Three, 'Writing at Play: Fantasy and Identity in Angela Carter'.)

Essays on Angela Carter

Where the texts discussed are not made obvious by the title, they are indicated in parentheses after the entry.

Almansi, Guido, 'In the Alchemist's Cave: Radio Plays', in Lorna Sage, ed., *Flesh and the Mirror: Essays on the Art of Angela Carter* (London: Virago Press, 1994), pp. 216–29.

Altevers, Nanette, 'Gender Matters in *The Sadeian Woman*', *The Review of Contemporary Fiction*, 14:3 (Fall 1994), pp. 18–23.

Armitt, Lucie, 'The Fragile Frames of *The Bloody Chamber*', in Joseph Bristow and Trev Lynn Broughton, eds, *The Infernal Desires of Angela Carter: Fiction, Femininity, Feminism* (Harlow: Addison Wesley Longman, 1997), pp. 88–99.

Armstrong, Isobel, 'Woolf by the Lake: Woolf at the Circus: Carter and Tradition', in Lorna Sage, ed., *Flesh and the Mirror: Essays on the Art of Angela Carter* (London: Virago Press, 1994), pp. 257–78. (*Nights at the Circus*.)

Atwood, Margaret, 'Running with the Tigers', in Lorna Sage, ed., *Flesh and the Mirror: Essays on the Art of Angela Carter* (London: Virago Press, 1994), pp. 117–35. (*The Sadeian Woman, The Bloody Chamber*.)

Bacchilega, Cristina, 'In the Eye of the Fairy Tale: Corinna Sargood and David Wheatley Talk about Working with Angela Carter', *Marvels and Tales: Journal of Fairy-Tale Studies*, 12:1 (1998), pp. 213–28. Reprinted in Danielle M. Roemer and Cristina Bacchilega, eds, *Angela Carter and the Fairy Tale* (Detroit, MI: Wayne State University Press, 2001), pp. 225–41.

Bannock, Sarah, 'Auto/Biographical Souvenirs in *Nights at the Circus*', in Joseph Bristow and Trev Lynn Broughton, eds, *The Infernal Desires of Angela Carter: Fiction, Femininity, Feminism* (Harlow: Addison Wesley Longman, 1997), pp. 198–215.

Barchilon, Jacques, 'Remembering Angela Carter', *Marvels and Tales: Journal of Fairy-Tale Studies*, 12:1 (1998), pp. 19–22. Reprinted in Danielle M. Roemer and Cristina Bacchilega, eds, *Angela Carter and the Fairy Tale* (Detroit, MI: Wayne State University Press, 2001), pp. 26–9. (*The Bloody Chamber*.)

Benson, Stephen, 'Angela Carter and the Literary Märchen: A Review Essay', *Marvels and Tales: Journal of Fairy-Tale Studies*, 12:1 (1998), pp. 23–51. Reprinted in Danielle M. Roemer and Cristina Bacchilega, eds, *Angela Carter and the Fairy Tale* (Detroit, MI: Wayne State University Press, 2001), pp. 30–58. (Survey of criticism published on *The Bloody Chamber*.)

Blodgett, Harriet, 'Fresh Iconography: Subversive Fantasy by Angela Carter', *The Review of Contemporary Fiction*, 14:3 (Fall 1994), pp.49–55. (*The Passion of New Eve, Nights at the Circus.*)

Boehm, Beth A., 'Wise Children: Angela Carter's Swan Song', *The Review of Contemporary Fiction*, 14:3 (Fall 1994), pp.84–9.

Bonca, Cornel, 'In Despair of the Old Adams: Angela Carter's *The Infernal Desire Machines of Dr.* [sic] *Hoffman*', *The Review of Contemporary Fiction*, 14:3 (Fall 1994), pp.56–62.

Britzolakis, Christina, 'Angela Carter's Fetishism', *Textual Practice*, 9:3 (Winter 1995), pp.459–75. (*Love, The Passion of New Eve*, 'Black Venus', *Nights at the Circus, Wise Children.*) Reprinted in Joseph Bristow and Trev Lynn Broughton, eds, *The Infernal Desires of Angela Carter: Fiction, Femininity, Feminism* (Harlow: Addison Wesley Longman, 1997), pp.43–58; and in Alison Easton, ed., *Angela Carter* (Basingstoke: Macmillan, 2000), pp.173–91.

Brown, Richard, 'Postmodern Americas: The Fiction of Angela Carter, Martin Amis and Ian McEwan', in Ann Massa and Alistair Stead, eds, *Forked Tongues?: Comparing British and American Literature* (London: Longman, 1994), pp.92–110. (*The Magic Toyshop, The Passion of New Eve.*)

Bruhl, Elise, and Gamer, Michael, 'Teaching Improprieties: *The Bloody Chamber* and the Reverent Classroom', *Marvels and Tales: Journal of Fairy-Tale Studies*, 12:1 (1998), pp.133–45. Reprinted in Danielle M. Roemer and Cristina Bacchilega, eds, *Angela Carter and the Fairy Tale* (Detroit, MI: Wayne State University Press, 2001), pp.145–58.

Bryant, Sylvia, 'Re-Constructing Oedipus Through "Beauty and the Beast"', *Criticism*, 31:4 (Fall 1989), pp.439–53.

Christensen, Peter, 'The Hoffman Connection: Demystification in Angela Carter's *The Infernal Desire Machines of Doctor Hoffman*', *The Review of Contemporary Fiction*, 14:3 (Fall 1994), pp.63–70.

Clark, Robert, 'Angela Carter's Desire Machine', *Women's Studies*, 14 (1987), pp.147–61. ('The Company of Wolves', *The Sadeian Woman, Heroes and Villains, The Infernal Desire Machines of Doctor Hoffman, The Passion of New Eve.*)

Coover, Robert, 'Entering Ghost Town', in Danielle M. Roemer and Cristina Bacchilega, eds, *Angela Carter and the Fairy Tale* (Detroit, MI: Wayne State University Press, 2001), pp.242–49. (Fictional tribute to Carter.)

Cronan Rose, Ellen, 'Through the Looking Glass: When Women Tell Fairy Tales', in Elizabeth Abel, Marianne Hirsch and Elizabeth Langland, eds, *The Voyage In: Fictions of Female Development* (Hanover, NH: University Press of New England, 1983), pp.209–27.

Crunell-Vanrigh, Anny, 'The Logic of the Same and *Différance*: "The Courtship of Mr Lyon"', *Marvels and Tales: Journal of Fairy-Tale Studies*, 12:1 (1998), pp.116–32. Reprinted in Danielle M. Roemer and Cristina Bacchilega, eds, *Angela Carter and the Fairy Tale* (Detroit, MI: Wayne State University Press, 2001), pp.128–44.

Ducornet, Rikki, 'A Scatalogical and Cannibal Clock: Angela Carter's "The Fall River Axe Murders"', *The Review of Contemporary Fiction*, 14:3 (Fall 1994), pp.37–42.

Duncker, Patricia, 'Re-Imagining the Fairy Tales: Angela Carter's Bloody Chambers', *Literature and History*, 10:1 (1984), pp. 3–14.

Fowl, Melinda G., 'Angela Carter's *The Bloody Chamber* Revisited', *Critical Survey*, 3:1 (1991), pp. 71–9.

Gass, Joanne M., 'Panopticism in Nights at the Circus', *The Review of Contemporary Fiction*, 14:3 (Fall 1994), pp. 71–6.

Hanson, Clare, 'Each Other: Images of Otherness in the Short Fiction of Doris Lessing, Jean Rhys and Angela Carter', *Journal of the Short Story in English*, 19 (Spring 1988), pp. 67–82. (*Black Venus*.)

Hanson, Clare, '"The Red Dawn Breaking Over Clapham": Carter and the Limits of Artifice', in Joseph Bristow and Trev Lynn Broughton, eds, *The Infernal Desires of Angela Carter: Fiction, Femininity, Feminism* (Harlow: Addison Wesley Longman, 1997), pp. 59–72. ('The Cabinet of Edgar Allan Poe', *Nights at the Circus, Wise Children*.)

Hardin, Michael, 'The Other Other: Self-Definition Outside Patriarchal Institutions in Angela Carter's *Wise Children*', *The Review of Contemporary Fiction*, 14:3 (Fall 1994), pp. 77–83.

Johnson, Heather L., 'Textualizing the Double-Gendered Body: Forms of the Grotesque in *The Passion of New Eve*', *The Review of Contemporary Fiction*, 14:3 (Fall 1994), pp. 43–8. Reprinted in Alison Easton, ed., *Angela Carter* (Basingstoke: Macmillan, 2000), pp. 127–35.

Johnson, Heather L., 'Unexpected Geometries: Transgressive Symbolism and the Transsexual Subject in Angela Carter's *The Passion of New Eve*', in Joseph Bristow and Trev Lynn Broughton, eds, *The Infernal Desires of Angela Carter: Fiction, Femininity, Feminism* (Harlow: Addison Wesley Longman, 1997), pp. 166–83.

Jordan, Elaine, 'Enthralment: Angela Carter's Speculative Fiction', in Linda Anderson, ed., *Plotting Change: Contemporary Women's Fiction* (London: Edward Arnold, 1990), pp. 19–40. (Detailed survey of Carter's *oeuvre*.)

Jordan, Elaine, 'Down the Road, or History Rehearsed', in Francis Barker, Peter Hulme and Margaret Iverson, eds, *Postmodernism and the Re-Reading of Modernity* (Manchester: Manchester University Press, 1992), pp. 159–79. (*The Passion of New Eve, Nights at the Circus*.)

Jordan, Elaine, 'The Dangers of Angela Carter', in Isobel Armstrong, ed., *New Feminist Discourse: Critical Essays on Theories and Texts* (London: Routledge, 1992), pp. 119–31. (*The Sadeian Woman, The Passion of New Eve, The Bloody Chamber, Nights at the Circus*.)

Jordan, Elaine, 'The Dangerous Edge', in Lorna Sage, ed., *Flesh and the Mirror: Essays on the Art of Angela Carter* (London: Virago Press, 1994), pp. 189–215. (*Heroes and Villains, The Infernal Desire Machines of Doctor Hoffman, The Passion of New Eve, Nights at the Circus*.)

Kaiser, Mary, 'Fairy Tale as Sexual Allegory: Intertextuality in Angela Carter's *The Bloody Chamber*', *The Review of Contemporary Fiction*, 14:3 (Fall 1994), pp. 30–6.

Kaveney, Roz, 'New New World Dreams: Angela Carter and Science Fiction', in Lorna Sage, ed., *Flesh and the Mirror: Essays on the Art of Angela Carter* (London: Virago Press, 1994), pp. 171–88. (*Heroes and Villains, The Passion of New Eve*.)

Keenan, Sally, 'Angela Carter's *The Sadeian Woman*: Feminism as Treason', in Joseph Bristow and Trev Lynn Broughton, eds, *The Infernal Desires of Angela Carter: Fiction, Femininity, Feminism* (Harlow: Addison Wesley Longman, 1997), pp. 132–48. Reprinted in Alison Easton, ed., *Angela Carter* (Basingstoke: Macmillan, 2000), pp. 37–57.

Kendrick, Walter, 'The Real Magic of Angela Carter', in Robert E. Hosmer, Jr, ed., *Contemporary British Women Writers: Texts and Strategies* (Basingstoke: Macmillan, 1993), pp. 66–84. (*The Sadeian Woman, Nights at the Circus*.)

Landon, Brooks, 'Eve at the End of the World: Sexuality and the Reversal of Expectations in Novels by Joanna Russ, Angela Carter, and Thomas Berger', in Donald Palumbo, ed., *Erotic Universe: Sexuality and Fantastic Literature* (New York: Greenwood Press, 1986), pp. 61–74.

Langlois, Janet L., 'Andrew Borden's Little Girl: Fairy-Tale Fragments in Angela Carter's "The Fall River Axe Murders" and "Lizzie's Tiger"', *Marvels and Tales: Journal of Fairy-Tale Studies*, 12:1 (1998), pp. 192–212. Reprinted in Danielle M. Roemer and Cristina Bacchilega, eds, *Angela Carter and the Fairy Tale* (Detroit, MI: Wayne State University Press, 2001), pp. 204–24.

Lee, Alison, 'Angela Carter's New Eve(lyn): De/Engendering Narrative', in Kathy Mezei, ed., *Ambiguous Discourse: Feminist Narratology and British Women Writers* (Chapel Hill: University of North Carolina Press, 1996), pp. 238–49.

Lee, Hermione, '"A Room of One's Own, Or a Bloody Chamber?": Angela Carter and Political Correctness', in Lorna Sage, ed., *Flesh and the Mirror: Essays on the Art of Angela Carter* (London: Virago Press, 1994), pp. 308–20.

Lewallen, Avis, 'Wayward Girls but Wicked Women?: Female Sexuality in Angela Carter's *The Bloody Chamber*', in Gary Day and Clive Bloom, eds, *Perspectives on Pornography: Sexuality in Film and Literature* (Basingstoke: Macmillan, 1988), pp. 144–58.

Magrs, Paul, 'Boys Keep Swinging: Angela Carter and the Subject of Men', in Joseph Bristow and Trev Lynn Broughton, eds, *The Infernal Desires of Angela Carter: Fiction, Femininity, Feminism* (Harlow: Addison Wesley Longman, 1997), pp. 184–97. ('The Executioner's Beautiful Daughter', 'The Loves of Lady Purple', 'The Bloody Chamber', *Shadow Dance, The Magic Toyshop, The Passion of New Eve, Nights at the Circus*.)

Mahoney, Elizabeth, 'But Elsewhere?: The Future of Fantasy in *Heroes and Villains*', in Joseph Bristow and Trev Lynn Broughton, eds, *The Infernal Desires of Angela Carter: Fiction, Femininity, Feminism* (Harlow: Addison Wesley Longman, 1997), pp. 73–87.

Makinen, Merja, 'Angela Carter's *The Bloody Chamber* and the Decolonization of Feminine Sexuality', *Feminist Review*, 42 (Autumn 1992), pp. 2–15. Reprinted in Alison Easton, ed., *Angela Carter* (Basingstoke: Macmillan, 2000), pp. 20–36.

Makinen, Merja, 'Sexual and Textual Aggression in *The Sadeian Woman* and *The Passion of New Eve*', in Joseph Bristow and Trev Lynn Broughton, eds, *The Infernal Desires of Angela Carter: Fiction, Femininity, Feminism* (Harlow: Addison Wesley Longman, 1997), pp. 149–65.

Manley, Kathleen E.B., 'The Woman in Process in Angela Carter's "The

Bloody Chamber"', *Marvels and Tales: Journal of Fairy-Tale Studies*, 12:1 (1998), pp.71–81. Reprinted in Danielle M. Roemer and Cristina Bacchilega, eds, *Angela Carter and the Fairy Tale* (Detroit, MI: Wayne State University Press, 2001), pp.83–93.

Matus, Jill, 'Blonde, Black and Hottentot Venus: Context and Critique in Angela Carter's "Black Venus"', *Studies in Short Fiction*, 28:4 (1991), pp.467–76. Reprinted in Alison Easton, ed., *Angela Carter* (Basingstoke: Macmillan, 2000), pp.161–72.

Mikkonen, Kai, 'The Hoffman(n) Effect and the Sleeping Prince: Fairy Tales in Angela Carter's *The Infernal Desire Machines of Doctor Hoffman*', *Marvels and Tales: Journal of Fairy-Tale Studies*, 12:1 (1998), pp.155–74. Reprinted in Danielle M. Roemer and Cristina Bacchilega, eds, *Angela Carter and the Fairy Tale* (Detroit, MI: Wayne State University Press, 2001), pp.167–86.

Moss, Betty, 'Desire and the Female Grotesque in Angela Carter's "Peter and the Wolf"', *Marvels and Tales: Journal of Fairy-Tale Studies*, 12:1 (1998), pp.175–91. Reprinted in Danielle M. Roemer and Cristina Bacchilega, eds, *Angela Carter and the Fairy Tale* (Detroit, MI: Wayne State University Press, 2001), pp.187–203.

Mulvey, Laura, 'Cinema Magic and the Old Monsters: Angela Carter's Cinema', in Lorna Sage, ed., *Flesh and the Mirror: Essays on the Art of Angela Carter* (London: Virago Press, 1994), pp.230–42.

Neale, Catherine, 'Pleasure and Interpretation: Film Adaptations of Angela Carter's Fiction', in Deborah Cartmell, I.Q. Hunter, Heidi Kaye and Imelda Whelehan, eds, *Pulping Fictions: Consuming Culture Across the Literature/Media Divide* (London: Pluto Press, 1996), pp.99–109.

Neumeier, Beate, 'Postmodern Gothic: Desire and Reality in Angela Carter's Writing', in Victor Sage and Allan Lloyd Smith, eds, *Modern Gothic: A Reader* (Manchester: Manchester University Press, 1996), pp.141–51. (*The Infernal Desire Machines of Doctor Hoffman, Nights at the Circus.*)

O'Day, Marc, 'Mutability is Having a Field Day: The Sixties Aura of Angela Carter's Bristol Trilogy', in Lorna Sage, ed., *Flesh and the Mirror: Essays on the Art of Angela Carter* (London: Virago Press, 1994), pp.24–58. (*Shadow Dance, Several Perceptions, Love.*)

Palmer, Paulina, 'From "Coded Mannequin" to Bird Woman: Angela Carter's Magic Flight', in Sue Roe, ed., *Women Reading Women's Writing* (Brighton: Harvester Press, 1987), pp.179–205. (*The Magic Toyshop, Heroes and Villains, The Passion of New Eve, The Bloody Chamber, Nights at the Circus.*)

Palmer, Paulina, 'Gender as Performance in the Fiction of Angela Carter and Margaret Atwood', in Joseph Bristow and Trev Lynn Broughton, eds, *The Infernal Desires of Angela Carter: Fiction, Femininity, Feminism* (Harlow: Addison Wesley Longman, 1997), pp.24–42. (*The Magic Toyshop, Nights at the Circus, Wise Children.*)

Punter, David, 'Essential Imaginings: The Novels of Angela Carter and Russell Hoban', in James Acheson, ed., *The British and Irish Novel Since 1960* (New York: St Martin's Press, 1991), pp.142–58. (General discussion of Carter's fiction.)

Renfroe, Cheryl, 'Initiation and Disobedience: Liminal Experience in Angela

Carter's "The Bloody Chamber"', *Marvels and Tales: Journal of Fairy-Tale Studies*, 12:1 (1998), pp. 82–94. Reprinted in Danielle M. Roemer and Cristina Bacchilega, eds, *Angela Carter and the Fairy Tale* (Detroit, MI: Wayne State University Press, 2001), pp. 94–106.

Robinson, Sally, 'The Anti-Hero as Oedipus: Gender and the Postmodern Narrative in *The Infernal Desire Machines of Doctor Hoffman*', in Alison Easton, ed., *Angela Carter* (Basingstoke: Macmillan, 2000), pp. 107–26.

Roe, Sue, 'The Disorder of Love: Angela Carter's Surrealist Collage', in Lorna Sage, ed., *Flesh and the Mirror: Essays on the Art of Angela Carter* (London: Virago Press, 1994), pp. 60–97.

Roemer, Danielle M., 'The Contextualization of the Marquis in Angela Carter's "The Bloody Chamber"', *Marvels and Tales: Journal of Fairy-Tale Studies*, 12:1 (1998), pp. 95–115. Reprinted in Danielle M. Roemer and Cristina Bacchilega, eds, *Angela Carter and the Fairy Tale* (Detroit, MI: Wayne State University Press, 2001), pp. 107–27.

Rubenstein, Roberta, 'Intersexions: Gender Metamorphosis in Angela Carter's *The Passion of New Eve* and Lois Gould's *A Sea-Change*', *Tulsa Studies in Women's Literature*, 12:1 (1993), pp. 103–18.

Sage, Lorna, 'Angela Carter: The Fairy Tale', *Marvels and Tales: Journal of Fairy-Tale Studies*, 12:1 (1998), pp. 52–68. Reprinted in Danielle M. Roemer and Cristina Bacchilega, eds, *Angela Carter and the Fairy Tale* (Detroit, MI: Wayne State University Press, 2001), pp. 65–82.

Sceats, Sarah, 'The Infernal Appetites of Angela Carter', in Joseph Bristow and Trev Lynn Broughton, eds, *The Infernal Desires of Angela Carter: Fiction, Femininity, Feminism* (Harlow: Addison Wesley Longman, 1997), pp. 100–15. (*The Magic Toyshop, Heroes and Villains, The Infernal Desire Machines of Doctor Hoffman, Nights at the Circus, Wise Children*.)

Smith, Patricia Juliana, 'All You Need is Love: Angela Carter's Novel of Sixties Sex and Sensibility', *The Review of Contemporary Fiction*, 14:3 (Fall 1994), pp. 24–9.

Suleiman, Susan Rubin, 'The Fate of the Surrealist Imagination in the Society of the Spectacle', in Lorna Sage, ed., *Flesh and the Mirror: Essays on the Art of Angela Carter* (London: Virago Press, 1994), pp. 98–116. (*The Infernal Desire Machines of Doctor Hoffman*.)

Vallorani, Nicoletta, 'The Body of the City: Angela Carter's *The Passion of New Eve*', *Science Fiction Studies*, 21:3 (1994), pp. 365–79.

Ward Jouve, Nicole, 'Mother is a Figure of Speech ...', in Lorna Sage, ed., *Flesh and the Mirror: Essays on the Art of Angela Carter* (London: Virago Press, 1994), pp. 136–70. (*The Passion of New Eve, The Bloody Chamber, Wise Children*.)

Warner, Marina, 'Angela Carter: Bottle Blonde, Double Drag', in Lorna Sage, ed., *Flesh and the Mirror: Essays on the Art of Angela Carter* (London: Virago Press, 1994), pp. 243–56. (*Nights at the Circus, Wise Children*.)

Warner, Marina, 'Ballerina: The Belled Girl Sends a Tape to an Impresario', in Danielle M. Roemer and Cristina Bacchilega, *Angela Carter and the Fairy Tale* (Detroit, MI: Wayne State University Press, 2001), pp. 250–7. (Short story written as a tribute to Angela Carter.)

Webb, Kate, 'Seriously Funny: *Wise Children*', in Lorna Sage, ed., *Flesh and the Mirror: Essays on the Art of Angela Carter* (London: Virago Press, 1994), pp. 279–307. Reprinted in Alison Easton, ed., *Angela Carter* (Basingstoke: Macmillan, 2000), pp. 192–215.

Wilson, Robert Rawdon, 'Slip Page: Angela Carter, In/Out/In the Postmodern Nexus', *Ariel: A Review of International English Literature*, 20:4 (October 1989), pp. 96–114. ('Lady of the House of Love'.)

Wisker, Gina, 'Weaving Our Own Web: Demythologising/Remythologising and Magic in the Work of Contemporary Women Writers', in Gina Wisker, ed., *It's My Party: Reading Twentieth Century Women's Writing* (London: Pluto Press, 1994), pp. 104–28. (*The Magic Toyshop, The Passion of New Eve*.)

Wisker, Gina, 'Revenge of the Living Doll: Angela Carter's Horror Writing', in Joseph Bristow and Trev Lynn Broughton, eds, *The Infernal Desires of Angela Carter: Fiction, Femininity, Feminism* (Harlow: Addison Wesley Longman, 1997), pp. 116–31. (*The Magic Toyshop, The Bloody Chamber*, 'The Fall River Axe Murders', 'The Loves of Lady Purple'.)

Wyatt, Jean, 'The Violence of Gendering: Castration Images in Angela Carter's *The Magic Toyshop, The Passion of New Eve*, and "Peter and the Wolf"', *Women's Studies*, 25:6 (1996), pp. 549–70. Reprinted in Alison Easton, ed., *Angela Carter* (Basingstoke: Macmillan, 2000), pp. 58–83.

Zipes, Jack, 'Crossing Boundaries with Wise Girls: Angela Carter's Fairy Tales for Children', *Marvels and Tales: Journal of Fairy-Tale Studies*, 12:1 (1998), pp. 147–54. Reprinted in Danielle M. Roemer and Cristina Bacchilega, eds, *Angela Carter and the Fairy Tale* (Detroit, MI: Wayne State University Press, 2001), pp. 159–66. (*Miss Z, The Dark Young Lady* and *The Donkey Prince*.)

ACKNOWLEDGEMENTS

The editor and publisher wish to thank the following for their permission to reprint copyright material: Virago (for material quoted from *Flesh and the Mirror*), Northcote House (for material quoted from Lorna Sage's *Angela Carter*), Macmillan (for material quoted from *Women in the House of Fiction, Contemporary Women's Fiction and the Fantastic,* Linden Peach's *Angela Carter,* and Alison Easton's *Angela Carter: Contemporary Critical Essays*), Edinburgh University Press (for material quoted from *Angela Carter: Writing From the Front Line*), *The Review of Contemporary Fiction* (for material quoted from 'All You Need is *Love*', '*Wise Children*: Angela Carter's Swan Song', and 'In Despair of the Old Adams'), Harvester (for material quoted from *Women Reading Women's Writing* and *Feminist Readings/Feminists Reading*), Manchester University Press (for material quoted from Aidan Day's *Angela Carter: The Rational Glass*), Edward Arnold (for material quoted from *Theorising the Fantastic*), Longman (for material quoted from *The Literature of Terror* and *The Infernal Desires of Angela Carter*), Routledge (for material quoted from *The Hidden Script, The Female Grotesque* and *(Un)Like Subjects: Women, Theory, Fiction*), *Women's Studies* (for material quoted from 'Angela Carter's Desire Machines'), University of North Carolina Press (for material quoted from *Ambiguous Discourse: Feminist Narratology and British Women Writers*), *Feminist Review* (for material quoted from 'Angela Carter's *The Bloody Chamber* and the Decolonization of Feminine Sexuality'), Polity Press (for material quoted from *The Pornography of Representation*), *Literature and History* (for material quoted from 'Re-Imagining the Fairy Tales'), University Press of New England (for material quoted from *The Voyage In*), *The Literary Review* (for material quoted from 'Magical Mannerist'), and *Studies in Short Fiction* (for material quoted from 'Blonde, Black and Hottentot Venus').

There are instances where we have been unable to trace or contact copyright holders before our printing deadline. If notified, the publisher will be pleased to acknowledge the use of copyright material.

The editor would like to thank Duncan Heath for his assistance in the preparation of this book, and my family (as usual) for their tolerance. I wish to dedicate it to Dr Bryan Burns of the University of Sheffield, who died in November 2000. Bryan was a greatly-valued mentor who urged me to read Carter's work many years ago, little knowing how much he was influencing the course of my subsequent academic career. He will be greatly missed by all his colleagues, students and friends.

Sarah Gamble is Senior Lecturer in English at the University of Sunderland, where she teaches modules in contemporary fiction and the history of women's writing. She is the author of *Angela Carter: Writing From the Front Line*, and editor of *The Routledge Companion to Feminism and Postfeminism*. Work in progress includes *Angela Carter: A Literary Life*, to be published by Palgrave Press.

INDEX

Ackroyd, Peter 88–9
alchemy/gender 91, 97–8
allegory 138
Alphaville film (Godard) 66
alterity 98
  see also difference
Altevers, Nanette
  The Sadeian Woman 113, 116–17
American Ghosts and Old World Wonders 134,
  183
  critics
    Day 184
    Gamble 184–5
    Peach 183
  'In Pantoland' 184–5
androgyny 91, 103–4
anti-essentialism 108
anti-mythology: *see* demythologising
Aquinas, Thomas 151
archetypes 64–5, 91
Armitt, Lucie
  Baudrillard 100, 101, 102, 103
  The Bloody Chamber 128–32
  'The Company of Wolves' 127
  formalist criticism 129–32
  Freud 46
  The Magic Toyshop 45–8
  The Passion of New Eve 100–5, 106–7
'Ashputtle' 134
Atwood, Margaret 110–11
  The Bloody Chamber and *The Sadeian
    Woman* 113, 121–3
Austen, Jane 29–31, 176, 183
authorial voice 9, 69, 89–90, 109
authority 174, 175
automata 55
  see also puppet imagery

Baartman, Saartjie 157, 198n54
Bacchilega, Cristina
  The Bloody Chamber 133
  fairy tales retold 132–4
Bakhtin, Mikhail
  carnivalesque 139, 141, 171–2, 179–80,
    184, 190–1n33
  dialogics 158
  difference 178
  grotesque 20, 140
  women 172
Ballard, J. G. 51, 111
Banville, Théodore de 157

Barker, Paul 8
Barthes, Roland 33, 119
  Japan 68
  myth 65, 66, 191n43
  objectivity 117
  reality 13
  text 49
Bataille, Georges 85, 86
Baudelaire, Charles 73, 86, 154, 157, 158
Baudrillard, Jean 100, 101, 102, 103, 105
'Beauty and the Beast' 125–7, 132, 133
Beauvoir, Simone de 39
Beckett, Samuel 22
Bedford, Les 49, 113–14
Benjamin, Jessica 42
Benjamin, Walter 153, 192n26
Bertens, Hans 75
Bettelheim, Bruno 124, 125–7
Bildungsroman 58
Birmingham Sun 115
Black Venus 134
  'Black Venus' 154–6, 159–61
  carnivalesque aspect 161–2
  critics
    Day 154–6
    Matus 156–9
    Peach 161–2
  'The Fall River Axe Murders' 159–61
'Black Venus' 154–6, 159–61
Blake, William 104
The Bloody Chamber 7, 12, 110, 137
  'Beauty and the Beast' 125–7
  'The Bloody Chamber' 131–2, 133
  'The Company of Wolves' 54, 87, 124,
    127, 130, 132
  'The Courtship of Mr Lyon' 125, 126
  critics
    Armitt 128–32
    Atwood 121–3
    Bacchilega 133
    Clark 124
    Cronan Rose 124–7, 128
    Duncker 120–1, 123–4
    Makinen 110–11
  'The Erl King' 130, 131
  eroticism 111–12, 121
  female sexuality 128–30
  intertextuality 128–9
  'The Lady of the House of Love' 131–2
  'Little Red Riding Hood' 121, 127, 132
  'Snow Child' 133
  subversiveness 132
  'The Tiger's Bride' 126
  voyeurism 124
  'The Werewolf' 127
  'Wolf-Alice' 133

'The Bloody Chamber' 131–2, 133
'Bluebeard' 132, 133
Boehm, Beth A.
    Wise Children 182–3
Bonca, Cornel
    The Infernal Desire Machines of Doctor
        Hoffman 85–7
Borden, Lizzie 159–61
Boston, Richard 27
Bouissac, Paul 151
Bradbury, Malcolm 165
bricoleur 167, 199n8
Bristol Trilogy 186n3
    critics
        Gamble 19–20
        O'Day 12–16
        Peach 20–4
        Sage 16–19
    Gothic 16, 20, 21
    intertextuality 24
    'Notes from the Front Line' 16
    plots 14–15
    setting 13–14, 15
    'Truly, it Felt Like Year One' 16
    see also Love; Several Perceptions; Shadow
        Dance
Bristow, Joseph 113
Brontë, Charlotte 41
Broughton, Trev Lynn 113
Broumas, Olga 124, 125
Brown, Norman O. 86
Butler, Judith 95–6, 181
Butter, P. H. 104
Byatt, A. S. 165

Cameron, Marsaili 115
camp 17, 19–20, 25, 99
carnivalesque
    Bakhtin 139, 141, 171–2, 179–80, 184,
        190–1n33
    Black Venus 161–2
    Nights at the Circus 139–41, 147
    sexuality 171–2
    Wise Children 168–72, 174
Carpentier, Alejo 74
Carr, Helen 137
Carter, Angela 7, 8, 182
    acclaim 8, 110, 136–7
    authorial voice 69, 89–90, 109
    as critic 11, 118–19
    demythologiser 10, 11, 90, 106, 116–17,
        123, 139, 197n41
    on The Infernal Desire Machines of Doctor
        Hoffman 70–1
    interviews 111–12, 137–8
        Bedford 49, 113–14

Clapp 164–5
Goldsworthy 155–6
Guardian 70
Haffenden 89–90, 138, 143
Katsavos 65
Kemp 164
Kenyon 32–3, 89
Sage 165–7
Stott 32
Watts 112
literary prizes 7, 32, 136
on The Magic Toyshop 43
on Nights at the Circus 143
obituaries 110–11
socialism 178
style changes 11, 72–3, 136–7
castration complex 41–2
Chodorow, Nancy 39
circus, semiotics of 151
Cixous, Hélène 63, 104, 114, 139, 194n11
Clapp, Susannah 164–5
Clark, Robert
    Armitt on 128
    The Bloody Chamber 124
    Heroes and Villains 53–6
    The Passion of New Eve 91
    rape 53–4
Clément, Catherine 104
Colette 145
commodification 89–90, 150, 175
'The Company of Wolves' 132
    critics
        Armitt 127
        Clark 124
    sexuality 54, 87, 127
    victims 130
'The Company of Wolves' film adaptation
    7–8, 136, 138
Connor, Steven 22
consciousness 23, 76
Cooke, Judith 165
'The Courtship of Mr Lyon' 125, 126
Crane, Richard 193n9
Cronan Rose, Ellen 8
    Armitt on 128
    The Bloody Chamber 124–7, 128
cross-dressing: see transvestism
Crow, Thomas 45
culture 33–4, 111, 175
Cuvier, Georges 157
cyborg 103–5

Day, Aidan
    American Ghosts and Old World Wonders
        184
    Black Venus 154–6

*The Infernal Desire Machines of Doctor
    Hoffman* 74–6
The Magic Toyshop 43–4
Nights at the Circus 143–9
The Passion of New Eve 107–8
Several Perceptions 27–8
Wise Children 184
Debord, Guy 82
deconstruction 139, 178–9
demythologising 10, 11, 90, 106, 116–17,
    123, 139, 197n41
difference 42, 178
    see also alterity
Dinesen, Isak 51
dominance, male 42, 53, 56, 68, 87, 148
double motif 34, 37
Duncker, Patricia
    Armitt on 128
    The Bloody Chamber 120–1, 123–4
    fairy tales 128
    The Sadeian Woman 119–21
DuPlessis, Rachel Blau 95
Duval, Jeanne 154–6, 158
Dworkin, Andrea 117, 120

Eco, Umberto 184, 185
Eisenstein, Sergei 91, 193n9
'The Erl King' 130, 131
Ernst, Max 51
eroticism 111–12, 121
evolution 107–8

fairy tales 15–16
    critics
        Bacchilega 132–4
        Duncker 128
        Peach 44–5
    feminism 124
    Freudian studies 124, 125–7
    Gothic literature 130–1
    rewritten 7, 10, 110, 124, 133
    sexuality 120–1
    Virago Press 110, 134
    Wise Children 162
'The Fall River Axe Murders' 159–61
fantasy/realism 10, 16, 37–8, 102, 137
fatalism 181–2
father figure 170, 174
femininity 62
    commodity 89–90, 150
    deconstructed 139
    masculinity 88, 92–3, 106
    The Passion of New Eve 88, 92–3, 106
    patriarchy 125–6, 141–2
feminism 11, 25
    fairy tales 124

pornography 113, 116
    readings 33, 35
feminist criticism 7, 10–11, 48, 95, 114–15
Fiedler, Leslie 21, 51
'Fin de Siècle' 72–3
Financial Times 115
Fireworks 67, 137
    afterword 21, 69–70
    critics
        Gamble 67–8, 69
        Peach 67
        Sage 68–9
    'Flesh and the Mirror' 69
flâneur 73, 192n26
'Flesh and the Mirror' 69
folk tales 21, 33, 112
Ford, John 183
formalist criticism 129–32, 171
Foucault, Michel 86, 112, 180–1
Fowles, John 74, 76, 107
Freud, Sigmund 33, 34, 46, 145, 189n45
    see also castration complex; Oedipus
        complex

Gallop, Jane 98
Gamble, Sarah
    American Ghosts and Old World Wonders
        184–5
    'Black Venus' 159–61
    Bristol Trilogy 19–20
    camp 19–20
    experimentation 72–3
    Fireworks 67–8, 69
    *The Infernal Desire Machines of Doctor
        Hoffman* 72–4
    magic realism 74
    The Passion of New Eve 105–6
    Several Perceptions 19–20
    Shadow Dance 19–20
    Wise Children 184–5
Garden of Eden story 33, 43, 45, 142
Gay News 89, 115
gaze 34–5, 60, 91, 97, 111, 131
    see also voyeurism
Geeraert, Jef 157
gender
    alchemy 97–8
    demythologising 197n41
    identity 87, 95–6
    myth 139
    performativity 95–6
    space/time 190n32
    subjectivity 76, 98, 133–4, 177
    violence 39, 53
genres 9, 11
Gerrard, Nicci 10, 137

Gilbert, Sandra M. 124
Godard, Jean-Luc 66
Godwin, William 146
Goldsworthy, Kerryn 155–6
Gothic literature
  Bristol Trilogy 16, 20, 21
  fairy tales 130–1
  Heroes and Villains 21, 49, 51–3
  psychoanalytical interpretation 46
  sensibility 30
  subversiveness 22
Graves, Robert 156
Gray, Stephen 157, 198n54
grotesque 26, 37, 140–1, 149–52, 190–1n33
Guardian 32, 70, 111, 135
Gubar, Susan 37, 124

Haffenden, John 89–90, 138, 143
Hamilton, Richard 45
Hanson, Clare
  Wise Children 178–81
Haraway, Donna 101, 103–4, 105
Heroes and Villains 12, 16, 137
  critics
    Clark 53–6
    Kaveney 50–1
    Mahoney 58–62
    Meaney 62–5
    Palmer 56–8
    Punter 51–3
    Sage 49
  demythologising 139
  Gothic literature 21, 49, 51–3
  irony 51
  Jewel 52, 54–5, 56–7, 59–61
  and *The Magic Toyshop* compared 58
  Marianne 51–3, 54–5, 56–7, 59–61
  mirror motif 61
  myth 65–6
  rape 52, 54–8, 59–60
  time 61–4
  and *Wise Children* compared 176–7
Hoffmann, E.T.A. 33, 34, 69
Holderness, Graham 175
Honeybuzzard: see Shadow Dance
Howarth, David 105
Hume, David 27, 187n47
Hutcheon, Linda 73

identity 95–6, 97, 98–9
incest 47–8, 68, 79
Independent on Sunday 164–5
The Infernal Desire Machines of Doctor Hoffman
  7, 67, 137
  Albertina 83–4
  critics

Bonca 85–7
  Day 74–6
  Gamble 72–4
  Jordan 70–2, 76
  Punter 76–81, 82
  Sage 70–1, 73–4, 76
  Suleiman 70, 80–4
Desiderio 74–6, 77, 78–80, 83–4, 86
incest 79
irony 82
metafiction 73
Minister of Determination 78–80, 83
parody 82
rape 83–4
sexual desire 77–9, 81, 82–3
voyeurism 83, 85
intertextuality 11, 24, 33, 128–9, 140
Irigaray, Luce 189n23
irony 19, 51, 64–5, 82

Japan 7, 66, 67–8, 84
Jarry, Alfred 145
Jefferies, Richard 50
Johnson, Heather L.
  The Passion of New Eve 97–100
Jordan, Elaine 11
  Armitt on 128
  *The Infernal Desire Machines of Doctor
    Hoffman* 70–2, 76
  Nights at the Circus 178
  The Passion of New Eve 90–1, 106–7, 108
  realism 72
Jordan, Neil 8, 136
jouissance 191n39
Joyce, James 174, 175–7

Kappeler, Susanne 117–19
Katsavos, Anna 65
Kaveney, Roz
  Heroes and Villains 50–1
Keats, John 44
Keenan, Sally
  The Sadeian Woman 113, 114–16, 117
Kemp, Peter 164
Kenyon, Olga 32–3, 89
Kingston, Maxine Hong 72
Klee, Paul 153
Kristeva, Julia
  Armitt on 128
  jouissance 191n39
  motherhood 114, 194–5n11
  thetic boundary 177
  time 62, 63, 190n32

Lacan, Jacques 133
'The Lady of the House of Love' 131–2

language 93–4, 181
Lanser, Susan 96
Late Show, BBC2 111
Lawrence, Karen 176
Leda motif 38, 39, 40, 148
Lee, Alison
   The Passion of New Eve 93–7, 100
Leno, Dan 145
lesbian relationship 142–3, 146
Lessing, Doris 63
Lewallen, Avis 124
liberation motif 142
literary prizes 7, 32, 136
The Literary Review 138, 163
'Little Red Riding Hood' 121, 127, 132
Llosa, Mario Vargas 74
Love 12, 15
   camp 19
   critics
      O'Day 31
      Peach 24
      Sage 18–19, 28
      Smith 30
   irony 19
   plot 14–15
   rape 29
   realism 23
   sadomasochism 15
   see also Bristol Trilogy
Lyotard, Jean-François 178–9, 199–200n43

MacAndrew, Elizabeth 22
McEwan, Ian 137–8
magic realism 10, 13, 23, 74, 137, 186n3
The Magic Toyshop 7, 12, 32, 137
   ambiguity of ending 44–5
   critics
      Armitt 45–8
      Day 43–4
      Palmer 33–5, 37
      Peach 44–5
      Sage 16, 37–9
      Wyatt 39–44
   demythologising 139
   feminist readings 48
   Finn 35, 36, 40–8
   and *Heroes and Villains* compared 58
   incest 47–8
   Margaret 37
   Melanie 34–7, 40–8
   patriarchy 46, 47
   rape 38, 40, 54, 58
   realism 37–8
   television version 8
   Uncle Philip 17, 34, 37, 40, 43, 47–8
   voyeurism 35, 60

woman as America 100
Mahoney, Elizabeth
   Heroes and Villains 58–62
Mailer, Norman 72
Maitland, Sara 115
Makinen, Merja
   Armitt on 128
   The Bloody Chamber 110–11
   Carter's success 136–7
   Nights at the Circus 178
Marcuse, Herbert 78, 80–2
Márquez, Gabriel García 74
masculinity 57, 71, 88, 92–3, 139, 183
materialism 10, 80, 112, 152–3
Matus, Jill
   Black Venus 156–9
Meaney, Gerardine
   gender/space/time 190n32
   Hanson on 179–80
   Heroes and Villains 62–5
   The Sadeian Woman 64
   Wise Children 174–8
Melville, Herman 21
metafiction 73
metaphysics/reality 77
Mill, John Stuart 144
Millard, Elaine 35–7
Miller, Jane 171
Miller, Walter 50
Mills, Sara 35–7
Milton, John 169–70
mirror motif 61, 69, 70, 91, 121, 133
misogyny 26, 124
Moorcock, Michael 51, 190n10
mother-goddesses 65
motherhood 114, 194–5n11, 198n46
Murdoch, Iris 165
myth 10, 15–16, 116–17
   archetypes 64–5
   Barthes 65, 66, 191n43
   culture 34
   gender 139
   Godard 66
   Graves 156
   Heroes and Villains 65–6
   irony 64–5
   The Passion of New Eve 89, 101
   The Sadeian Woman 64, 65–6
   Venus 157–8
   violence 34
   see also demythologising

New Society 111, 112
New York Times 135, 163
New York Times Book Review 27
Nights at the Circus 7, 136, 137

allegory 138
carnivalesque 139–41, 147
critical response 135–6
critics
    Day 143–9
    Jordan 178
    Makinen 178
    Nye 135
    O'Day 13
    Palmer 138–43, 147, 152–3
    Russo 149–52
    See 135–6
    Suleiman 153
Fevvers 135, 139, 144, 145–6, 149–50,
    151, 153
historical context 144–7
intertextuality 140
lesbian relationship 142–3, 146
liberation motif 142
Lizzie 142, 153
postmodernism 143–4
Walser 135, 145, 146, 151–2
'Notes for a Theory of Sixties Style' 72–3
'Notes from the Front Line' 9, 16, 33, 90,
    181
Nothing Sacred 73
Nye, Robert
    Nights at the Circus 135

Oakley, Ann 115
Oates, Joyce Carol 163
Observer 110–11
O'Day, Marc
    Bristol Trilogy 12–16
    Love 31
    Nights at the Circus 13
    Sage on 16
    Several Perceptions 13
    Shadow Dance 13, 31
Oedipus complex 39, 48, 77, 125–6, 189n23
O'Faolain, Julia 115
'Once More into the Mangle' 84
oral history 112
Ovid 40

Paglia, Camille 85
pain/pleasure 84
Palmer, Paulina 48
    Heroes and Villains 56–8
    The Magic Toyshop 33–5, 37
    Nights at the Circus 138–43, 147, 152–3
'In Pantoland' 184–5
parody 51, 52, 53, 82, 176–7
The Passion of New Eve 7, 90–1, 137
    critics
        Ackroyd 88–9

Armitt 100–5, 106–7
Clark 91
Day 107–8
Gamble 105–6
Johnson 97–100
Jordan 90–1, 106–7, 108
Lee 93–7
Peach 183
Punter 91–3
Sage 89, 109
demythologising 90, 106, 139
ending 105–6
Evelyn/Eve 91–5, 97–8, 99–100, 104–5
femininity/masculinity 88, 92–3, 106
gender identity 87
Mother 96
motherhood 194–5n11
myth 89, 101
rape 94–5
surrealism 88
Tristessa 96, 99, 106
Zero 93–5, 96, 100
patriarchy 25
    effects 43, 114
    femininity 125–6, 141–2
    hierarchy 34, 35, 36
    imaginary 39–40
    The Magic Toyshop 46, 47
    male dominance 148
    male transgression 173–4
    sexual violence 53
Peach, Linden
    American Ghosts and Old World Wonders 183
    Black Venus 161–2
    Bristol Trilogy 20–4
    fairy tales 44–5
    Fireworks 67
    Love 24
    The Magic Toyshop 44–5
    The Passion of New Eve 183
    pornographic style 84–5
    realism 22–4
    Several Perceptions 26, 27
Peake, Mervyn 51
Pearce, Lynne 35–7
peep-show metaphor 74–5, 76, 83, 84, 86
Perrault, Charles 91, 110, 120
'Peter and the Wolf' 134
pleasure 73, 84
Poe, Edgar Allan 21, 69, 86
poisoning 173
political correctness 11
pornographic style 84–5, 86–7
pornography 25
    feminism 113, 116
    Japan 68

Kappeler 117–19
  moral pornographer 116, 119
  power relations 119
  readings 57–8
  de Sade 17, 112, 187n18
  sexual violence 35
  Shadow Dance 17
  victims 117
post-apocalyptic novels 50
postmodernism 101
  deconstruction 178–9
  fairy tales retold 133
  female subjectivity 133–4
  Nights at the Circus 143–4
  relativism 107
  representation/reality 75
power relations 119, 181
Puck character 161–2
Punter, David 8
  Heroes and Villains 51–3
  *The Infernal Desire Machines of Doctor
    Hoffman* 76–81, 82
  The Passion of New Eve 91–3
  Suleiman on 81
puppet imagery 34, 139, 197n36
Pynchon, Thomas 51

rape
  Clark 53–4
  Heroes and Villains 52, 54–8, 59–60
  *The Infernal Desire Machines of Doctor
    Hoffman* 83–4
  Leda 38, 39, 40, 148
  'Little Red Riding Hood' 121
  Love 29, 53–4
  The Magic Toyshop 38, 40, 54, 58
  The Passion of New Eve 94–5
  Wise Children 171–2
readings
  feminist 33, 35
  masculine 92
  materialist/utopian 152–3
  moral response 25
  multi-layered 8–9, 11, 22
  'Notes from the Front Line' 33
  pornography 57–8
  retrospective 88
  voyeurism 53–4
realism
  critics
    Jordan 72
    Peach 22–4
  fantasy 10, 16, 37–8, 102, 137
  Love 23
  magic 10, 13, 23, 74, 137, 186n3
  The Magic Toyshop 37–8

social 15
  theatricality 27, 187n47
reality 13, 75, 77, 79
referent/sign 77
Reich, Wilhelm 78
relativism/postmodernism 107
representations 75, 79
Richard, Renée 98
Richlin, Amy 40
Rickford, Frankie 57
Rimmon-Kenan, Shlomith 93
Ross, Andrew 19–20, 20
Rubin, Gayle 42
Rushdie, Salman 111, 163–4
Russo, Mary
  grotesque 26, 149–52, 190–1n33
  Nights at the Circus 149–52
  on Palmer 152–3
  The Sadeian Woman 150

Sade, Marquis de 10, 84, 113–14, 118–19,
    121–3
  radical pornographer 17, 112, 187n18
  style 84–5, 86
The Sadeian Woman
  critical reception 112–13, 115
  critics
    Altevers 113, 116–17
    Atwood 121–3
    Duncker 119–21
    Keenan 113, 114–16, 117
    Meaney 64
    Peach 84–5
    Russo 150
    Sage 71, 113
  cultural determinism 111
  female sexuality 114–15
  feminist criticism 114, 115
  mythologising of women 64, 65–6
  voyeurism 150
sadism 68, 86
sadomasochism 15, 85
Sage, Lorna
  Bristol Trilogy 16–19
  Carter 8–9, 110, 182
  experimentation 72
  Fireworks 68–9
  Heroes and Villains 49
  *The Infernal Desire Machines of Doctor
    Hoffman* 70–1, 73–4, 76
  interview 165–7
  Love 18–19, 28
  The Magic Toyshop 16, 37–9
  obituary 111
  on O'Day 16
  The Passion of New Eve 89, 109

The Sadeian Woman 71, 113
Shadow Dance 16–18, 25, 28
science-fiction genre 50–1, 102, 137
Scott, Walter 91
See, Carolyn
  Nights at the Circus 135–6
self-alienation 54–5
self-consciousness 69, 72–3
self-referentiality 68
semiotics 77, 151, 177
sensibility 30
sequence novel 22
Several Perceptions 7, 12, 27
  camp 19–20
  critics
    Day 27–8
    Gamble 19–20
    O'Day 13
    Peach 26, 27
  male consciousness 23
  plot 15
  see also Bristol Trilogy
Sexton, Anne 124, 125
sexual desire 28–9
  female 58, 61, 62, 176–7
  *The Infernal Desire Machines of Doctor
    Hoffman* 77–9, 81, 82–3
  masculinity 57
sexual violence 28–9, 31, 35, 53–4, 190n29
  see also rape
sexuality
  adolescent 45
  animal aspects 120, 122–3, 126
  carnivalesque 171–2
  'The Company of Wolves' 54, 87, 127
  fairy tales 120–1
  female 22, 26, 114–15, 128–30
  Foucault 112
  male 120–1
Shadow Dance 12
  campness 17, 19–20, 25
  critics
    Gamble 19–20
    O'Day 13, 31
    Sage 16–18, 25, 28
  Ghislaine 17, 18, 25–6
  Honeybuzzard 17, 25, 26
  male consciousness 23
  plot 14–15
  pornography 17
  setting 14
  sixties 17–18
  violence 25–6
  see also Bristol Trilogy
Shakespeare, William
  All's Well That Ends Well 182

Carter on 165–7
  Cymbeline 166
  Hamlet 166
  King Lear 166
  Love's Labours Lost 167
  Measure for Measure 182
  A Midsummer Night's Dream 161–2, 167,
    175, 182
  Othello 166
  The Tempest 51
  Twelfth Night 183
  The Winter's Tale 27
  and *Wise Children* 162, 174, 175, 182–3
Shelley, Mary 50
Sidney, Sir Philip 51
sign/referent 77
Sladek, John 51
Smith, Patricia Juliana 29–31
Smith, Ricarda 81
'Snow Child' 133
socialism 10, 178
Sontag, Susan 17
spatiality 105
Spaull, Sue 35–7
Spectator 88–9
speculative novels 70–1
Stoller, Robert 99
Stone, Sandy 97
Stott, Catherine 32
subjectivity
  Barthes 117
  culture 33–4
  decentred 64
  erased 36, 39
  gender 76, 98, 133–4, 177
  split 34–5
subversiveness 22, 111, 132
Suleiman, Susan Rubin
  *The Infernal Desire Machines of Doctor
    Hoffman* 70, 80–4
  Nights at the Circus 153
  on Punter 81
Sunday Times 138
surrealism 68, 81, 88, 102, 137
symbolism/semiotics 177

theatricality/realism 27, 187n47
thetic boundary 177
'The Tiger's Bride' 126
time 61–4, 105, 190n32
Todd, Janet 30
Toulouse-Lautrec, Henri 145
tragedy 179, 180
transsexuality 95, 97, 98–9
transvestism 89–90, 95, 99, 183
'Truly, it Felt Like Year One' 16, 20

Truss, Lynne 163

utopia, feminist 27–8, 171

vampire imagery 17, 131–2
Venus myth 157–8
victims
    'The Company of Wolves' 130
    Japan 84
    pornography 117
    self-alienation 54–5
    women 82–3, 84, 100, 114, 117
violence
    gender 39, 53
    myth 34
    race 102
    sexual 28–9, 35, 53–4, 190n29
    Shadow Dance 25–6
    surrealism 68
Virago Press 110, 134, 137
voyeurism
    The Bloody Chamber 124
    *The Infernal Desire Machines of Doctor
        Hoffman* 83, 85
    The Magic Toyshop 35, 60
    readings 53–4
    The Sadeian Woman 150

Warner, Marina 21, 134
Watts, Helen Cagney 112
Waugh, Patricia 73
Webb, Kate
    Wise Children 168–74, 179
'The Werewolf' 127
Wise Children 8, 87, 164
    carnivalesque 168–72, 174
    critical response 163–4
    critics
        Boehm 182–3
        Day 184

Gamble 184–5
Meaney 174–8
Webb 168–74, 179
Dora 175–8, 180, 182
dualism 179
fairy tales 162
fatalism 181–2
father figure 170, 174
Grandma Chance 180
and *Heroes and Villains* compared 176–7
interviews 164–5
Joyce 174, 175–7
Melchior 175, 180
Nora 175–8, 182
parody 176–7
Peregrine 175–6, 183
rape/seduction 171–2
Saskia 173
Shakespeare 162, 174, 175, 182–3
tragedy 179, 180
wish-fulfilment 102
Wisker, Gina 8
'Wolf-Alice' 133
Wollstonecraft, Mary 146
women
    Bakhtin 172
    language 93–4
    myth 64, 65–6
    suffrage 144–6
    victims 82–3, 84, 100, 114, 117
Women Who Run with the Wolves 117
Women's Report 115
Wood, James 25
Wyatt, Jean 32
    The Magic Toyshop 39–44

Yeats, William Butler 40

Zola, Émile 157

Printed in the United States
112711LV00001B/305/A